Cambridge School Shakespeare

中文详注剑桥莎士比亚精选

理查三世

原版创始主编：[英] 瑞克斯·吉布森（Rex Gibson）
原版主编：[英] 瑞查德·安褚斯（Richard Andrews）
　　　　　[英] 维姬·维南德（Vicki Wienand）
原版编注：[英] 琳孜·布雷迪（Linzy Brady）
　　　　　[英] 珍·科尔兹（Jane Coles）
总主编：陈国华
分册主编：张洪瑞

社图号 20117

Cambridge School Shakespeare: King Richard III [Third edition] [978-1-108-45606-7] was first published by Cambridge University Press in 2015. All rights reserved.

This Simplified Chinese edition for the People's Republic of China is published by arrangement with the Press Syndicate of the University of Cambridge, Cambridge, United Kingdom.

© Cambridge University Press & Beijing Language and Culture University Press 2020.

This book is in copyright. No reproduction of any part may take place without the written permission of Cambridge University Press or Beijing Language and Culture University Press.

本书版权由剑桥大学出版社和北京语言大学出版社共同所有。本书任何部分之文字及图片，如未获得出版者书面同意，不得用任何方式抄袭、节录或翻印。

This edition is for sale in the People's Republic of China (excluding Hong Kong SAR, Macao SAR and Taiwan Province) only. 此版本仅限在中华人民共和国境内销售。

北京市版权局著作权合同登记图字：01-2020-3275 号

图书在版编目（CIP）数据

中文详注剑桥莎士比亚精选. 理查三世：英文 / 陈国华总主编；张洪瑞分册主编. -- 北京：北京语言大学出版社，2020.10

书名原文：Cambridge School Shakespeare：King Richard III

ISBN 978-7-5619-5724-0

Ⅰ. ①中… Ⅱ. ①陈… ②张… Ⅲ. ①历史剧－剧本－英国－中世纪－英文 Ⅳ. ① I561.33

中国版本图书馆 CIP 数据核字（2020）第 152210 号

中文详注剑桥莎士比亚精选：理查三世
ZHONGWEN XIANG ZHU JIANQIAO SHASHIBIYA JINGXUAN: LICHA SAN SHI

项目策划： 李　亮	**责任编辑：** 孙冠群
封面设计： 乔　剑	**排版制作：** 北京创艺涵文化发展有限公司
责任印制： 武晓东		

出版发行：	北京语言大学出版社
社　　址：	北京市海淀区学院路 15 号，100083
网　　址：	www.blcup.com
电子信箱：	service@blcup.com
电　　话：	编 辑 部　8610-82301019/0178
	发 行 部　8610-82303650/3591/3648
	北语书店　8610-82303653
	网购咨询　8610-82303908
印　　刷：	北京博海升彩色印刷有限公司

版　次： 2020 年 10 月第 1 版	**印　次：** 2020 年 10 月第 1 次印刷
开　本： 787 毫米 × 1092 毫米 1/16	**印　张：** 17.75
字　数： 536 千字		
定　价： 89.00 元		

PRINTED IN CHINA

序

　　由于观察角度不同，评判标准不同，关于哪个国家哪位诗人或小说家的成就最大，世人可能难以达成一致；可是说到剧作家，大家的共识是，莎士比亚不仅是英语国家有史以来最伟大的剧作家，也是全世界最伟大的剧作家，在知名度、影响力和传世作品的数量上，没有任何一位剧作家可以与之比肩。正是由于其公认的文学成就和人文精神，在过去400多年里，莎士比亚戏剧的演出在英语国家和许多非英语国家经久不衰，莎剧的阅读和鉴赏已成为这些国家英文教学的必选内容。

　　莎剧进入中国，已经有100多年历史，莎士比亚全集已经有了四个中文译本。不懂英文的人可以通过译本来欣赏莎士比亚剧作。然而文学作品的语言，尤其是诗歌的语言，具有相当程度的不可译性，而几乎所有莎剧的大部分台词都是素体诗（blank verse）。例如《哈姆雷》（*Hamlet*）里主人翁的名言"To be, or not to be, that is the question"，不论怎样译，都难以完全再现原文的深刻内涵和形式特点。要想真正欣赏莎士比亚的语言和戏剧艺术，还得阅读其英文原作。最早由剑桥大学出版社出版的这套莎剧精选，收录了最受读者和观众喜爱的14部剧目，涵盖莎剧的各个类别，以其独具匠心的设计和编排，成为所有英文原版莎剧中最适合英语学习者阅读、最适合戏剧爱好者排演的莎剧选集。

　　本选集的创始主编瑞克斯·吉布森（Rex Gibson）在本书引言（Introduction）里指出："不论做什么，都要记住，莎士比亚写下他的剧本是为了演出、观看和享受的。"秉承这一宗旨，这一新版莎剧选集有四个鲜明的区别性特点：

　　一、书的开本和页面的宽高比例特别适合学校的老师和学生以及剧团的导演和演员在排练莎剧时把书打开，拿在手里，随时参阅，而且左边页面上有许多有关排演活动的建议。

　　二、书中配有大量世界各国莎剧演出的彩色剧照，为莎剧爱好者和剧团排演莎剧提供了灵感。

　　三、书的正文部分打开后，右页是未经删减、原汁原味的剧本原文，左页是多种不同栏目，包括导演技巧（Stagecraft）、剧中语言（Language in the play）、人物分析（Characters）、主题分析（Themes）、写作练习（Write about it）及词语注释等。每幕之间（本幕回顾）和最后一幕后（本剧回顾）有与剧情相关的各种思考题。

　　四、在剧本之后有各种针对全剧的专题论述，以《哈姆雷》为例，包括视角与主题（Perspectives and themes）、人物分析（Characters）、《哈姆雷》的语言（The language of *Hamlet*）、《哈姆雷》的演出（*Hamlet* in performance）、笔论莎士比亚（Writing about Shakespeare）、笔论《哈姆雷》（Writing about *Hamlet*），还有一份莎翁年表（William Shakespeare 1564–1616）。

　　左页上的栏目对于解读和排演莎剧特别有帮助，剧本后面的专题论述对于撰写有关莎士比亚的文章特别有帮助，而参加莎剧排演，背诵台词，撰写论文，又是提高英语水平的极好途径。

i

为了方便更多的中国读者阅读、欣赏、排演莎士比亚原作，北京语言大学出版社携手剑桥大学出版社，将这套莎剧精选引入中国。我有幸应邀担任这套书的中文版总主编，组织起一个团队，对原版进行一定程度的改编和汉化，以适应中国读者的需求。我们不仅将原版提供的关键注释基本译成了中文，而且针对中国英语学习者和莎剧爱好者阅读理解上的难点，主要做了以下四件事：

一、参考 The Oxford Dictionary of Original Shakespearean Pronunciation (David Crystal 2016)、Oxford Dictionary of Pronunciation for Current English (Clive Upton 2003) 和 Shakespeare's Names: A Pronouncing Dictionary (Helge Kökeritz 1950)，给每个剧本前面人物表里的人名加上了国际音标。为了便于读者识别，我们将第一本发音词典里一般中国读者不认识的个别音标替换成了大家熟悉的近似音标。

二、为左页顶端的剧情简介添加中文译文。

三、左页中以及剧本后面论文部分里有一些具有挑战性的词和术语（如tableau），我们为其中的大部分添加了相应的中文释义。

四、适当增加了原版里没有的词语注释。

给剧中人物的名字加了国际音标之后，我们发现，现有莎剧中文译本里一些人名的中文译名与原文的读音差别较大且互不相同。根据定名不咎、译音循本、音义兼顾、音系对应的原则，我们给出了新译名。根据前两个原则，我们将剧本 Julius Caesar /ˈdʒuːlɪəs ˈsiːzə(r)/ 译成《儒略·恺撒》，而没有采用《尤利/力乌斯·恺撒》《裘利/力斯·凯撒》《居里厄斯·恺撒》等现成译名中的任何一个，因为从公元前1世纪到公元16世纪西方使用的儒略历（Julian calendar）就是以这位 Julius Caesar（拉丁文读音是 /ˈjuːlɪ.ʊs ˈkaɛsaɪ/）命名的。根据音义兼顾的原则，我们将剧本 Hamlet /ˈ(h)amlət/ 译成《哈慕雷》而不是《哈姆莱特》或《哈姆雷特》，因为"慕雷"比"姆莱"或"姆雷"更适合用来给男子起名，结尾的辅音 /t/ 在实际说话中往往不发音。根据音系对应的原则，我们借鉴了曹禺的译法，将剧本 Romeo and Juliet 译成《柔密欧与茱丽叶》，没有将 Romeo 译成更常见的"罗密欧"，因为"柔 /rou/"比"罗 /luo/"更接近原名 Romeo /ˈroːmɪoː/ 的读音；同时我们将 Juliet /ˈdʒuːlɪət/ 译成"茱丽叶"而不是"朱丽叶"，因为这样做不容易让人误以为这个女孩姓"朱"。

这套经过改编并且带中文注释的《中文详注剑桥莎士比亚精选》不仅可以用作中国高中和大学的英文教材，而且适合中国所有具有较高英语能力的莎剧爱好者阅读和欣赏，将戏剧从书中提升到自己心中，将剧本从课堂搬演到戏台。

相信《中文详注剑桥莎士比亚精选》会带给中国广大英语爱好者一个惊喜。

北京外国语大学
2020年5月于英国剑桥家中

Contents 目录

Introduction 引言	iv
Photo gallery 剧照精选	v
Shakespeare's history plays 莎士比亚的历史剧	1
The world of the play 剧中世界	2

King Richard III 《理查三世》

List of characters 人物表	4
Act 1 第1幕	7
Act 2 第2幕	69
Act 3 第3幕	97
Act 4 第4幕	149
Act 5 第5幕	199
Perspectives and themes 视角与主题	230
The contexts of *King Richard III* 《理查三世》的创作背景	236
Characters 人物分析	239
The language of *King Richard III* 《理查三世》的语言	248
King Richard III in performance 《理查三世》的演出	252
Writing about Shakespeare 笔论莎士比亚	262
Writing about *King Richard III* 笔论《理查三世》	264
Royal family tree 王室家谱图	266
William Shakespeare 1564–1616 莎翁年表	267
Acknowledgements 鸣谢	268

Introduction 引言

This *King Richard III* is part of the **Cambridge School Shakespeare** series. Like every other play in the series, it has been specially prepared to help all students in schools and colleges.

The **Cambridge School Shakespeare** *King Richard III* aims to be different. It invites you to lift the words from the page and to bring the play to life in your classroom, hall or drama studio. Through enjoyable and focused activities, you will increase your understanding of the play. Actors have created their different interpretations of the play over the centuries. Similarly, you are invited to make up your own mind about *King Richard III*, rather than having someone else's interpretation handed down to you.

Cambridge School Shakespeare does not offer you a cut-down or simplified version of the play. This is Shakespeare's language, filled with imaginative possibilities. You will find on every left-hand page: a summary of the action, an explanation of unfamiliar words, and a choice of activities on Shakespeare's stagecraft, characters, themes and language.

Between each act and in the pages at the end of the play, you will find notes, illustrations and activities. These will help to encourage reflection after every act and give you insights into the background and context of the play as a whole.

This edition will be of value to you whether you are studying for an examination, reading for pleasure or thinking of putting on the play to entertain others. You can work on the activities on your own or in groups. Many of the activities suggest a particular group size, but don't be afraid to make up larger or smaller groups to suit your own purposes. Please don't think you have to do every activity: choose those that will help you most.

Although you are invited to treat *King Richard III* as a play, you don't need special dramatic or theatrical skills to do the activities. By choosing your activities, and by exploring and experimenting, you can make your own interpretations of Shakespeare's language, characters and stories.

Whatever you do, remember that Shakespeare wrote his plays to be acted, watched and enjoyed.

Rex Gibson
Founding editor

This new edition contains more photographs, more diversity and more supporting material than previous editions, whilst remaining true to Rex's original vision. Specifically, it contains more activities and commentary on stagecraft and writing about Shakespeare, to reflect contemporary interest. The glossary has been enlarged too. Finally, this edition aims to reflect the best teaching and learning possible, and to represent not only Shakespeare through the ages, but also the relevance and excitement of Shakespeare today.

Richard Andrews and Vicki Wienand
Series editors

This edition of *King Richard III* uses the text of the play established by Janis Lull in **The New Cambridge Shakespeare**.

▶ In this play, Shakespeare dramatises a slice of English history as he charts Richard of Gloucester's murderous progress to kingship. All who thwart (阻挠；挫败) Richard's royal ambition learn, to their cost, that beneath his charismatic (魅力超凡) personality lurks a lethal killer.

▼ The play opens at the end of one of the decisive battles in the Wars of the Roses (蔷薇战争). The victory goes to the Yorkist Edward (second from the left), who has defeated his Lancastrian enemies and assumed the English throne to become King Edward IV.

Richard's first step to the throne is to get rid of his older brother George, Duke of Clarence, who stands between Richard and the crown. Edward and Clarence are at odds with each other, and Richard swears to help Clarence reconcile (和解) with the King. At the same time, Richard orchestrates (精心策划) Clarence's death.

The dying King Edward seeks to secure peace and stability for his family and country by continuing his royal line through his eldest son. But Richard plans to kill both of Edward's young sons and seize the crown for himself.

As part of his plan to take the throne, Richard persuades Anne Neville to become his wife. Richard admits that he killed Anne's husband and father-in-law, but gives such a dazzling performance in wooing Anne that her loathing (厌恶) turns first to confusion and then to acceptance.

Margaret is the widow of the Lancastrian Henry VI. Her long life and enduring memory remind certain characters – especially Richard – of their bloody past, as she calls for justice and revenge to redress (纠正；补救) old wrongs committed against her family.

When King Edward dies, his son is hailed as Edward V. However, the boy's mother fears for his safety because he is so young and under the protection of his manipulative (操控别人的) and evil uncle.

Richard plays the jovial (快活) and harmless uncle with the young King and his brother. But secretly he plans their imprisonment and murder.

Richard's next steps to the throne involve getting rid of courtiers (朝臣) and nobles who do not support his claim to it. One of these is Lord Hastings, a faithful supporter of Edward IV and his sons. Hastings is unaware of Richard's plans to seize the throne and he is led into a trap and executed.

Richard also gathers support from influential nobles such as Buckingham, who is willing to do anything to ensure that Richard becomes King.

With the help of Buckingham, Richard stages a performance in which he plays a saintly man who is more concerned with praying than ruling England. He pretends to refuse the crown, but makes a show of being forced to take it for the sake of the country and its citizens.

▲ Richard finally fulfils his ambitions and gains the throne. In order to secure his position, he makes plans to murder the two young princes, Edward and Richard. He tests Buckingham's loyalty by asking him to kill them. Buckingham refuses and tries to flee, but he is captured and beheaded.

▲ Richard is still working out ways to secure his throne. With Anne dead, he seeks to marry the daughter of Edward IV and Elizabeth to consolidate (巩固) his position as King. But Elizabeth is unimpressed (不为所动) and secretly makes plans to marry her daughter to someone else.

▼ News of Richard's villainy (恶行) has reached the Earl of Richmond. He wages war to take back the throne and re-establish order, while also asserting the Lancastrian claim to the throne. Richard and his dwindling (人数减少) army prepare to defend the crown.

▼ On the eve of the decisive Battle of Bosworth, where he is to meet Richmond, Richard dreams that he is cursed by the ghosts of his eleven victims. Appearing in the order of their deaths, the ghosts make repeated demands for revenge on Richard. They are a forceful reminder of his past crimes and guilt.

▶ Richmond's defeat of Richard ends the cycle of murder and revenge that has fuelled the Wars of the Roses. Richmond unites the houses of Lancaster and York by marrying Princess Elizabeth. In doing so, he founds a new dynasty – the Tudors (都铎王朝) – and establishes peace in England.

Shakespeare's history plays 莎士比亚的历史剧
The movement of the English crown through the plays

King Richard III is the last of eight plays that Shakespeare wrote to dramatise the historical events leading up to the reign of the Tudors in England. The plays are Shakespeare's version of the struggle for the crown that culminated (达到高潮) in the civil war known as the Wars of the Roses. These wars were skirmishes (小冲突) over the right to the throne between two branches of the House of Plantagenet (/plænˈtædʒɪˌnet/)(金雀花家族), a royal dynasty in England: Lancaster (represented by a red rose) and York (represented by a white rose). The wars ended when the Lancastrian Henry Tudor defeated the Yorkist Richard III. Henry married Elizabeth of York so that their descendants would unite the two branches and ensure peace. This new Tudor line was symbolised by a red and white rose.

King Richard II
Richard II is a weak and ineffectual (无能) ruler. Henry Bullingbrook becomes Henry IV.

King Henry IV Parts 1 and 2
Henry IV's son Hal, after spending his youth with Falstaff in London taverns, turns over a new leaf when he becomes King Henry V.

King Henry V
King Henry V wins an important victory over the French at Agincourt. He extends England's territory and marries a French princess.

King Henry VI Parts 1, 2 and 3
Henry VI loses English possessions in France and sees his kingdom racked by civil war (the Wars of the Roses) as the house of York challenges his right to rule. Edward IV emerges from these wars as the new King.

King Richard III
When King Edward dies, the crown passes to his son, the young Prince Edward; the old King's brother, Richard, is made Lord Protector (摄政大臣) until Edward is old enough to rule. However, Richard seizes the throne and murders all who get in the way, including his young nephews. He is finally overthrown by the Earl of Richmond (Henry Tudor), who becomes King Henry VII. Henry unites the two warring families and begins the line of Tudor monarchs.

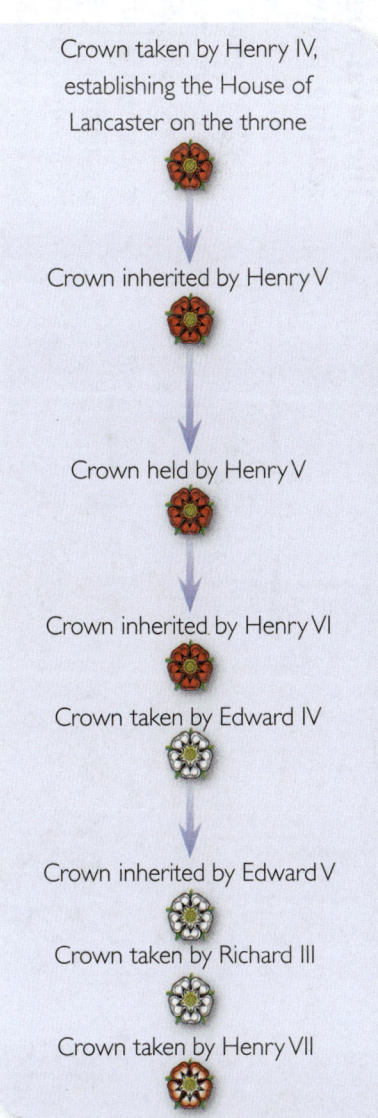

Crown taken by Henry IV, establishing the House of Lancaster on the throne

Crown inherited by Henry V

Crown held by Henry V

Crown inherited by Henry VI

Crown taken by Edward IV

Crown inherited by Edward V

Crown taken by Richard III

Crown taken by Henry VII

King Richard III
理查三世

The royal rogue (流氓；无赖): a pre-reading activity

You are in the court of a new king towards the end of the Wars of the Roses. The crown has just been taken from the previous king, who died in battle along with his sons. Now a new king, with his newly made royal family and trusted courtiers, comes to London. Imagine there is a clever but isolated member of this new royal family. He is determined to become king one day – no matter what the cost. In groups, compile a list of actions this 'royal rogue' might use to manoeuvre his way (施展手腕) to the throne. Start with the following: intimidate; flatter; seduce; murder; marry; imprison; bribe.

What else can you add? Remember, the royal rogue cannot be too obvious or his actions might alienate the people of London and start another civil war. Assign roles to every member of the group so that you simulate this new court:

- the new king
- the new king's wife
- the new king's brother
- the new king's young son (the heir to the throne)
- the old king's wife
- the old king's daughter-in-law
- the new king's trusted courtier.

Then take turns as the royal rogue to decide which action you would use for each of the people listed above. Remember to give your reasons and to think about the consequences of the actions you take.

The world of the play 剧中世界

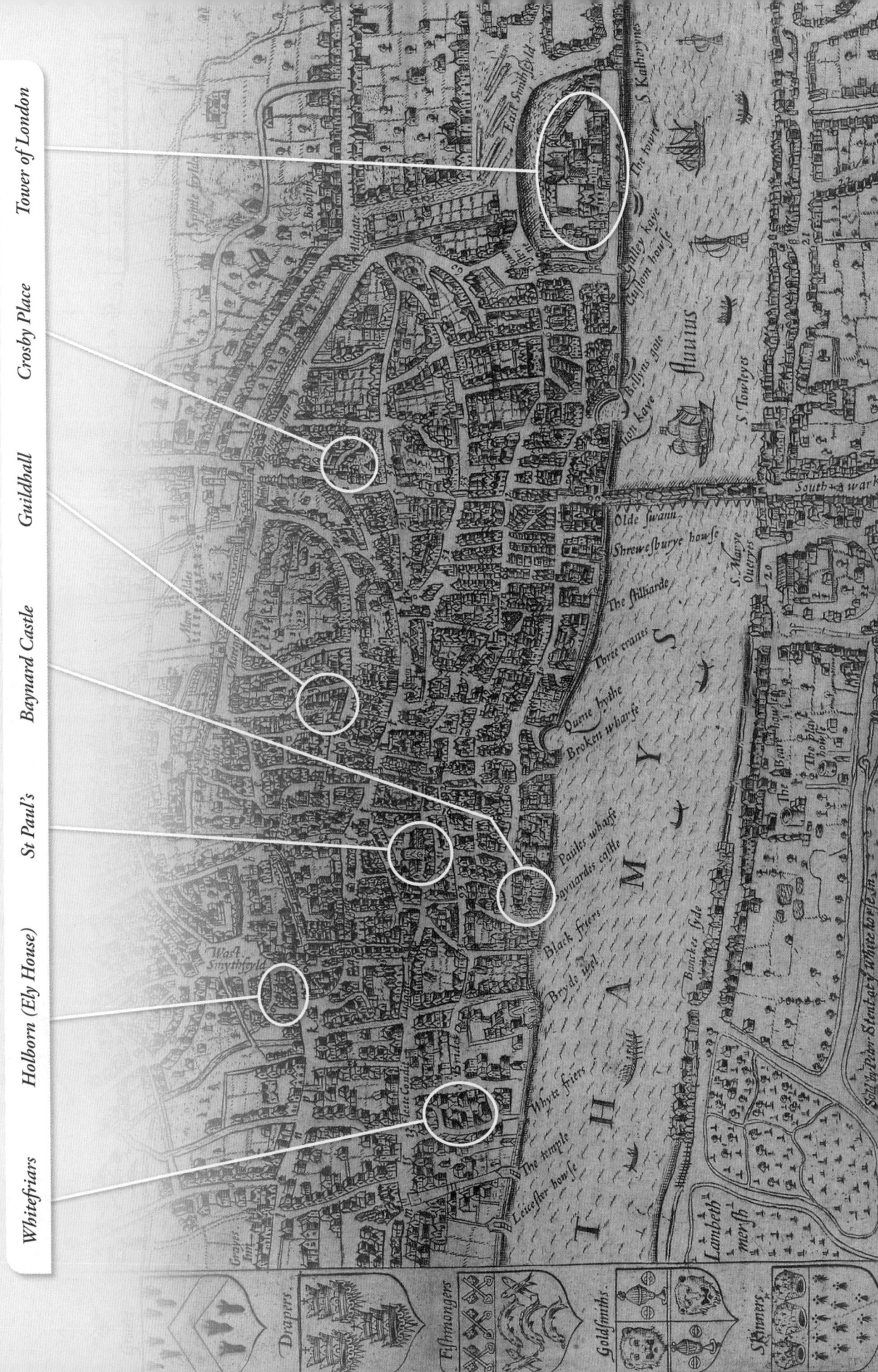

King Richard III
理查三世

List of characters 人物表

The royal family 王室

RICHARD /ˈrɪtʃə(r)d/ (理查), Duke of Gloucester /ˈglɒstə(r)/ (格劳斯特公爵) (later King Richard III)
DUCHESS OF YORK /jɔː(r)k/ (约克公爵夫人) Richard's mother
KING EDWARD /ˈedwə(r)d/ IV (爱德华四世) ⎫
CLARENCE /ˈklærəns/ (克莱润) ⎬ Richard's brothers
ANNE /æn/ (安娜) Richard's wife (earlier betrothed [订婚] to Prince Edward, son of King Henry VI)
QUEEN ELIZABETH /əˈlɪzəˌbeθ/ (伊丽莎白王后) wife of King Edward IV
PRINCE EDWARD (爱德华王子) ⎫ sons of Queen Elizabeth
DUKE OF YORK (约克公爵) ⎬ (the princes in the Tower)
BOY ⎫
GIRL ⎬ Clarence's children
QUEEN MARGARET /ˈmɑː(r)grɪt/ (玛格蕊王后) widow of King Henry VI
EARL OF RICHMOND /ˈrɪtʃmənd/ (瑞奇蒙伯爵) later King Henry VII

The Woodvilles /ˈwʊdvɪlz/ 伍德威尔家族

MARQUESS OF DORSET /ˈdɔː(r)sət/ (多塞侯爵) ⎫
LORD GREY /greɪ/ (格瑞勋爵) ⎬ sons of Queen Elizabeth
LORD RIVERS /ˈrɪvə(r)z/ (瑞沃勋爵) brother of Queen Elizabeth
VAUGHAN /ˈvɔːən/ (沃恩)

Nobles, church and court 贵族，教会和宫廷

LORD HASTINGS /ˈhæstɪŋz/ (海斯廷勋爵)
BISHOP OF ELY /ˈiːlɪ/ (伊利主教)
DUKE OF BUCKINGHAM /ˈbʌkɪŋəm/ (白金汉公爵)
ARCHBISHOP OF YORK (约克大主教)
LORD STANLEY /ˈstænlɪ/ (斯坦雷勋爵), Earl of Derby /ˈdɑː(r)bɪ/ (达比伯爵)
LORD CARDINAL (红衣主教), Archbishop of Canterbury (坎特伯雷大主教)
BRAKENBURY /ˈbrækənbrɪ/ (布莱肯布瑞)
SIR CHRISTOPHER URSWICK /ˈkrɪstəfə(r) ˈɜː(r)swɪk/ (克瑞斯特夫·额斯维爵士)
LORD LOVELL /ˈlʌvəl/ (拉沃尔勋爵)
EARL OF OXFORD /ˈɒksfə(r)d/ (牛津伯爵)
SIR RICHARD RATCLIFFE /ˈrætklɪf/ (理查·拉克利夫爵士)
EARL OF SURREY /ˈsʌrɪ/ (萨里伯爵)
SIR WILLIAM CATESBY /ˈwɪljəm ˈkeɪtsbɪ/ (威廉·凯茨贝爵士)
SIR WALTER HERBERT /ˈwɔːltə(r) ˈhɑː(r)bə(r)t/ (沃尔特·哈博爵士)
JAMES TYRREL /ˈdʒeɪmz ˈtɪrəl/ (杰慕·提若尔)
SIR JAMES BLUNT /blʌnt/ (杰慕·布琅爵士)
TRESSEL /ˈtresəl/ (揣瑟尔) ⎫
DUKE OF NORFOLK /ˈnɔː(r)fək/ (诺福克公爵)
BERKELEY /ˈbɑː(r)klɪ/ (巴克雷) ⎬ attendants of Lady Anne

List of characters

The people 庶民

KEEPER OF THE TOWER (伦敦塔看守)
LORD MAYOR OF LONDON (伦敦市长大人)
THREE CITIZENS (三市民)
TWO MURDERERS (二杀手)

SCRIVENER (文书)
SHERIFF (郡长)
PURSUIVANT (传令随从)
PRIEST (神父)

Ghosts 鬼魂

(Who appear to Richard and Richmond at Bosworth /ˈbɒzwə(r)θ/)

PRINCE EDWARD (son of King Henry VI)
KING HENRY VI
CLARENCE
RIVERS
GREY

VAUGHAN
HASTINGS
ANNE
BUCKINGHAM
THE PRINCES IN THE TOWER

Lords, Attendants, Halberds (执戟尉), Messengers (信使), Soldiers, Servants, Citizens, Gentlemen, Page (侍从), Guards, two Bishops.

The action of the play takes place in various locations in England.

Richard soliloquises on the end of the civil war and the pleasure of peace. He mocks his brother's sexual games and regrets he cannot enjoy similar pleasures.

 剧情简介：理查独白，评论内战的结束与和平带来的快乐。他一面嘲弄哥哥的荒淫游戏，一面却懊恼自己无法享受同样的快乐。

Stagecraft 导演技巧

A dramatic opening (in pairs)

The play opens dramatically with Richard, Duke of Gloucester's **soliloquy** (独白). He describes the change from war to peace that has taken place since his brother Edward, the new Yorkist king, has assumed the throne. He then goes on to paint a verbal portrait of himself.

a Read through Richard's soliloquy together, taking turns with the three main sections (lines 1–13, 14–27 and 28–41). Then work out how you would stage the lines to achieve the greatest dramatic effect, highlighting the following features in the script:

- His dramatic opening, capturing the audience's attention with the word 'Now'.
- His repetition of the word 'Our' and his use of **alliteration*** (words with the same letter sounds at the start) in lines 6–8.
- His use of **personification** (拟人) (giving human attributes to non-human things) – for example, describing war as a soldier who has replaced his warlike behaviour with that of a lover.
- From line 14 onwards, Richard repeatedly uses the personal pronoun ('I') and shifts the attention to himself.

b Choose a block of four lines to memorise. Explore different ways of saying it in order to bring out the drama and the meaning.

c In role as director, make notes to advise the actor playing Richard at the start of this scene. Keep a Director's Journal as an ongoing record of your ideas about this play in performance. This is where you will explore aspects of stagecraft, actors' perspectives and dramatic possibilities.

1 Visual images (in small groups)

Richard makes use of vivid visual **imagery** (see p. 250) through his choice of words.

a Look through the soliloquy and find examples of visual images of flirtation, deformity, pleasure and war. Then create a series of tableaux (亮相；舞台造型) ('freeze-frames' [演员全部静止不动]) to represent Richard's images for each example.

b Discuss which is more effective: Richard's description in words or your embodiment of the ideas in the form of frozen pictures? Give reasons for your decision.

---

1 **this son of York** （即新国王爱德华四世，理查之兄）
2 **loured** 降临；横眉立目
3 **bruisèd arms** 破损的兵器
4 **monuments** 纪念品
5 **alarums** 号角
6 **dreadful** 令人恐惧
7 **measures** 舞步
8 **front** 眉头
9 **barbèd steeds** 铁甲战马
10 **fearful** 令人胆寒
11 **lascivious pleasing** 淫乐之声
12 **shaped for sportive tricks** 有荒淫嬉戏的身材
13 **rudely stamped** 被匆匆打造出来
14 **want** 缺少
15 **wanton** 轻浮
16 **ambling** 迈着舞步
17 **nymph** 美少女
18 **curtailed of this fair proportion** 匀称的身材被裁短
19 **Cheated of feature** 被剥夺了相貌
20 **dissembling** 欺骗，伪装
21 **sent before my time** 不到时间就被打发出来
22 **unfashionable** 不时髦
23 **halt** 跛行
24 **piping time of peace** 太平盛世
25 **descant on** 诉说

* **alliteration** 头韵，指诗句里两个或多个词的第一个辅音相同，如 sing a song of sixpence，类似中文的双声。

King Richard III

Act 1 Scene 1

Outside the Tower of London

Enter RICHARD DUKE OF GLOUCESTER

RICHARD
Now is the winter of our discontent
Made glorious summer by this son of York[1],
And all the clouds that loured[2] upon our house
In the deep bosom of the ocean buried.
Now are our brows bound with victorious wreaths, 5
Our bruisèd arms[3] hung up for monuments[4],
Our stern alarums[5] changed to merry meetings,
Our dreadful[6] marches to delightful measures[7].
Grim-visaged war hath smoothed his wrinkled front[8],
And now, instead of mounting barbèd steeds[9] 10
To fright the souls of fearful[10] adversaries,
He capers nimbly in a lady's chamber
To the lascivious pleasing[11] of a lute.
But I that am not shaped for sportive tricks[12]
Nor made to court an amorous looking-glass, 15
I that am rudely stamped[13] and want[14] love's majesty
To strut before a wanton[15] ambling[16] nymph[17],
I that am curtailed of this fair proportion[18],
Cheated of feature[19] by dissembling[20] nature,
Deformed, unfinished, sent before my time[21] 20
Into this breathing world scarce half made up,
And that so lamely and unfashionable[22]
That dogs bark at me as I halt[23] by them,
Why, I, in this weak piping time of peace[24],
Have no delight to pass away the time, 25
Unless to see my shadow in the sun
And descant on[25] mine own deformity.

Richard resolves to be evil. He tells the audience that he has arranged for King Edward to see his brother Clarence as a threat and imprison him in the Tower. He jokes about Clarence's plight.

剧情简介：理查决心作恶。他告诉观众自己已设法让爱德华国王把哥哥克莱润视作威胁并把他囚禁于伦敦塔。他还拿克莱润的处境开玩笑。

Stagecraft 导演技巧

Richard's soliloquy (in fours)

Richard's opening soliloquy falls into three main parts:

- **Lines 1–13** His comments about the change from war to peace and the character of the new monarch, Edward ('this son of York').
- **Lines 14–27** How Richard feels about the way he looks.
- **Lines 28–41** How he plans to gain power.

A major decision for any director of the play is how to stage this important speech. The conventional way of playing a soliloquy is for the actor to speak directly to the audience, as if inviting them to share his innermost thoughts. In the 1996 movie version starring Ian McKellen, however, Richard speaks the first ten lines as if making a public speech at a state banquet. The rest of the soliloquy is delivered in private in the men's toilet. What ideas do *you* have for staging this speech?

a One member of your group takes the role of director; the other members each choose one of the three sections listed above and read the lines aloud one after the other. Think about how you might create contrasts between voice, gesture and body language as you swap over from section to section.

b What particular words or images give you clues about how you might play the part? Compile a list in your groups.

1 entertain 享受
2 determinèd 决心
3 inductions 谋划
4 libels 流言蜚语
5 subtle 狡猾
6 false 不忠
7 mewed up 囚禁
8 About a prophecy 由于一个预言
9 Dive 下潜，下来，下去
10 guarded 被押解
11 Tend'ring 照顾，挂念
12 conduct 递解；护卫
13 the Tower 伦敦塔（既是王室住所，又是国家监狱）
14 Alack 天啊
15 belike 也许
16 protest 说实话
17 hearkens 倾听
18 cross-row 字母表
19 issue 子嗣
20 toys 奇想
21 commit 监禁

1 Dramatic irony （戏剧反讽）(in threes)

Richard has just told the audience how he is plotting to destroy his brother George, the Duke of Clarence, so almost all of what Richard says to Clarence's face is filled with **dramatic irony** (when the audience knows more than a character on stage, see p. 251). Richard pretends to be innocent, but he already knows the answers to the questions he asks.

- Two members of the group take the parts of Richard and Clarence and read through the script opposite from line 43. The third person voices Richard's hidden thoughts at appropriate points. For example, when Richard says, 'Brother, good day', does he mean this? What is he really thinking? Practise reading the script in this way up to line 61, then share your presentation with the rest of the class.

And therefore, since I cannot prove a lover
To entertain[1] these fair well-spoken days,
I am determinèd[2] to prove a villain   30
And hate the idle pleasures of these days.
Plots have I laid, inductions[3] dangerous,
By drunken prophecies, libels[4], and dreams
To set my brother Clarence and the king
In deadly hate the one against the other.   35
And if King Edward be as true and just
As I am subtle[5], false[6], and treacherous,
This day should Clarence closely be mewed up[7]
About a prophecy[8] which says that 'G'
Of Edward's heirs the murderer shall be.   40
Dive[9], thoughts, down to my soul, here Clarence comes.

    Enter CLARENCE *and* BRAKENBURY, *guarded*[10]

Brother, good day. What means this armèd guard
That waits upon your grace?
CLARENCE   His majesty,
Tend'ring[11] my person's safety, hath appointed
This conduct[12] to convey me to the Tower[13].   45
RICHARD Upon what cause?
CLARENCE   Because my name is George.
RICHARD Alack[14], my lord, that fault is none of yours.
He should for that commit your godfathers.
Oh, belike[15] his majesty hath some intent
That you should be new christened in the Tower.   50
But what's the matter, Clarence? May I know?
CLARENCE Yea, Richard, when I know, but I protest[16]
As yet I do not. But as I can learn,
He hearkens[17] after prophecies and dreams,
And from the cross-row[18] plucks the letter 'G',   55
And says a wizard told him that by 'G'
His issue[19] disinherited should be.
And for my name of George begins with 'G',
It follows in his thought that I am he.
These, as I learn, and suchlike toys[20] as these   60
Hath moved his highness to commit[21] me now.

Richard claims that Queen Elizabeth has caused King Edward to imprison Clarence, and that she and Jane Shore have become powers behind the throne. Brakenbury's unease is dismissed with innuendo and sexual puns.

 剧情简介：理查称是王后伊丽莎白让爱德华国王将克莱润下狱的，并且她和姬嫣·肖已经成为左右王权的力量。布莱肯布瑞的不自在被理查用暗示和淫秽的双关语打消了。

Themes 主题分析

Richard's attitude to women

Richard comments that 'men are ruled by women' (line 62). He blames Queen Elizabeth and Clarence blames King Edward's mistress, Jane Shore, for having Clarence sent to the Tower. In line 64, Richard sneeringly refers to Queen Elizabeth as 'My lady Grey' because before her marriage to Edward in 1464 she was the widow of Sir Thomas Grey. Elizabeth used her position as Queen to gain power and influence for her large family, the Woodvilles, and in so doing aroused much jealousy. In the course of the play, Richard frequently refers to both Jane Shore and Elizabeth as sources of trouble, as if they pose a threat to him in his pursuit of power.

- Look through the script opposite and make a list of all the words Richard uses that are insulting to women. As you work through the play, keep in mind Richard's attitude to women and consider the true extent of women's power and influence in this society.

1 Making Brakenbury feel inferior (自卑)? (in threes)

Brakenbury (the courtier who is taking Clarence to the Tower) addresses Richard and Clarence as 'your graces' (line 84) because they are royal dukes, but Richard calls him 'man' (指仆人) (line 90) and makes jokes at Brakenbury's expense. How might you show their different status on stage?

a Number each group member 1 to 3, where 1 is someone of very high status, 2 is someone of middle status and 3 is someone of low status. Experiment with how these people relate to one another:

- How do you look at one another?
- How do you say hello to one another?
- How do you sit down, walk around and so on?

b Take Richard's line 90 ('We speak no treason, man') and freeze the action in role as Richard, Clarence and Brakenbury. Show your tableau to the rest of the class. Can they guess who is who, using clues from positioning, body language and facial expressions?

c Compile a list of reasons why Richard might enjoy trying to make Brakenbury feel inferior. Do you think he succeeds?

1 worship 德高望重
2 kindred 亲戚
3 night-walking heralds 夜间行走的传令官
4 trudge betwixt 奔波于……之间 (betwixt = between)
5 suppliant 乞求者
6 delivery 释放
7 her deity 她的神祇 (指姬嫣·肖的邪恶精灵)
8 Lord Chamberlain 内廷大臣 (即海斯廷 [Hastings])
9 livery 官服 (指仆人的制服)
10 o'er-worn 年老色衰
11 widow (指伊丽莎白王后)
12 dubbed 册封
13 beseech your graces 恳请大人们 (beseech: 恳求，恳请)
14 straitly given in charge 严词责令
15 conference 谈话
16 Of what degree soever 无论什么级别
17 please your worship 如果阁下您愿意
18 partake of 分享
19 Well struck in years 上岁数
20 bonny 美丽
21 passing pleasing tongue 嘴巴格外甜
22 nought = nothing (nought与naught读音相同, naught = naughtiness [坏事])
23 doth naught 做坏事

King Richard III Act 1 Scene 1
理查三世

RICHARD	Why, this it is when men are ruled by women.
	'Tis not the king that sends you to the Tower.
	My lady Grey, his wife, Clarence, 'tis she
	That tempts him to this harsh extremity.
	Was it not she and that good man of worship[1],
	Anthony Woodville, her brother there,
	That made him send Lord Hastings to the Tower,
	From whence this present day he is delivered?
	We are not safe, Clarence, we are not safe.
CLARENCE	By heaven, I think there is no man secure
	But the queen's kindred[2] and night-walking heralds[3]
	That trudge betwixt[4] the king and Mistress Shore.
	Heard you not what an humble suppliant[5]
	Lord Hastings was for her delivery[6]?
RICHARD	Humbly complaining to her deity[7]
	Got my Lord Chamberlain[8] his liberty.
	I'll tell you what, I think it is our way,
	If we will keep in favour with the king,
	To be her men and wear her livery[9].
	The jealous, o'er-worn[10] widow[11] and herself,
	Since that our brother dubbed[12] them gentlewomen,
	Are mighty gossips in our monarchy.
BRAKENBURY	I beseech your graces[13] both to pardon me;
	His majesty hath straitly given in charge[14]
	That no man shall have private conference[15],
	Of what degree soever[16], with your brother.
RICHARD	Even so. And please your worship[17], Brakenbury,
	You may partake of[18] any thing we say.
	We speak no treason, man. We say the king
	Is wise and virtuous, and his noble queen
	Well struck in years[19], fair, and not jealous.
	We say that Shore's wife hath a pretty foot,
	A cherry lip, a bonny[20] eye, a passing pleasing tongue[21],
	And that the queen's kindred are made gentlefolks.
	How say you, sir? Can you deny all this?
BRAKENBURY	With this, my lord, myself have nought[22] to do.
RICHARD	Naught to do with Mistress Shore? I tell thee, fellow,
	He that doth naught[23] with her (excepting one)
	Were best to do it secretly alone.

65

70

75

80

85

90

95

100

Richard promises to do any service he can to ensure Clarence's release. Alone on stage, Richard reveals that he really seeks Clarence's death. Hastings swears vengeance on those who caused his imprisonment.

剧情简介：理查许诺尽全力救出克莱润。然而当他独自留在台上时，他又透露自己其实想让克莱润死掉。海斯廷发誓要向那些让他入狱的人复仇。

1 Saying one thing but meaning another (in pairs)

A major feature of Richard's language is that his words frequently have double meanings. Listeners hear one thing, but he means something else. Most of what he says to Clarence has a meaning that Clarence does not perceive. For example, when Richard says 'Brother, farewell', Clarence probably hears a friendly voice, but Richard may mean 'Goodbye for ever because you'll soon be dead'.

- As one person slowly speaks lines 107–16, pausing frequently, the other person says in each pause what Richard probably means.

Characters 人物分析

Who's who? (in pairs)

- Draw up a list of who's who in the play so far and show their relationships to one another. Use the list of characters on pages 4–5 and devise symbols, or a colour code, to show status and relationships between the people who have appeared so far in the scene.
- Where would you fit Lord Hastings? Hastings is a faithful supporter of the House of York, but he is much opposed to Queen Elizabeth and the rest of the Woodville family. Hastings's influence weakened during the illness of his patron King Edward, and that loss of power may have led to his imprisonment. Hastings was Jane Shore's lover, however, and she may have used her influence with the King to secure his early release from prison.

Language in the play 剧中语言

Birds of prey (by yourself)

Throughout the play, the imagery of birds and animals is often used to describe Richard.

a Who is Hastings referring to when he talks of 'the eagles' (line 133) and 'kites and buzzards' (鸢和秃鹰，喻指贪婪卑鄙的小人) (line 134)?

b Write a paragraph describing Shakespeare's use of animal imagery in this part of the play and its effect on characterisation and atmosphere. Remember to refer to the script in detail and to use embedded quotations.

1 withal 还有
2 Forbear 停止，克制
3 abjects 不受待见的人（理查用这个词来对应subject）
4 widow （依然指伊丽莎白王后，理查又在嘲讽她）
5 enfranchise 使……自由
6 lie for you 替您坐牢
7 perforce 别无选择
    （patience perforce为谚语，意为"无可救药"）
8 Exeunt （剧本中的说明，两个以上演员）退场，下场
9 new-delivered 刚获释的
10 brooked 熬过
11 to give them thanks 答谢他们（这里指报复）
12 cause of my imprisonment （海斯廷暗指伍德威尔家族）

King Richard III Act 1 Scene 1
理查三世

BRAKENBURY	What one, my lord?	
RICHARD	Her husband, knave. Wouldst thou betray me?	
BRAKENBURY	I do beseech your grace to pardon me, and withal[1]	
	Forbear[2] your conference with the noble duke.	
CLARENCE	We know thy charge, Brakenbury, and will obey.	105
RICHARD	We are the queen's abjects[3] and must obey.	
	Brother, farewell. I will unto the king,	
	And whatsoe'er you will employ me in,	
	Were it to call King Edward's widow[4] 'sister',	
	I will perform it to enfranchise[5] you.	110
	Meantime, this deep disgrace in brotherhood	
	Touches me deeper than you can imagine.	
CLARENCE	I know it pleaseth neither of us well.	
RICHARD	Well, your imprisonment shall not be long.	
	I will deliver you or else lie for you[6].	115
	Meantime, have patience.	
CLARENCE	I must perforce[7]. Farewell.	

Exeunt[8] Clarence[, Brakenbury, and guards]

RICHARD	Go, tread the path that thou shalt ne'er return.	
	Simple, plain Clarence, I do love thee so	
	That I will shortly send thy soul to heaven,	120
	If heaven will take the present at our hands.	
	But who comes here? The new-delivered[9] Hastings?	

Enter LORD HASTINGS

HASTINGS	Good time of day unto my gracious lord.	
RICHARD	As much unto my good Lord Chamberlain.	
	Well are you welcome to this open air.	125
	How hath your lordship brooked[10] imprisonment?	
HASTINGS	With patience, noble lord, as prisoners must.	
	But I shall live, my lord, to give them thanks[11]	
	That were the cause of my imprisonment[12].	
RICHARD	No doubt, no doubt, and so shall Clarence too,	130
	For they that were your enemies are his	
	And have prevailed as much on him as you.	
HASTINGS	More pity that the eagles should be mewed	
	While kites and buzzards play at liberty.	
RICHARD	What news abroad?	135

13

Hastings says Edward is near to death. Richard blames the King's lifestyle. Alone on stage, Richard hopes that Edward will not die until Clarence has been executed. He reveals his plan to marry Anne.

剧情简介：海斯廷透露爱德华将不久于人世。理查将这归罪于国王的生活方式。独自一人在戏台上时，理查表示希望国王在克莱润被处决后再死。他还透露了自己要迎娶安娜的计划。

1 What is King Edward like?

On every page of the play so far, there have been clues to King Edward's character. 'Oh, he hath kept an evil diet long' (line 140) suggests that for a long time Edward has lived wildly.

- Look back at what Richard, Clarence and Hastings have said about Edward so far in Scene 1. Compile a list of between six and ten words that sum up your impression of the King.

Characters 人物分析

Richard's revelations (in pairs)

The soliloquy that ends this scene (lines 146–63) offers many opportunities to explore Richard's wicked revelations through a range of dramatic choices regarding changes in voice inflection, emphasis, tone, pitch, pause and gesture.

a Sometimes actors play the lines with a lot of humour. In line 153, 'bustle' (be busy) often gains a laugh as it catches the obvious roguishness (流氓性) of Richard's character. Take turns to speak the lines with actions that might be used to provoke laughter.

b Sometimes actors play the lines with a sense of outrageous evil. Lines 149–58, in particular, provoke a response in audiences. Take turns to speak the lines in a way that will most shock the audience.

c In role as an actor, write notes about how you intend to speak this soliloquy and what aspects of Richard's character you want to portray at each line or two.

1 **fear him** 替他的性命担忧
2 **by Saint John** 向圣约翰发誓
3 **diet** 饮食起居
4 **packed with post-horse** 立马打发
5 **steeled** 强化
6 **deep** 高深莫测
7 **bustle** 自由自在
8 **Warwick's youngest daughter** （指安娜）
9 **What though** = What if
10 **her father** 她公公（剧中的亨利六世）
11 **wench** 妞儿
12 **secret close intent** 隐秘企图
13 **run … market** 操之过急

King Richard III Act 1 Scene 1
理查三世

HASTINGS	No news so bad abroad as this at home:	
	The king is sickly, weak, and melancholy,	
	And his physicians fear him[1] mightily.	
RICHARD	Now by Saint John[2], that news is bad indeed.	
	Oh, he hath kept an evil diet[3] long	140
	And over-much consumed his royal person.	
	'Tis very grievous to be thought upon.	
	Where is he, in his bed?	
HASTINGS	He is.	
RICHARD	Go you before, and I will follow you.	145

Exit Hastings

He cannot live, I hope, and must not die
Till George be packed with post-horse[4] up to heaven.
I'll in to urge his hatred more to Clarence
With lies well steeled[5] with weighty arguments,
And if I fail not in my deep[6] intent,   150
Clarence hath not another day to live:
Which done, God take King Edward to his mercy
And leave the world for me to bustle[7] in!
For then I'll marry Warwick's youngest daughter[8].
What though[9] I killed her husband and her father[10]?   155
The readiest way to make the wench[11] amends
Is to become her husband and her father,
The which will I, not all so much for love
As for another secret close intent[12]
By marrying her which I must reach unto.   160
But yet I run before my horse to market[13].
Clarence still breathes, Edward still lives and reigns;
When they are gone, then must I count my gains.   *Exit*

Lady Anne mourns over the corpse of Henry VI. She curses Richard for killing Henry and her husband, Prince Edward, Henry's son.

 剧情简介：安娜王妃对着亨利六世的遗体哀悼。她诅咒理查不得好死，因为他杀害了亨利和亨利的儿子，即她的丈夫爱德华王子。

Stagecraft 导演技巧

'The corpse of KING HENRY VI is carried in'

The dead body of the former King is on stage throughout Scene 2 as a dramatic reminder of Anne's grief and loss. Imagine you are the stage designer. How do you deal with the body on stage? Compile notes and/or sketches in your Director's Journal. Remember that the body:

- is royal (but this is not a state funeral)
- is of the Lancastrian dynasty (兰开斯特王朝)
- has been on view for some time as Anne grieves over it
- has to be transported across the stage.

Language in the play 剧中语言

Anne's grief and anger (in pairs)

a Together, read Anne's speech and pick out one key word or short phrase per line. Keeping these key words or phrases in their original order, devise a dramatic presentation of your shortened script. Experiment with different drama strategies, such as tone of voice, choral speech, mime (哑剧), movement or tableaux. Remember, you cannot add any other words. Share your performances with the rest of the class. Which one is the most effective and why?

b As an extension to this activity, you could choose some background music that you feel captures the mood and tone of the speech. Be prepared to explain why you think it is suitable.

Write about it 写作练习

Curses

During the course of the play, several prophecies and curses are made – some of which come true in bitterly ironic ways. In lines 14–28, Anne utters a series of vengeful curses against the man who murdered her husband and his father.

- Write two paragraphs summarising Anne's curses and commenting on the language she uses. For example, think about the kinds of creatures she refers to and which words she repeats in the course of her speech.

1 HALBERDS 执戟尉
2 shrouded 装殓
3 hearse 棺椁
4 obsequiously 按吊唁的礼仪
5 lament 哀悼，悲伤
6 Th'untimely = The untimely (过早的)
7 key-cold 冰凉
8 figure 身躯
9 blood 血脉
10 Be it = Let it be
11 invocate 请出
12 the selfsame 那同一个
13 Lo = Look
14 windows 伤口
15 let forth 释放
16 helpless balm 无助的香脂，这里指眼泪（下葬前通常将尸体加香料做防腐处理）
17 holes 伤口
18 More direful hap betide 更可怕的命运落在……身上 (hap = happen)
19 wretch 卑鄙小人
20 creeping venomed thing 有毒的爬虫
21 abortive 夭折
22 Prodigious 畸形
23 thee (指亨利六世)
24 Chertsey 切特西（伦敦西南一城，城中有一修道院）
25 Paul's 圣保罗大教堂（前任国王没有得到在该教堂举行的国葬仪式）
26 interrèd 埋葬
27 weary of 倦于……

Act 1 Scene 2
Near the Tower of London

The corpse of KING HENRY VI *is carried in accompanied by* LADY ANNE, HALBERDS[1], TRESSEL, BERKELEY *and other gentlemen*

ANNE   Set down, set down your honourable load,
       If honour may be shrouded[2] in a hearse[3],
       Whilst I awhile obsequiously[4] lament[5]
       Th'untimely[6] fall of virtuous Lancaster.
       Poor key-cold[7] figure[8] of a holy king,   5
       Pale ashes of the house of Lancaster,
       Thou bloodless remnant of that royal blood[9],
       Be it[10] lawful that I invocate[11] thy ghost
       To hear the lamentations of poor Anne,
       Wife to thy Edward, to thy slaughtered son,   10
       Stabbed by the selfsame[12] hand that made these wounds.
       Lo[13], in these windows[14] that let forth[15] thy life,
       I pour the helpless balm[16] of my poor eyes.
       Oh, cursèd be the hand that made these holes[17],
       Cursed the heart that had the heart to do it,   15
       Cursed the blood that let this blood from hence.
       More direful hap betide[18] that hated wretch[19]
       That makes us wretched by the death of thee
       Than I can wish to wolves, to spiders, toads,
       Or any creeping venomed thing[20] that lives.   20
       If ever he have child, abortive[21] be it,
       Prodigious[22], and untimely brought to light,
       Whose ugly and unnatural aspèct
       May fright the hopeful mother at the view,
       And that be heir to his unhappiness.   25
       If ever he have wife, let her be made
       More miserable by the death of him
       Than I am made by my young lord and thee[23].
       Come now towards Chertsey[24] with your holy load,
       Taken from Paul's[25] to be interrèd[26] there.   30
       And still as you are weary of[27] this weight,
       Rest you while I lament King Henry's corpse.

Richard orders the guards to set down the coffin. He threatens violence if they disobey him. Anne accuses Richard of being a devil. Henry's wounds open and begin to bleed. Anne calls for Richard's death.

 剧情简介：理查命令护卫们放下棺材。他以暴力威胁违抗他命令的人。安娜指责理查的恶魔行径。亨利伤口裂开，开始流血。安娜诅咒理查遭报应。

Stagecraft 导演技巧

Power-play (in large groups)

Richard's entrance (入场，上场) changes the mood of the scene and creates a moment of dramatic tension between Richard, Anne and the men accompanying her.

a Create a series of three tableaux using the following lines:
- 'Stay, you that bear the corpse' (line 33)
- 'Unmannered dog, stand thou when I command' (line 39)
- 'What, do you tremble? Are you all afraid?' (line 43)

Think about the ways in which various characters react to these lines – what gestures might the speaker make? Who looks at whom and in what way? Where is each character positioned – at a distance or closer together? Place a line of chairs to denote where the corpse is stationed at each line and consider what difference it makes if Anne is accompanied by three or four men, or ten.

b Share your tableaux with the class. Class members can take it in turn to tap various characters on the shoulder and ask them to voice their thoughts at this precise moment.

c Discuss which tableau suggests the highest moment of dramatic tension and why. Then write a note in your Director's Journal explaining how you would stage this part of the scene.

1 conjures up 招来
2 Unmannered 没有教养，没有礼貌
3 halberd 戟
4 to my foot 到地上
5 spurn 踩
6 Avaunt 滚（通常用于驱鬼）
7 minister 代理人
8 but 只有
9 curst 恶毒；凶狠
10 hence 走开
11 exclaims 呐喊
12 heinous 邪恶
13 Henry's … afresh 亨利结痂的伤口又开始流血了（人们当时相信尸体会在凶手出现时再次流血）
14 exhales 吸出
15 deluge 洪流
16 mad'st 创造
17 quick 活生生
18 charity 基督教教义

Characters 人物分析

Anne's view of Richard

Read through the script opposite, paying particular attention to all the different words Anne uses to describe Richard. List Anne's descriptions in a table similar to the one below, and then consider what impression this gives of Richard. Add to this table as you continue working through Scene 2.

Description	Line	Impression of Richard
'fiend' (恶魔)	34	He's evil
'devil'	45	He's a creature from hell

18

Enter RICHARD DUKE OF GLOUCESTER

RICHARD	Stay, you that bear the corpse, and set it down.
ANNE	What black magician conjures up¹ this fiend
	To stop devoted charitable deeds?
RICHARD	Villains, set down the corpse, or by Saint Paul,
	I'll make a corpse of him that disobeys.
GENTLEMAN	My lord, stand back and let the coffin pass.
RICHARD	Unmannered² dog, stand thou when I command.
	Advance thy halberd³ higher than my breast,
	Or by Saint Paul, I'll strike thee to my foot⁴
	And spurn⁵ upon thee, beggar, for thy boldness.
ANNE	What, do you tremble? Are you all afraid?
	Alas, I blame you not, for you are mortal,
	And mortal eyes cannot endure the devil.
	Avaunt⁶, thou dreadful minister⁷ of hell.
	Thou hadst but⁸ power over his mortal body;
	His soul thou canst not have. Therefore be gone.
RICHARD	Sweet saint, for charity, be not so curst⁹.
ANNE	Foul devil, for God's sake hence¹⁰, and trouble us not,
	For thou hast made the happy earth thy hell,
	Filled it with cursing cries and deep exclaims¹¹.
	If thou delight to view thy heinous¹² deeds,
	Behold this pattern of thy butcheries.
	O gentlemen, see, see, dead Henry's wounds
	Open their còngealed mouths and bleed afresh¹³.
	Blush, blush, thou lump of foul deformity,
	For 'tis thy presence that exhales¹⁴ this blood
	From cold and empty veins where no blood dwells.
	Thy deeds inhuman and unnatural
	Provokes this deluge¹⁵ most unnatural.
	O God, which this blood mad'st¹⁶, revenge his death.
	O earth, which this blood drink'st, revenge his death.
	Either heav'n with lightning strike the murd'rer dead,
	Or earth gape open wide and eat him quick¹⁷,
	As thou dost swallow up this good king's blood,
	Which his hell-governed arm hath butcherèd.
RICHARD	Lady, you know no rules of charity¹⁸,
	Which renders good for bad, blessings for curses.

Anne continues to curse Richard, accusing him of murder. He asks for an opportunity to defend himself. He denies killing her husband but admits trying to kill Queen Margaret and killing King Henry.

剧情简介：安娜继续诅咒理查，指控他犯了谋杀罪。理查恳求给他一个机会为自己辩护。他否认杀死了安娜的丈夫，但是承认企图谋杀玛格蕊王后并且杀死了亨利王。

Language in the play 剧中语言

Tennis-match language (in pairs, then whole class)

In lines 68–118, Anne's and Richard's words move rhythmically back and forth like the ball in a tennis rally. The technical term for this rapid alternating exchange of lines is **stichomythia** (交互对白) (see p. 249). The same words are sometimes repeated, or words with opposite meanings are flung back at the first speaker.

a Draw two columns on a sheet of paper, one headed 'Anne', the other headed 'Richard'. Collect examples of matched repetitions or contrasts. Three have been given below – how many more can you find?

Anne	Richard
'No beast so fierce but knows some touch of pity' (line 71)	'But I know none, and therefore am no beast' (line 72)
'devils tell the truth' (73)	'angels are so angry' (line 74)
'Vouchsafe, diffused infection of man' (line 78)	'Vouchsafe, divine perfection of a woman' (line 75)

b Collate (对照；整理) a whole-class version of this table. Divide the class into two lines (A and B), facing each other as if opponents: line A is Anne, line B is Richard. The line taking the role of Anne starts by saying together 'No beast so fierce …'. Richard's line then answers it. Experiment with different ways of saying the lines – for example, whispered, shouted, hissed, angrily hurled, calmly stated and so on. Try changing the pace, just as in a real tennis rally, and see how your opponent reacts.

c As a class, discuss which style of delivery works best and why.

1 Vouchsafe 准许
2 supposèd 子虚乌有的
3 leave 允许
4 circumstance 事实情况
5 acquit 为……开脱
6 diffused 广为流传（像传染病一样）
7 èxcuse current 说得通的借口
8 slew 杀死
9 Nay = No
10 Edward （即理查的哥哥）
11 falchion （中世纪的）弯刀
12 smoking in his blood 在他的血泊里冒着热气
13 bend 刺向
14 sland'rous 恶意中伤
15 aught = anything
16 ye = you （您）
17 hedgehog 刺儿头（对理查的辱骂）

King Richard III Act 1 Scene 2
理查三世

ANNE	Villain, thou know'st nor law of God nor man.	70
	No beast so fierce but knows some touch of pity.	
RICHARD	But I know none, and therefore am no beast.	
ANNE	Oh, wonderful, when devils tell the truth!	
RICHARD	More wonderful, when angels are so angry.	
	Vouchsafe[1], divine perfection of a woman,	75
	Of these supposèd[2] crimes to give me leave[3]	
	By circumstance[4] but to acquit[5] myself.	
ANNE	Vouchsafe, diffused[6] infection of man,	
	Of these known evils but to give me leave	
	By circumstance to curse thy cursèd self.	80
RICHARD	Fairer than tongue can name thee, let me have	
	Some patient leisure to excuse myself.	
ANNE	Fouler than heart can think thee, thou canst make	
	No èxcuse current[7] but to hang thyself.	
RICHARD	By such despair I should accuse myself.	85
ANNE	And by despairing shalt thou stand excused	
	For doing worthy vengeance on thyself,	
	That didst unworthy slaughter upon others.	
RICHARD	Say that I slew[8] them not.	
ANNE	Then say they were not slain.	90
	But dead they are, and, devilish slave, by thee.	
RICHARD	I did not kill your husband.	
ANNE	Why, then he is alive.	
RICHARD	Nay[9], he is dead, and slain by Edward's[10] hands.	
ANNE	In thy foul throat thou liest. Queen Margaret saw	95
	Thy murd'rous falchion[11] smoking in his blood[12],	
	The which thou once didst bend[13] against her breast,	
	But that thy brothers beat aside the point.	
RICHARD	I was provokèd by her sland'rous[14] tongue,	
	That laid their guilt upon my guiltless shoulders.	100
ANNE	Thou wast provokèd by thy bloody mind,	
	That never dream'st on aught[15] but butcheries.	
	Didst thou not kill this king?	
RICHARD	I grant ye[16].	
ANNE	Dost grant me, hedgehog[17]? Then God grant me too	105
	Thou mayst be damnèd for that wicked deed.	
	Oh, he was gentle, mild, and virtuous.	

Anne wishes Richard in hell but he offers himself as her new husband. He claims that her beauty caused him to kill. She curses her beauty and him, hoping for revenge.

剧情简介：安娜一心希望理查下地狱，但理查却提出要做她的新任丈夫，声称是她的美貌害得他大开杀戒。她诅咒他和自己的美貌，并想要复仇。

1 An unlikely wooing scene (in pairs)

Act 1 Scene 2 is often referred to as 'the wooing scene' because this is where Richard attempts to propose marriage to Anne.

- Read through the whole script opposite. Then list all the ways that this scene differs from conventional 'wooing scenes' in which a lover talks of marriage. In particular, consider such scenes in any other Shakespeare plays you are familiar with. Think about setting and context, as well as the words spoken by the couple.

2 'Your bedchamber' (in pairs)

Look again at Richard's line 115, where he tells Anne he wants to share her bed. On stage this can be a truly shocking moment. Think carefully about what Anne's reaction might be to Richard's advances. For example, might she be:

- visibly repulsed (憎恶)
- wrong-footed (乱了阵脚) and confused
- angry and confident
- fearful and intimidated
- sexually attracted to Richard (despite not liking him)?

a Try different ways of acting out this part of the scene (from line 109 up to Richard's 'I know so' at line 119).

b It is easy to forget that, according to the stage directions, Richard's proposition takes place in public, with pall bearers (抬棺人), soldiers and others all looking on. Do you think that makes it more or less shocking?

▼ How would you interpret this moment between Anne and Richard?

1 holp = helped
2 thither = there
3 Ill rest betide 愿……噩梦连连
4 timeless 过早的
5 Thou … effect 你就是罪魁祸首
6 To … world 杀尽天下人
7 homicide 杀人凶手
8 rend 撕破
9 wrack 毁灭
10 blemish 损害
11 Black … life 你的白天被黑夜覆盖，你的生命也尽是死亡（注意第136行的两处对比：黑夜/白天；死亡/生命）
12 bereft 掠夺，抢劫

King Richard III Act 1 Scene 2
理查三世

RICHARD	The better for the king of heaven that hath him.	
ANNE	He is in heaven, where thou shalt never come.	
RICHARD	Let him thank me, that holp[1] to send him thither[2],	110
	For he was fitter for that place than earth.	
ANNE	And thou unfit for any place but hell.	
RICHARD	Yes, one place else, if you will hear me name it.	
ANNE	Some dungeon.	
RICHARD	Your bedchamber.	115
ANNE	Ill rest betide[3] the chamber where thou liest.	
RICHARD	So will it, madam, till I lie with you.	
ANNE	I hope so.	
RICHARD	I know so. But gentle Lady Anne,	
	To leave this keen encounter of our wits	120
	And fall something into a slower method,	
	Is not the causer of the timeless[4] deaths	
	Of these Plantagenets, Henry and Edward,	
	As blameful as the executioner?	
ANNE	Thou wast the cause and most accursed effect[5].	125
RICHARD	Your beauty was the cause of that effect:	
	Your beauty, that did haunt me in my sleep	
	To undertake the death of all the world[6],	
	So I might live one hour in your sweet bosom.	
ANNE	If I thought that, I tell thee, homicide[7],	130
	These nails should rend[8] that beauty from my cheeks.	
RICHARD	These eyes could not endure that beauty's wrack[9].	
	You should not blemish[10] it if I stood by.	
	As all the world is cheerèd by the sun,	
	So I by that. It is my day, my life.	135
ANNE	Black night o'ershade thy day, and death thy life[11].	
RICHARD	Curse not thyself, fair creature; thou art both.	
ANNE	I would I were, to be revenged on thee.	
RICHARD	It is a quarrel most unnatural	
	To be revenged on him that loveth thee.	140
ANNE	It is a quarrel just and reasonable	
	To be revenged on him that killed my husband.	
RICHARD	He that bereft[12] thee, lady, of thy husband	
	Did it to help thee to a better husband.	
ANNE	His better doth not breathe upon the earth.	145

Richard tells Anne that he could love her better than Edward, her former husband. He claims that Anne has the power to make him weep when other griefs leave him unmoved. He continues to woo her.

剧情简介：理查承诺安娜，说他会比她的前夫爱德华更爱她。他声称别的伤心事他都能无动于衷，但安娜却有本领让他流泪。理查继续追求安娜。

1 Why Plantagenet?

Plantagenet was the family name of the kings of England between 1154 and 1485. Both the houses of York and Lancaster, which fought in the Wars of the Roses, were Plantagenets. This is the second time in this scene that Richard has used his family name (the first is in line 123).

- Why do you think he uses the name Plantagenet again here to refer to himself?

2 'Why dost thou spit at me?' (in small groups)

Richard's 'Here' (line 149) seems to be the trigger for Anne's strong reaction. Is it this word alone that so angers Anne, or are there other reasons for her contemptuous (轻蔑的) response?

a Carefully read the three or four lines leading up to Anne's reaction and discuss what you think they mean.

b What gesture do you think Richard makes as he says 'Here'? Try out a few and see which you think works best.

c Pool your ideas on what the action of spitting at someone means and how this might vary in different cultures. How might some of the items on your list help you to advise Anne how to play her line 150? Add your notes to your Director's Journal.

3 Richard's audacity (厚颜无耻)

Richard's quick-witted wordplay continues. His lines 156–71 turn Anne's image of the eyes of a monster into his own eyes, which weep for Anne's beauty but are unable to weep at tragic events such as the death of Rutland and of his own father. (Rutland was Richard's younger brother, murdered in 1470.)

- Look again at lines 150–9, which show how Richard reverses Anne's intended insults ('poison', 'infect', 'dead', 'die', 'kill' and 'eyes') in his audacious (大胆的) attempt to win her affection. Make two lists – one of Anne's insults and another of Richard's clever answers.

1	mortal	致命的
2	basilisks	巴西利斯（一种目光能杀人的蛇怪）
3	a living death	活受罪，半死不活
4	aspècts	样子
5	Rutland	拉特兰（理查的亡弟）
6	warlike	骁勇
7	bedashed	被浸湿
8	sued to	求助于
9	smoothing	奉承
10	proposed	（作为……）付给
11	sues	乞求；为……辩护

King Richard III Act 1 Scene 2
理查三世

RICHARD	He lives that loves thee better than he could.
ANNE	Name him.
RICHARD	Plantagenet.
ANNE	Why, that was he.
RICHARD	The selfsame name, but one of better nature.
ANNE	Where is he?
RICHARD	Here.

[She] spits at him

                Why dost thou spit at me?

ANNE	Would it were mortal[1] poison for thy sake.	150
RICHARD	Never came poison from so sweet a place.	
ANNE	Never hung poison on a fouler toad.	
	Out of my sight. Thou dost infect mine eyes.	
RICHARD	Thine eyes, sweet lady, have infected mine.	
ANNE	Would they were basilisks'[2], to strike thee dead.	155
RICHARD	I would they were, that I might die at once,	
	For now they kill me with a living death[3].	
	Those eyes of thine from mine have drawn salt tears,	
	Shamed their aspècts[4] with store of childish drops.	
	These eyes, which never shed remorseful tear,	160
	No, when my father York and Edward wept	
	To hear the piteous moan that Rutland[5] made	
	When black-faced Clifford shook his sword at him,	
	Nor when thy warlike[6] father, like a child,	
	Told the sad story of my father's death	165
	And twenty times made pause to sob and weep,	
	That all the standers-by had wet their cheeks	
	Like trees bedashed[7] with rain. In that sad time	
	My manly eyes did scorn an humble tear.	
	And what these sorrows could not thence exhale	170
	Thy beauty hath, and made them blind with weeping.	
	I never sued to[8] friend nor enemy.	
	My tongue could never learn sweet smoothing[9] word.	
	But now thy beauty is proposed[10] my fee,	
	My proud heart sues[11] and prompts my tongue to speak.	175

She looks scornfully at him

          Teach not thy lip such scorn, for it was made
          For kissing, lady, not for such contempt.

25

Richard offers Anne the opportunity to stab him. He admits he killed King Henry and Prince Edward. Anne refuses to use the dagger, so Richard offers to kill himself. He places his ring on Anne's finger.

  剧情简介： 理查给安娜机会刺死他。他承认杀害了亨利王和爱德华王子。安娜拒绝接过匕首，于是理查提出自杀。他把自己的戒指戴在了安娜的手指上。

1 Anne seduced? (in pairs)

Richard's delight in clever wordplay is revealed through the return to the language of stichomythia (see p. 20), but Anne's replies now seem less confident than earlier, and, unlike at the beginning of the scene, she is no longer abusive.

a Read lines 197–205 aloud, experimenting with the way Richard and Anne speak. For instance, is Anne:

- angry
- calmly confident
- scared or nervous
- humouring (迁就) Richard just to get rid of him
- genuinely seduced by Richard's charms
- confused?

b Consider a range of ways to read Richard's part, then discuss which reading works best and why.

c Why do you think Anne does not take the opportunity to kill Richard?

▼ Choose a line from the script opposite that you think would work as a caption (说明文字) for this image.

1	*lays his breast open*	解开衬衣露出胸膛
2	*offers at*	对准
3	*dispatch*	动手
4	*falls* = drops	
5	*dissembler*	虚伪小人
6	*bid*	吩咐
7	*àccessary*	帮凶
8	*figured*	表现
9	*put up*	收起
10	Vouchsafe	答应
11	Look how	正如
12	encompasseth	套住

If thy revengeful heart cannot forgive,
Lo, here I lend thee this sharp-pointed sword,
Which if thou please to hide in this true breast 180
And let the soul forth that adoreth thee,
I lay it naked to the deadly stroke
And humbly beg the death upon my knee.
  He lays his breast open[1][;] *she offers at*[2] *with his sword*
Nay, do not pause, for I did kill King Henry,
But 'twas thy beauty that provokèd me. 185
Nay, now dispatch[3]; 'twas I that stabbed young Edward,
But 'twas thy heavenly face that set me on.
    She falls[4] *the sword*
Take up the sword again, or take up me.

ANNE Arise, dissembler[5]; though I wish thy death,
I will not be thy executioner. 190

RICHARD Then bid[6] me kill myself, and I will do it.

ANNE I have already.

RICHARD   That was in thy rage.
Speak it again, and even with the word,
This hand, which for thy love did kill thy love,
Shall for thy love kill a far truer love. 195
To both their deaths shalt thou be àccessary[7].

ANNE I would I knew thy heart.

RICHARD 'Tis figured[8] in my tongue.

ANNE I fear me both are false.

RICHARD Then never man was true. 200

ANNE Well, well, put up[9] your sword.

RICHARD Say then my peace is made.

ANNE That shalt thou know hereafter.

RICHARD But shall I live in hope?

ANNE All men, I hope, live so. 205

RICHARD Vouchsafe[10] to wear this ring.
Look how[11] my ring encompasseth[12] thy finger.
Even so thy breast encloseth my poor heart.
Wear both of them, for both of them are thine.
And if thy poor devoted servant may 210
But beg one favour at thy gracious hand,
Thou dost confirm his happiness forever.

ANNE What is it?

Richard persuades Anne to stop mourning and allow him to take charge of King Henry's funeral. He exults at his success but predicts he will soon abandon Anne.

 剧情简介：理查劝安娜节哀，并让他负责亨利王的葬礼。他对自己的成功洋洋自得，却透露很快会抛弃安娜。

1 Richard the hypocrite (伪君子) (whole class)

As soon as Anne leaves the stage, Richard drops his public mask and becomes the schemer and master planner. In his soliloquy (which continues up to line 267), Richard revels in his triumph in successfully wooing the woman whose handsome husband, Edward, he has murdered. The rhythm and energy of the lines reveal his pleasure at having carried off such a coup (成功之举).

a Form a large circle. Read Richard's soliloquy round the class, handing over to the next person at each punctuation mark. Then repeat the reading, but more quickly this time. Say aloud each phrase or line with as much energy and glee (欢喜) as you can. Add an appropriate gesture suggested by the words.

b Split into small groups and look more closely at the punctuation of this speech. Richard includes a number of questions and exclamations. What dramatic effect do these have? In your groups, suggest some ideas and then come back together as a class and share your thoughts.

Write about it 写作练习

Advice to Anne

a Imagine that after the engagement of Anne and Richard has been announced at court, a shocked friend of Anne's writes to her pointing out all the reasons why she should not marry Richard. Write the letter. You might want to include:

- the circumstances surrounding her former husband's death
- the history of their families
- the timing of the engagement
- Anne's emotional state
- Richard's appearance
- Richard's reputation.

b As an additional challenge, you could write a second letter to Anne in the guise of another friend, this time persuading her that it is a shrewd (精明) diplomatic move to marry Richard. You might want to use the same prompts as above, but draw different conclusions from that information.

1	sad designs	悼念（为亨利六世办葬礼）
2	presently	马上
3	repair to	去往
4	Crosby House	（理查在伦敦的住所）
5	interred	安葬
6	expedient	迅速
7	divers	几个
8	unknown	不便明言
9	boon	愿望
10	penitent	悔过，愧疚
11	Whitefriars	（伦敦的一座修道院，位置见本书第3页的地图）
12	humour	心情
13	bleeding witness	（指亨利六世流血的尸体）
14	by	眼前
15	bars	障碍
16	suit	追求
17	all the world to nothing	诸事不利
18	brave	高贵
19	Framed … nature	人中龙凤
20	right	真正

RICHARD	That it may please you leave these sad designs[1]
	To him that hath most cause to be a mourner	215
	And presently[2] repair to[3] Crosby House[4],
	Where, after I have solemnly interred[5]
	At Chertsey monast'ry this noble king
	And wet his grave with my repentant tears,
	I will with all expedient[6] duty see you.	220
	For divers[7] unknown[8] reasons, I beseech you,
	Grant me this boon[9].
ANNE	With all my heart, and much it joys me, too,
	To see you are become so penitent[10].
	Tressel and Berkeley, go along with me.	225
RICHARD	Bid me farewell.
ANNE	'Tis more than you deserve,
	But since you teach me how to flatter you,
	Imagine I have said farewell already.

Exeunt two with Anne

| GENTLEMAN | Towards Chertsey, noble lord? |
| RICHARD | No, to Whitefriars[11]; there attend my coming. | 230 |

Exeunt [all but Richard with the] corpse

Was ever woman in this humour[12] wooed?
Was ever woman in this humour won?
I'll have her, but I will not keep her long.
What, I that killed her husband and his father,
To take her in her heart's extremest hate, 235
With curses in her mouth, tears in her eyes,
The bleeding witness[13] of my hatred by[14],
Having God, her conscience, and these bars[15] against me,
And I no friends to back my suit[16] withal
But the plain devil and dissembling looks? 240
And yet to win her, all the world to nothing[17]!
Ha!
Hath she forgot already that brave[18] prince,
Edward, her lord, whom I some three months since
Stabbed in my angry mood at Tewkesbury? 245
A sweeter and a lovelier gentleman,
Framed in the prodigality of nature[19],
Young, valiant, wise, and (no doubt) right[20] royal,
The spacious world cannot again afford.

Richard marvels at Anne's acceptance of him, in spite of his unattractive outward appearance. Elizabeth and her relatives discuss King Edward's illness.

剧情简介: 理查惊叹于安娜竟然不顾他相貌丑陋接受了他。伊丽莎白与其近臣谈论爱德华王的病情。

1 The mask slips? (in pairs)

Imagine you are an actor and director in rehearsal. The actor playing Richard argues that in lines 250–8, Richard reveals genuine feelings of self-disgust and should speak the lines in such a way as to gain sympathy from the audience. The director disagrees, claiming that Richard is cynically mocking his own appearance, glorying in having seduced Anne in such an outrageous way. He believes that Richard should speak triumphantly.

a One person reads the lines as the actor suggests, the other as the director feels is right. Afterwards, talk together about which style seems the more successful.

b In your Director's Journal, write a paragraph outlining your ideas about the way this part of the speech should be played. Explain your conclusions, with reference to what you already know of Richard.

1 abase 垂下，低下
2 cropped 毁掉
3 Edward's moiety 爱德华的零头
4 beggarly 区区
5 denier 丹尼尔（面值十分之一便士的硬币，相当于一文钱）
6 marv'lous 令人惊叹
7 proper 英俊
8 be at charges for 买
9 entertain 雇
10 fashions 时髦衣服
11 turn yon fellow in 把那个家伙（对亨利六世尸体的蔑称）倒进
12 glass 镜子
13 accustomed 往常
14 quick 活泼
15 goodly 英俊，漂亮

Characters 人物分析

Richard in images

In the final couplet of the soliloquy, Richard picks up the contrasting images of sun and shadow once more, suggesting that he is made to cast a permanent shadow.

- Look back over Act 1 Scene 2 and pick out some of the most striking images Anne has used to describe Richard. Create a collage (拼贴画) of these images, using pictures from newspapers, magazines and the Internet.

Stagecraft 导演技巧

A change of scene

Scene 3 offers a sharp change of scene and characters. There were no lights on Shakespeare's stage, nor were there the resources to build complicated sets. New characters were indicated by means of costumes and simple props.

- If you were directing a stage version of the play with limited resources at your disposal, how would you let your audience know that the scene has shifted to the royal palace? Consider music or other sounds, costumes, simple furniture, actions and gestures. Write your ideas in your Director's Journal.

      And will she yet abase[1] her eyes on me, 250
      That cropped[2] the golden prime of this sweet prince
      And made her widow to a woeful bed?
      On me, whose all not equals Edward's moiety[3]?
      On me, that halts and am misshapen thus?
      My dukedom to a beggarly[4] denier[5], 255
      I do mistake my person all this while.
      Upon my life, she finds (although I cannot)
      Myself to be a marv'lous[6] proper[7] man.
      I'll be at charges for[8] a looking-glass
      And entertain[9] a score or two of tailors 260
      To study fashions[10] to adorn my body.
      Since I am crept in favour with myself,
      I will maintain it with some little cost.
      But first I'll turn yon fellow in[11] his grave
      And then return lamenting to my love. 265
      Shine out, fair sun, till I have bought a glass[12],
      That I may see my shadow as I pass.

                                                 Exit

Act 1 Scene 3
London: a room in King Edward's palace

        Enter QUEEN ELIZABETH, LORD RIVERS, LORD GREY *and the*
                       MARQUESS OF DORSET

RIVERS   Have patience, madam. There's no doubt his majesty
             Will soon recover his accustomed[13] health.
GREY   In that you brook it ill, it makes him worse.
             Therefore, for God's sake, entertain good comfort,
             And cheer his grace with quick[14] and merry eyes. 5
ELIZABETH If he were dead, what would betide on me?
GREY   No other harm but loss of such a lord.
ELIZABETH The loss of such a lord includes all harms.
GREY   The heavens have blessed you with a goodly[15] son
             To be your comforter when he is gone. 10

Elizabeth claims that Richard, soon to be Protector, hates her and her family. Buckingham says that the dying King Edward wants reconciliation between the factions. Richard condemns those who complain of him to the King.

剧情简介：伊丽莎白声称，即将做摄政大臣的理查仇视她和她的家人。白金汉说垂死的爱德华王希望促成各派别和睦相处。理查谴责那些向国王说他坏话的人。

1 Concerns for the future (in pairs)

All of the Woodville family faction (派别) hope the King will recover, as do Buckingham and Stanley. Elizabeth expresses her concerns for the future.

- Copy the diagram below and collect together all the troubles that are on Elizabeth's mind from line 6 to line 41 (add more circles if you need to).

1. his minority 他年幼（无法执政）
2. trust 监护
3. Protector 摄政大臣
4. determined, not concluded yet 协商一致，但未做决定
5. miscarry 死亡
6. arrogance 傲慢
7. envious slanders 恶意中伤
8. wayward sickness 顽疾（此处指抑郁）
9. grounded malice 存心为恶
10. amendment 康复
11. grant 赐予
12. confer with 与……谈话
13. atonement 和解
14. warn 召唤
15. forsooth 确实
16. stern 无情
17. holy Paul 圣保罗
18. his grace （指爱德华四世）
19. lightly 几乎不
20. dissentious 扰乱人心

2 Enter Richard (in groups of six or seven)

Just as we learn that there is hope for reconciliation between the various warring factions, Richard suddenly makes an appearance and introduces a new note of conflict.

a   Remind yourselves who is on stage at the moment of Richard's entrance, and share out the roles. Using the information you have gathered from the play so far, group the characters according to their allegiances (效忠). Freeze the action at line 42 ('They do me wrong and I will not endure it'). Decide how to show the delicate political situation from the way people stand or sit, the space between them and the direction of their gaze.

b   Discuss who Richard might be addressing. For example, do you think line 42 is part of his ongoing conversation with Hastings? Or is he openly addressing the whole room?

c   Look back over the concerns voiced by Elizabeth (see Activity 1 above), and discuss how she might react to Richard's surprise entrance.

King Richard III Act 1 Scene 3

理查三世

ELIZABETH	Ah, he is young, and his minority[1]
	Is put unto the trust[2] of Richard Gloucester,
	A man that loves not me nor none of you.
RIVERS	Is it concluded he shall be Protector[3]?
ELIZABETH	It is determined, not concluded yet[4],
	But so it must be if the king miscarry[5].

Enter BUCKINGHAM *and* [STANLEY EARL OF] DERBY

GREY	Here come the lords of Buckingham and Derby.
BUCKINGHAM	Good time of day unto your royal grace.
STANLEY	God make your majesty joyful, as you have been.
ELIZABETH	The Countess Richmond, good my lord of Derby,
	To your good prayer will scarcely say amen.
	Yet Derby, not withstanding she's your wife
	And loves not me, be you, good lord, assured
	I hate not you for her proud arrogance[6].
STANLEY	I do beseech you, either not believe
	The envious slanders[7] of her false accusers,
	Or if she be accused on true report,
	Bear with her weakness, which I think proceeds
	From wayward sickness[8] and no grounded malice[9].
ELIZABETH	Saw you the king today, my lord of Derby?
STANLEY	But now the Duke of Buckingham and I
	Are come from visiting his majesty.
ELIZABETH	What likelihood of his amendment[10], lords?
BUCKINGHAM	Madam, good hope. His grace speaks cheerfully.
ELIZABETH	God grant[11] him health. Did you confer with[12] him?
BUCKINGHAM	Ay, madam. He desires to make atonement[13]
	Between the Duke of Gloucester and your brothers,
	And between them and my Lord Chamberlain,
	And sent to warn[14] them to his royal presence.
ELIZABETH	Would all were well, but that will never be.
	I fear our happiness is at the height.

Enter RICHARD [*and* HASTINGS]

RICHARD	They do me wrong, and I will not endure it.
	Who is it that complains unto the king
	That I, forsooth[15], am stern[16] and love them not?
	By holy Paul[17], they love his grace[18] but lightly[19]
	That fill his ears with such dissentious[20] rumours.

Richard claims the Woodvilles report ill of him to the King. Elizabeth says the King sends for him to find the truth. Richard implies that the Woodvilles are commoners. Elizabeth denies responsibility for Clarence's imprisonment.

 剧情简介：理查认定是伍德威尔族人向国王告他的恶状。伊丽莎白澄清是国王派人调查真相。理查暗示伍德威尔家族都是些平民。伊丽莎白否认自己和克莱润入狱有关。

1 'I cannot flatter and look fair' (in pairs)

Richard complains that he is an honest man, unfairly accused of being untrustworthy because of his looks. This is another example of dramatic irony (see p. 8).

- Look closely at the way Richard describes himself in lines 47–53, then find examples from Scenes 1 or 2 that appear to prove the opposite. Record your ideas in a table similar to the one below.

Richard claims he cannot …	But …
'flatter and look fair'	In Scene 2, he uses charm and flattery to win over Anne, when he says …
'Smile in men's faces'	He jokes and smiles when he bumps into Clarence, even though …
'smooth, deceive and cog'	

Write about it 写作练习

Who is telling the truth?

In lines 58–86, Richard makes accusations against the Woodvilles that Elizabeth refutes.

a Identify the lines in which the following accusations and refutations are made:
- What wrongs have I ever done to your dishonest family?
- Your faction has complained against me to the dying King.
- It was the King's own wish to send for you to find the reason for the hatred you show to my family.
- Commoners are being ennobled.
- You're envious that my supporters have achieved higher social status.
- Clarence is imprisoned because of you, I'm in disgrace, nobles are scorned and people of no rank are becoming nobles.
- I swear by God I never provoked Edward against Clarence. I've argued against his imprisonment.

b Decide which statements are true, which false and which cannot be proved. Write two or three paragraphs outlining the claims and counterclaims. Give your opinion of who is most likely to be believed, based on your understanding of the characters so far.

1 look fair 假装一副迷人的样子
2 smooth 恭维
3 cog 作伪
4 Duck 屈身
5 French nods 法式点头（指假装优雅的举止）
6 apish courtesy 装模作样的礼节
7 rancorous 可憎
8 plain 诚实，脚踏实地
9 silken 女里女气
10 insinuating 曲意逢迎
11 jacks 庶民
12 nor … nor = neither … nor
13 injured 伤害
14 scarce a breathing while 连喘口气的工夫也没有
15 lewd 粗俗
16 on his own royal disposition 以他自己的君王秉性
17 suitor 游说的人，寻求恩宠的人
18 belike 也许
19 Makes him to send 让他派人找（你）
20 the ground 此中缘由
21 I cannot tell 我的确不知道
22 wrens 鹪鹩（非常小的鸟）
23 advancement 擢升，飞黄腾达
24 ennoble 授衔（如授予勋爵头衔）
25 noble 诺布尔（旧时英格兰使用的金币）
26 careful 劳心费神
27 hap 运势，（好）命
28 advocate 辩护者

King Richard III Act 1 Scene 3
理查三世

	Because I cannot flatter and look fair[1],	
	Smile in men's faces, smooth[2], deceive, and cog[3],	
	Duck[4] with French nods[5] and apish courtesy[6],	
	I must be held a rancorous[7] enemy.	50
	Cannot a plain[8] man live and think no harm,	
	But thus his simple truth must be abused	
	With silken[9], sly, insinuating[10] jacks[11]?	
GREY	To who in all this presence speaks your grace?	
RICHARD	To thee, that hast nor honesty nor[12] grace.	55
	When have I injured[13] thee? When done thee wrong?	
	Or thee? Or thee? Or any of your faction?	
	A plague upon you all. His royal grace,	
	Whom God preserve better than you would wish,	
	Cannot be quiet scarce a breathing while[14]	60
	But you must trouble him with lewd[15] complaints.	
ELIZABETH	Brother of Gloucester, you mistake the matter.	
	The king, on his own royal disposition[16],	
	And not provoked by any suitor[17] else,	
	Aiming, belike[18], at your interior hatred,	65
	That in your outward action shows itself	
	Against my children, brothers, and myself,	
	Makes him to send[19], that he may learn the ground[20].	
RICHARD	I cannot tell[21]. The world is grown so bad	
	That wrens[22] make prey where eagles dare not perch.	70
	Since every jack became a gentleman,	
	There's many a gentle person made a jack.	
ELIZABETH	Come, come, we know your meaning, brother Gloucester.	
	You envy my advancement[23] and my friends'.	
	God grant we never may have need of you.	75
RICHARD	Meantime, God grants that I have need of you.	
	Our brother is imprisoned by your means,	
	My self disgraced, and the nobility	
	Held in contempt, while great promotions	
	Are daily given to ennoble[24] those	80
	That scarce some two days since were worth a noble[25].	
ELIZABETH	By Him that raised me to this careful[26] height	
	From that contented hap[27] which I enjoyed,	
	I never did incense his majesty	
	Against the Duke of Clarence, but have been	85
	An earnest advocate[28] to plead for him.	

Richard continues to accuse and insult Elizabeth. She swears to inform the King of his scornful behaviour. Queen Margaret enters silently, and quietly rails against both Richard and Elizabeth.

 剧情简介： 理查继续谴责、侮辱伊丽莎白。她发誓要向国王状告他这种无礼行为。玛格蕊王后悄悄登场，暗中痛斥理查和伊丽莎白。

1 The argument gains pace (in threes)

Richard's sustained taunting of Elizabeth is too much for Grey and Rivers to bear. But once they step into the argument, Richard just shifts into a new gear and throws their words back at them.

- To gain a sense of the bitter exchange of views here, take parts as Richard, Rivers and Elizabeth and read lines 89–109 aloud, emphasising Richard's repetitions and Elizabeth's indignant response. Try to avoid leaving a gap where one person finishes speaking and the other responds – in a real argument, people often start speaking before the first person has finished.

Stagecraft 导演技巧

The entrance of 'old QUEEN MARGARET' (in pairs)

Queen Margaret (the widow of Henry VI) enters unseen by the other characters. She proceeds to comment on the conversation between Richard and Elizabeth in a series of **asides** (旁白) to the audience. An aside is a stage convention that allows a character to voice his or her thoughts to the audience without other characters overhearing.

a Read the script from Margaret's entrance at line 110 up to line 161. Imagine you are directing a new stage production of the play. How are you going to present Margaret? How will she enter so that she can talk to the audience while remaining unseen by the other characters, until line 155 when she fully reveals herself and begins to speak directly to them?

- How does she enter, and where does she stand at first? (For example, she could stand right at the front of the stage, or she might stand on a gallery above, then come down the stairs to join the other characters. Or she could emerge from the audience.)
- What does she look like? Is she finely dressed to denote her royal status? Or is she dressed in rags to show that she has lost everything?
- How does she behave? Is she calm and authoritative or on the edge of insanity? Realistic or slightly ghost-like?

b Once you have played around with some ideas, make notes in your Director's Journal about the way you would stage this part of the play and why you have made those decisions.

1	injury	不公正
2	suspects	嫌疑
3	mean	执行者
4	preferments	提拔
5	lay … desert	声称那些荣誉是您正当赢得的
6	marry	马利亚啊（圣母马利亚 [Virgin Mary] 的简称，功能与今天的Jesus相似，表示对事实的感叹或惊奇、义愤等情感；这里表示对事实的感叹）
7	marry	（表示惊奇）
8	stripling	小伙子
9	wis	知道
10	grandam	祖母
11	blunt upbraidings	粗鲁的斥责
12	scoffs	嘲笑，讥讽
13	acquaint	禀告
14	oft	= often
15	with this condition	像这样
16	baited	折磨（纵狗撕咬拴着的熊为bait，斗熊）
17	state	等级，社会地位
18	seat	王位
19	is due to me	本应属于我
20	avouch't	申诉
21	adventure to be	冒……风险
22	pains	功劳
23	Ere	= Before
24	pack-horse	负重的牲口，干重活的工人
25	royalise his blood	把他扶上王位
26	spent mine own	呕心沥血，鞠躬尽瘁

	My lord, you do me shameful injury[1]	
	Falsely to draw me in these vile suspècts[2].	
RICHARD	You may deny that you were not the mean[3]	
	Of my Lord Hastings' late imprisonment.	90
RIVERS	She may, my lord, for –	
RICHARD	She may, Lord Rivers, why, who knows not so?	
	She may do more, sir, than denying that.	
	She may help you to many fair preferments[4],	
	And then deny her aiding hand therein,	95
	And lay those honours on your high desert[5].	
	What may she not? She may, ay, marry[6], may she.	
RIVERS	What, marry[7], may she?	
RICHARD	What, marry, may she? Marry with a king,	
	A bachelor, and a handsome stripling[8] too.	100
	I wis[9] your grandam[10] had a worser match.	
ELIZABETH	My lord of Gloucester, I have too long borne	
	Your blunt upbraidings[11] and your bitter scoffs[12].	
	By heaven, I will acquaint[13] his majesty	
	Of those gross taunts that oft[14] I have endured.	105
	I had rather be a country servant maid	
	Than a great queen with this condition[15],	
	To be so baited[16], scorned, and stormèd at.	
	Small joy have I in being England's queen.	

Enter old QUEEN MARGARET

MARGARET	[*Aside*] And lessened be that small, God I beseech him.	110
	Thy honour, state[17], and seat[18] is due to me[19].	
RICHARD	What? Threat you me with telling of the king?	
	I will avouch't[20] in presence of the king.	
	I dare adventure to be[21] sent to th'Tower.	
	'Tis time to speak. My pains[22] are quite forgot.	115
MARGARET	[*Aside*] Out, devil. I do remember them too well.	
	Thou kill'dst my husband, Henry, in the Tower,	
	And Edward, my poor son, at Tewkesbury.	
RICHARD	Ere[23] you were queen, ay, or your husband king,	
	I was a pack-horse[24] in his great affairs,	120
	A weeder-out of his proud adversaries,	
	A liberal rewarder of his friends.	
	To royalise his blood[25] I spent mine own[26].	

1 Queen Margaret

Margaret eventually reveals herself to Richard and the Woodvilles. How is Margaret portrayed in the production pictured here? Consider her clothes, her hair, the look on her face, the way she stands.

How do you imagine Queen Margaret? Do you think she could be portrayed in a different way?

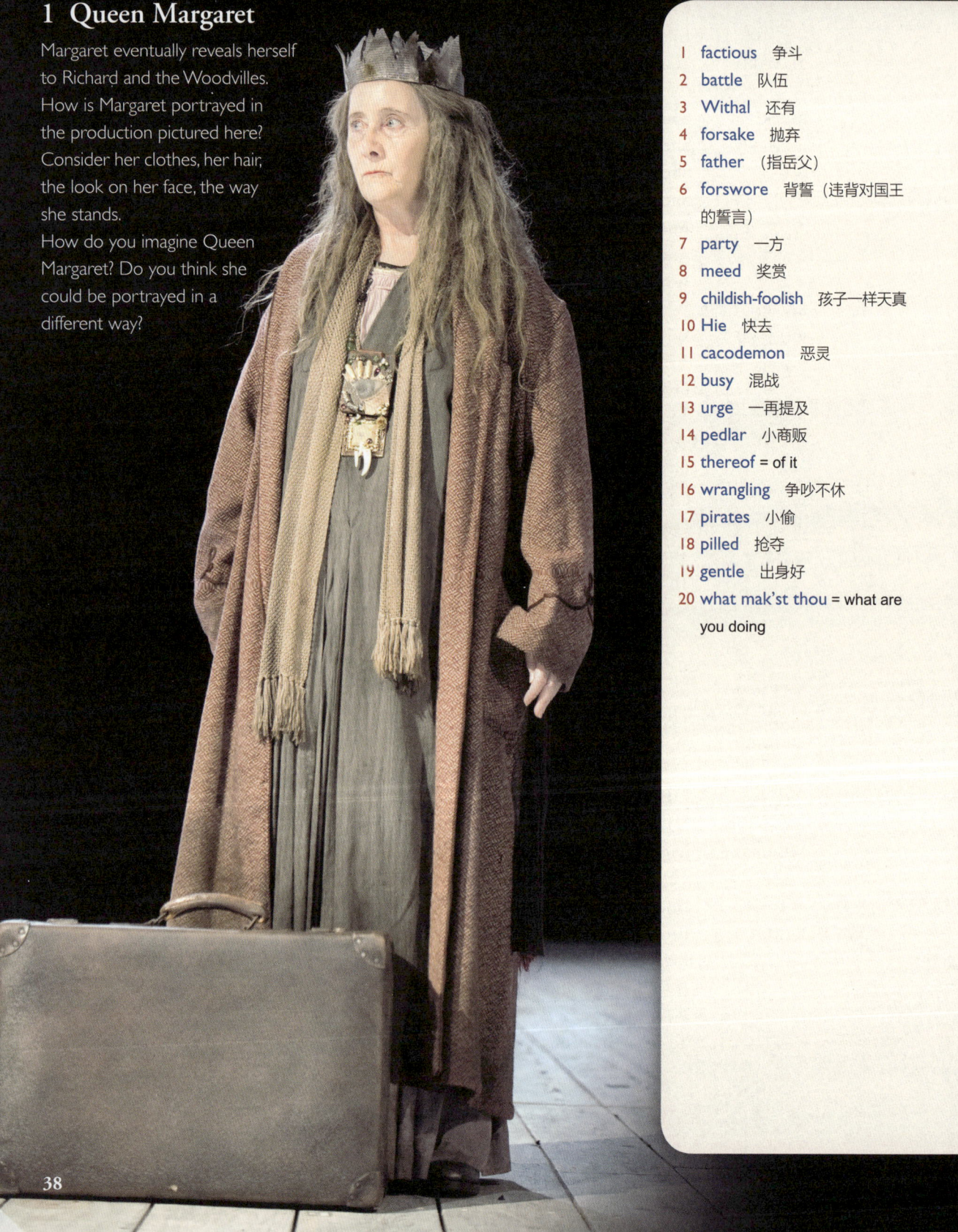

1 factious 争斗
2 battle 队伍
3 Withal 还有
4 forsake 抛弃
5 father （指岳父）
6 forswore 背誓（违背对国王的誓言）
7 party 一方
8 meed 奖赏
9 childish-foolish 孩子一样天真
10 Hie 快去
11 cacodemon 恶灵
12 busy 混战
13 urge 一再提及
14 pedlar 小商贩
15 thereof = of it
16 wrangling 争吵不休
17 pirates 小偷
18 pilled 抢夺
19 gentle 出身好
20 what mak'st thou = what are you doing

King Richard III Act 1 Scene 3
理查三世

MARGARET	[*Aside*] Ay, and much better blood than his or thine.	
RICHARD	In all which time, you and your husband Grey	125
	Were factious[1] for the house of Lancaster,	
	And, Rivers, so were you. Was not your husband	
	In Margaret's battle[2] at Saint Albans slain?	
	Let me put in your minds, if you forget,	
	What you have been ere this, and what you are;	130
	Withal[3], what I have been, and what I am.	
MARGARET	[*Aside*] A murderous villain, and so still thou art.	
RICHARD	Poor Clarence did forsake[4] his father[5] Warwick,	
	Ay, and forswore[6] himself, which Jesu pardon.	
MARGARET	[*Aside*] Which God revenge.	135
RICHARD	To fight on Edward's party[7] for the crown.	
	And for his meed[8], poor lord, he is mewed up.	
	I would to God my heart were flint, like Edward's,	
	Or Edward's soft and pitiful, like mine.	
	I am too childish-foolish[9] for this world.	140
MARGARET	[*Aside*] Hie[10] thee to hell for shame, and leave this world,	
	Thou cacodemon[11]. There thy kingdom is.	
RIVERS	My lord of Gloucester, in those busy[12] days	
	Which here you urge[13] to prove us enemies,	
	We followed then our lord, our sovereign king.	145
	So should we you, if you should be our king.	
RICHARD	If I should be? I had rather be a pedlar[14].	
	Far be it from my heart, the thought thereof[15].	
ELIZABETH	As little joy, my lord, as you suppose	
	You should enjoy were you this country's king,	150
	As little joy you may suppose in me	
	That I enjoy, being the queen thereof.	
MARGARET	[*Aside*] A little joy enjoys the queen thereof,	
	For I am she, and altogether joyless.	
	I can no longer hold me patient –	155
	Hear me, you wrangling[16] pirates[17], that fall out	
	In sharing that which you have pilled[18] from me.	
	Which of you trembles not that looks on me?	
	If not that I am queen, you bow like subjects,	
	Yet that by you deposed, you quake like rebels.	160
	Ah, gentle[19] villain, do not turn away.	
RICHARD	Foul wrinkled witch, what mak'st thou[20] in my sight?	

Margaret demands the return of her throne. Richard tells how she pitilessly taunted his father. Everyone condemns that deed, but Margaret begins to curse them, prophesying deaths and sorrows ahead.

剧情简介：玛格蕊要求归还她的王位。理查讲述她如何毫无怜悯地戏弄他的父亲。所有人都谴责玛格蕊，她却开始诅咒众人，预言他们会死得很惨。

1 A complicated family feud (in large groups)

From lines 125 to 152, Richard, Elizabeth and the Woodvilles trade insults about their parts in their often violent recent history. Since various characters changed sides and switched loyalties more than once during the Wars of the Roses, Richard enjoys exposing his opponents' hypocrisies. However, once Margaret joins the argument (line 155), the relationship between those on stage shifts a little. Are there now three factions? Does Margaret have any allies? Who was loyal to whom and who behaved treacherously?

- You will need at least fifteen people for this activity, so clear a space in your classroom or drama studio. Check that you are allowed to use masking tape on the floor. Divide the floor space into three sections – one each for York, Lancaster and neutral/unknown. Turn to the family tree on page 266 and allocate parts for the people listed. First decide in which space you would place Henry VI, Queen Margaret and their son, Edward, when they ruled England. Then place Richard, Clarence and Rutland along with their father the Duke of York. Next, Elizabeth and her brothers take up a space. Where do you think Hastings, Rivers, Dorset and Buckingham might stand before Henry VI was defeated?
- Now read from line 125 (any members of the class who have not taken roles could read the script in turn) and follow the various accusations as they are made. For example, in lines 125–6, Richard accuses Elizabeth and her former husband of originally supporting the Lancastrians; they fought against Margaret and Henry (line 128), resulting in the death of Elizabeth's husband (line 127–8). As each accusation is made, or piece of history recounted, the identified person should decide whether they move, stay or die. Which characters switch allegiance?

1	repetition	重申
2	marred	毁坏
3	That	(指重申的内容)
4	Wert thou	= Were you
5	on pain of death	违令则处死
6	abode	逗留于此
7	thou	(指伊丽莎白王后)
8	allegiance	忠诚
9	usurp	僭夺
10	crown … paper	(玛格蕊曾羞辱被俘的约克公爵，令其佩戴纸王冠)
11	drew'st	引出
12	clout	破布
13	faultless	无辜
14	plagued	永恒地惩罚
15	that babe	(指年幼的拉特兰)
16	No man but	= Everybody
17	prophesied	料到
18	snarling	怒骂
19	catch … throat	与祂死掐
20	but answer for	抵得上
21	peevish brat	愚蠢的臭小子
22	quick	尖刻
23	surfeit	纵欲

Characters 人物分析

Who hates whom most? (in eights)

- Consider Margaret's line 188, 'turn you all your hatred now on me?' and decide where loyalties lie at this moment. Freeze this moment on stage and show where each character is standing and what that reveals about their allegiance (or self interest).
- As an extra challenge, some of the characters in the tableaux could come alive and voice their thoughts at this moment.

MARGARET	But repetition[1] of what thou hast marred[2],	
	That[3] will I make before I let thee go.	
RICHARD	Wert thou[4] not banishèd on pain of death[5]?	165
MARGARET	I was. But I do find more pain in banishment	
	Than death can yield me here by my abode[6].	
	A husband and a son thou ow'st to me –	
	And thou[7] a kingdom – all of you allegiance[8].	
	This sorrow that I have by right is yours,	170
	And all the pleasures you usurp[9] are mine.	
RICHARD	The curse my noble father laid on thee	
	When thou didst crown his warlike brows with paper[10]	
	And with thy scorns drew'st[11] rivers from his eyes,	
	And then to dry them gav'st the duke a clout[12]	175
	Steeped in the faultless[13] blood of pretty Rutland –	
	His curses then, from bitterness of soul	
	Denounced against thee, are all fall'n upon thee,	
	And God, not we, hath plagued[14] thy bloody deed.	
ELIZABETH	So just is God, to right the innocent.	180
HASTINGS	Oh, 'twas the foulest deed to slay that babe[15],	
	And the most merciless, that e'er was heard of.	
RIVERS	Tyrants themselves wept when it was reported.	
DORSET	No man but[16] prophesied[17] revenge for it.	
BUCKINGHAM	Northumberland, then present, wept to see it.	185
MARGARET	What? Were you snarling[18] all before I came,	
	Ready to catch each other by the throat[19],	
	And turn you all your hatred now on me?	
	Did York's dread curse prevail so much with heaven	
	That Henry's death, my lovely Edward's death,	190
	Their kingdom's loss, my woeful banishment,	
	Should all but answer for[20] that peevish brat[21]?	
	Can curses pierce the clouds, and enter heaven?	
	Why then, give way, dull clouds, to my quick[22] curses.	
	Though not by war, by surfeit[23] die your king,	195
	As ours by murder to make him a king.	
	Edward thy son, that now is Prince of Wales,	
	For Edward our son, that was Prince of Wales,	
	Die in his youth by like untimely violence.	
	Thyself a queen, for me that was a queen,	200
	Outlive thy glory, like my wretched self.	

Margaret continues her prophetic cursing, wishing grief on Elizabeth and early deaths on Rivers, Dorset and Hastings. Her most powerful curse is on Richard. He turns her words against her.

 剧情简介：玛格蕊继续她预言般的诅咒，希望悲伤降临到伊丽莎白身上，希望瑞沃、多塞和海斯廷死于非命。她对理查下的诅咒最恶毒。理查反唇相讥。

Write about it 写作练习

Awards and censures (谴责)

A committee of disabled people is awarding prizes to the films, plays and TV programmes that have portrayed disabled people most accurately. The awards also censure those that have portrayed the handicapped badly or ignored the problem of physical disability. Margaret's lines (226–31) are 'politically incorrect' in that they equate Richard's disability with his evil nature.

- Write a letter to the awarding committee, in which you complain about the offensive nature of the lines. Consider whether you agree with Queen Margaret's opinion that Richard's disability is a reflection of his evil character.
- Write the reply that the committee might make.

1 Decked 装扮
2 stalled 占据
3 unlooked 没有料到
4 charm 妖术
5 hag 妖婆
6 grievous 严重
7 begnaw 噬咬
8 elvish-marked 被魔鬼打上烙印
9 abortive 天生畸形
10 rooting hog 吃土的猪
11 sealed 打上封泥
12 nativity 生下来
13 heavy 怀孕
14 rag 一文不值的渣子
15 I cry thee mercy 我请你原谅
16 period 完结

1 Curses and prophecies

Some of Queen Margaret's curses are colourful and vindictive (怀恨在心), especially when directed towards Richard. Other curses are mixed with realistic prophecies.

- Read through the lines in which she curses some of the other characters (lines 195 to 231). Make a list of each person she curses and what she curses them with. Copy the following table and, in the final column, make notes on how likely you think it is that this curse will be fulfilled in the course of the play.

The person addressed	Queen Margaret's curse	How likely is it that this curse will be fulfilled?
King Edward		
Prince Edward		
Queen Elizabeth		
Rivers and Dorset		
Richard		

	Long mayst thou live to wail thy children's death	
	And see another, as I see thee now,	
	Decked[1] in the rights, as thou art stalled[2] in mine.	
	Long die thy happy days before thy death,	205
	And after many lengthened hours of grief,	
	Die neither mother, wife, nor England's queen.	
	Rivers and Dorset, you were standers-by,	
	And so wast thou, Lord Hastings, when my son	
	Was stabbed with bloody daggers. God I pray him,	210
	That none of you may live his natural age,	
	But by some unlooked[3] accident cut off.	
RICHARD	Have done thy charm[4], thou hateful, withered hag[5].	
MARGARET	And leave out thee? Stay, dog, for thou shalt hear me.	
	If heaven have any grievous[6] plague in store	215
	Exceeding those that I can wish upon thee,	
	Oh, let them keep it till thy sins be ripe	
	And then hurl down their indignation	
	On thee, the troubler of the poor world's peace.	
	The worm of conscience still begnaw[7] thy soul.	220
	Thy friends suspect for traitors while thou liv'st,	
	And take deep traitors for thy dearest friends.	
	No sleep close up that deadly eye of thine,	
	Unless it be while some tormenting dream	
	Affrights thee with a hell of ugly devils.	225
	Thou elvish-marked[8], abortive[9], rooting hog[10],	
	Thou that wast sealed[11] in thy nativity[12]	
	The slave of nature and the son of hell.	
	Thou slander of thy heavy[13] mother's womb,	
	Thou loathèd issue of thy father's loins,	230
	Thou rag[14] of honour, thou detested –	
RICHARD	Margaret.	
MARGARET	Richard.	
RICHARD	Ha?	
MARGARET	I call thee not.	
RICHARD	I cry thee mercy[15] then, for I did think	235
	That thou hadst called me all these bitter names.	
MARGARET	Why so I did, but looked for no reply.	
	Oh, let me make the period[16] to my curse.	
RICHARD	'Tis done by me, and ends in 'Margaret'.	

Margaret predicts that Elizabeth will come to curse Richard. She rebukes Hastings, Rivers and Dorset, and sorrows for her dead son. She calls on God to punish the house of York.

剧情简介：玛格蕊预言伊丽莎白有一天也会诅咒理查。她痛斥海斯廷、瑞沃和多塞特，并为自己死掉的儿子伤心。她请求上帝惩罚约克家族。

1 Who's who? (in large groups)

a Work out who is mentioned in this section by taking parts as Margaret, Hastings, Rivers, Dorset and Richard. Speak lines 240–63 slowly. As each person (or persons) is mentioned, point to them.

b How would you want to group the characters on stage to show their relationships to each other and to reveal where their loyalties lie? For example, in lines 259–60, Margaret observes that the higher the rank, the greater the consequences of a fall as she talks to Dorset (Queen Elizabeth's son, who has only recently been raised to high status). Where would you place Dorset to reflect his recent change of rank?

Language in the play 剧中语言
Imagery of authority and nobility

In lines 263–5, Richard compares the house of York's position at the top of the tree to that of an eagle. It was believed to be a sign of the eagle's noble nature that it could gaze into the sun unblinded. Richard claims that, like the eagle, the house of York 'scorns the sun'.

a Look back at the 'Language' box on page 12. Now consider further how imagery can enhance the audience's understanding of Richard's character and add to the tension of a scene. Add another paragraph to your earlier one, in which you outline your responses to the imagery in the script opposite.

b What other animal imagery might be appropriate for Richard (and any other characters of your choice) at this point in the play?

Themes 主题分析
Lancaster or York: the right to rule?

Margaret accuses Richard of causing the death of her son – 'turns the sun to shade' (line 266) – and accuses the house of York of unjustly stealing Lancaster's high status: 'Your aerie buildeth in our aerie's nest' (line 270).

- Write out in your own words how the crown has passed from the house of Lancaster to the house of York and back again since the time of Richard II. Who do you think really has the right to rule England?

---

1 **painted** 画出来的；假的
2 **vain flourish of my fortune** 我命中一现的昙花
3 **bottled** 滚圆
4 **ensnareth** = ensnares（诱捕入网）
5 **whet'st** 磨
6 **bunch-backed** 驼背
7 **False-boding** 胡说八道
8 **Were you well served** = If you were well served（假如您得到了您应得的）
9 **Teach me to be** 把我当……伺候
10 **master** 少爷（对小男孩的称呼，是对多塞的羞辱）
11 **malapert** 无礼，放肆
12 **Your … current** 您的新头衔就像新铸的钱币，还未合法流通
13 **young** 新得的
14 **blasts** 强风
15 **born so high** 生来就如此高贵
16 **aerie** 鹰巢
17 **cedar** 雪松（一种高大长寿的乔木，象征着高贵）
18 **dallies with** 与……嬉戏
19 **suffer** 容许
20 **Peace** 住嘴

ELIZABETH	Thus have you breathed your curse against yourself.	240
MARGARET	Poor painted[1] queen, vain flourish of my fortune[2],	
	Why strew'st thou sugar on that bottled[3] spider	
	Whose deadly web ensnareth[4] thee about?	
	Fool, fool, thou whet'st[5] a knife to kill thyself.	
	The day will come that thou shalt wish for me	245
	To help thee curse this poisonous bunch-backed[6] toad.	
HASTINGS	False-boding[7] woman, end thy frantic curse,	
	Lest to thy harm thou move our patience.	
MARGARET	Foul shame upon you. You have all moved mine.	
RIVERS	Were you well served[8], you would be taught your duty.	250
MARGARET	To serve me well, you all should do me duty,	
	Teach me to be[9] your queen, and you my subjects;	
	Oh, serve me well and teach yourselves that duty.	
DORSET	Dispute not with her. She is lunatic.	
MARGARET	Peace, master[10] marquess, you are malapert[11].	255
	Your fire-new stamp of honour is scarce current[12].	
	Oh, that your young[13] nobility could judge	
	What 'twere to lose it and be miserable.	
	They that stand high have many blasts[14] to shake them,	
	And if they fall, they dash themselves to pieces.	260
RICHARD	Good counsel, marry. Learn it, learn it, marquess.	
DORSET	It touches you, my lord, as much as me.	
RICHARD	Ay, and much more. But I was born so high[15].	
	Our aerie[16] buildeth in the cedar's[17] top,	
	And dallies with[18] the wind and scorns the sun.	265
MARGARET	And turns the sun to shade, alas, alas.	
	Witness my son, now in the shade of death,	
	Whose bright out-shining beams thy cloudy wrath	
	Hath in eternal darkness folded up.	
	Your aerie buildeth in our aerie's nest.	270
	O God that seest it, do not suffer[19] it;	
	As it is won with blood, lost be it so.	
BUCKINGHAM	Peace[20], peace, for shame, if not for charity.	
MARGARET	Urge neither charity nor shame to me.	
	Uncharitably with me have you dealt,	275
	And shamefully my hopes by you are butchered.	
	My charity is outrage, life my shame,	
	And in that shame still live my sorrow's rage.	

Margaret extends friendship to Buckingham and warns him against Richard. He rejects her and she prophesies his downfall. Richard expresses sympathy for Margaret and those who imprisoned Clarence.

剧情简介：玛格蕊向白金汉示好，提醒他提防理查，被拒绝后便预言白金汉的败落。理查对玛格蕊和那些让克莱润下狱的人表达自己的怜悯。

1 Buckingham disappoints Margaret (in pairs)

Margaret, having accused everyone of responsibility for the bloody deeds of the civil war, now turns to Buckingham. She says he had no part in harming her family and therefore he is the only one she does not curse.

- Take parts as Buckingham and Margaret, and speak lines 279–94, indicating how Margaret pleads with Buckingham in her first two speeches.
- Then speak their lines 296–304, exploring how Margaret's tone might change as Buckingham does not respond in the way she hopes.
- What does Buckingham's reply in line 296 reveal about his character?

Stagecraft 导演技巧

Margaret's stage business (戏台动作)

In line 295, Richard says: 'What doth she say, my lord of Buckingham?' But what does this mean? Is Margaret whispering to Buckingham, or is Richard simply suggesting that people who matter (such as himself) have stopped listening to her?

- In your Director's Journal, write your own stage direction to describe what would be going on at this point if you were directing the play.

1	princely Buckingham	（白金汉是爱德华三世最小的儿子格劳斯特公爵托马斯 [Thomas] 的后人）
2	league	结盟
3	amity	友谊
4	fair befall	好运降临
5	compass	范围
6	pass	脱离
7	will not think but	只相信
8	Look	提防
9	venom	有毒
10	rankle	使……溃烂
11	ministers	群魔
12	counsel	劝告
13	soothe	安抚，奉承
14	muse	想知道
15	God's holy mother	圣母马利亚在上
16	vantage	好处
17	hot	热心
18	somebody	（指爱德华国王）
19	franked up	像猪一样关在圈里
20	scathe	伤害

BUCKINGHAM	Have done, have done.	
MARGARET	O princely Buckingham[1], I'll kiss thy hand	280
	In sign of league[2] and amity[3] with thee.	
	Now fair befall[4] thee and thy noble house.	
	Thy garments are not spotted with our blood,	
	Nor thou within the compass[5] of my curse.	
BUCKINGHAM	Nor no one here, for curses never pass[6]	285
	The lips of those that breathe them in the air.	
MARGARET	I will not think but[7] they ascend the sky	
	And there awake God's gentle sleeping peace.	
	O Buckingham, take heed of yonder dog.	
	Look[8] when he fawns, he bites; and when he bites,	290
	His venom[9] tooth will rankle[10] to the death.	
	Have not to do with him; beware of him.	
	Sin, death, and hell have set their marks on him,	
	And all their ministers[11] attend on him.	
RICHARD	What doth she say, my lord of Buckingham?	295
BUCKINGHAM	Nothing that I respect, my gracious lord.	
MARGARET	What, dost thou scorn me for my gentle counsel[12]	
	And soothe[13] the devil that I warn thee from?	
	Oh, but remember this another day,	
	When he shall split thy very heart with sorrow,	300
	And say poor Margaret was a prophetess.	
	Live each of you the subjects to his hate,	
	And he to yours, and all of you to God's.	*Exit*
BUCKINGHAM	My hair doth stand on end to hear her curses.	
RIVERS	And so doth mine. I muse[14] why she's at liberty.	305
RICHARD	I cannot blame her, by God's holy mother[15],	
	She hath had too much wrong, and I repent	
	My part thereof that I have done to her.	
ELIZABETH	I never did her any to my knowledge.	
RICHARD	Yet you have all the vantage[16] of her wrong.	310
	I was too hot[17] to do somebody[18] good	
	That is too cold in thinking of it now.	
	Marry, as for Clarence, he is well repaid;	
	He is franked up[19] to fatting for his pains.	
	God pardon them that are the cause thereof.	315
RIVERS	A virtuous and a Christian-like conclusion,	
	To pray for them that have done scathe[20] to us.	

Catesby informs the Queen and courtiers that King Edward has sent for them. Alone on stage, Richard discloses his techniques for deceiving others. He instructs the Murderers to kill Clarence quickly, without pity.

剧情简介：凯茨贝通知王后和朝臣爱德华王要召见他们。独自留在戏台上的理查透露了他如何欺骗了众人。他吩咐杀手们立刻干掉克莱润，不许手软。

1 Mock innocence and false piety (in pairs)

In lines 324–38, Richard tells the audience how he uses Derby, Hastings and Buckingham and persuades them that the Queen has caused Clarence's imprisonment. When his 'gulls' urge him to take revenge on the Woodvilles, he uses the Bible ('scripture', 'holy writ') to pretend he pardons his enemies. Part of Richard's style is mock innocence and false piety (pretending to be very religious), often tinged with menace.

- In modern English, improvise (即兴表演) a conversation between Richard and one of these gullible (易上当) courtiers to imitate his style of saintly innocence and forgiveness. Remember that actors playing Richard often try to bring out his humorous delight in clever play-acting, unnoticed by those on stage.

Stagecraft 导演技巧

Murder and manipulation (in small groups)

a Prepare a dramatic reading of Richard's conversation with the Murderers (lines 339–55). Use the following questions to help you:

- Would Richard be seated while the Murderers stand, or would all stand?
- Would Richard remain hidden in shadows or would he tower above the Murderers?
- Would he have freedom of movement and a wide vocal range to show his power over the Murderers, who fearfully stay in one place on the stage?
- Would the Murderers be restless, wild and violent men, or would they be cold and calculating?
- What stage business might be created around the warrant (通行证，许可证) (line 344) to make the audience smile, and to remind them of Richard's duplicity (奸诈，口是心非)?

b Make notes about the reasons for your performance choices in your Director's Journal. Use these notes to script a conversation between the director and the actor playing Richard or one of the Murderers. Explain their motives and actions to the actor. Imagine how the actor might respond – would he agree or have alternative suggestions?

1 well advised 小心谨慎
2 brawl 叫嚣
3 mischiefs 灾祸
4 The … others 我暗中策动的阴谋会让别人来承担罪责
5 cast in darkness 投入监狱或判处死刑
6 beweep 抹眼泪
7 gulls 傻瓜
8 whet 唆使，怂恿
9 do good for evil 以德报怨（这是理查老掉牙的说辞之一）
10 odd 零碎
11 ends 只言片语
12 soft 且慢
13 hardy 勇敢
14 resolvèd 坚定
15 sudden 麻利
16 obdurate 狠下心来
17 mark 听（……说话）

RICHARD	So do I ever, being well advised[1].	
	(*Speaks to himself*) For had I cursed now, I had cursed myself.	

Enter CATESBY

CATESBY	Madam, his majesty doth call for you,	320
	And for your grace, and you, my gracious lord.	
ELIZABETH	Catesby, I come. Lords, will you go with me?	
RIVERS	We wait upon your grace.	

Exeunt all but Gloucester

RICHARD	I do the wrong, and first begin to brawl[2].	
	The secret mischiefs[3] that I set abroach	325
	I lay unto the grievous charge of others[4].	
	Clarence, who I indeed have cast in darkness[5],	
	I do beweep[6] to many simple gulls[7],	
	Namely to Derby, Hastings, Buckingham,	
	And tell them 'tis the queen and her allies	330
	That stir the king against the duke my brother.	
	Now they believe it, and withal whet[8] me	
	To be revenged on Rivers, Dorset, Grey.	
	But then I sigh, and with a piece of scripture	
	Tell them that God bids us do good for evil[9].	335
	And thus I clothe my naked villainy	
	With odd[10] old ends[11] stol'n forth of holy writ,	
	And seem a saint when most I play the devil.	

Enter two MURDERERS

	But soft[12], here come my executioners –	
	How now, my hardy[13], stout, resolvèd[14] mates,	340
	Are you now going to dispatch this thing?	
FIRST MURDERER	We are, my lord, and come to have the warrant	
	That we may be admitted where he is.	
RICHARD	Well thought upon, I have it here about me.	
	When you have done, repair to Crosby Place.	345
	But, sirs, be sudden[15] in the execution,	
	Withal obdurate[16]. Do not hear him plead,	
	For Clarence is well spoken and perhaps	
	May move your hearts to pity if you mark[17] him.	

Richard dismisses the Murderers to kill Clarence. In the Tower, Clarence recounts his dream of escaping to Burgundy by boat, from which he was pushed overboard by Richard.

剧情简介：理查派杀手去杀克莱润。伦敦塔里，克莱润讲述他梦到自己坐船逃往勃艮第，却被理查推下甲板。

1 'Go, go, dispatch'

The word 'dispatch' is a **pun** (双关语) – a play on words that have more than one meaning or that look or sound the same (see p. 250). Here, 'dispatch' could mean either 'kill' or 'go quickly'.

- Invent gestures that Richard might use to accompany his words in the shared line 355. Then write a detailed stage direction to advise the actors playing Richard and the Murderers at this point.

2 Symbolising the Tower

Three of the four scenes in Act 1 are set outside, near or in the Tower of London. Some directors of the play use this famous building as a symbol of Richard's cruel regime. Elizabethan staging would have indicated the play's location through dialogue. Modern stage productions, however, often use sophisticated scenery, props (道具) or set design.

- Imagine you are the set designer for a modern stage production. Look for clues about location and other stage properties in the dialogue.
- Sketch how you would present the Tower to symbolise its atmosphere and gruesome (阴森) associations. You might like to make use of some of the imagery in this scene (for example, line 353, where Richard suggests that the Murderers are so hard that if they wept, they would weep stones rather than tears).

3 Clarence's nightmare

In lines 9–63 of Scene 4, Clarence recounts a dream in which he escaped from the Tower and, while sailing to Burgundy, was pushed into the sea by Richard. Drowning, he experiences the terrors of death as he goes to hell. There, he is accused of perjury (背信弃义) and murder, and is taken to be tortured.

He wakes, thinking he is in hell.

- Find a copy of the image of 'Doom' in the Guild Chapel in Stratford-upon-Avon, which Shakespeare would have seen often as a child. List the similarities between Clarence's nightmare and this scene.
- Describe in your own words why Shakespeare's visual imagery is more frightening or alarming. Identify some of the vivid images of death, torture and hell as you do so.

1	prate	聊闲天
2	millstones	磨石
3	fall	滴下
4	straight	马上
5	dispatch	去办事
6	heavily	闷闷不乐
7	Christian faithful man	虔诚的基督徒
8	dismal	沉闷
9	tempted	说服
10	hatches	甲板
11	cited up	回忆起
12	heavy	艰难
13	giddy	摇摇晃晃
14	stay	稳住
15	tumbling billows	汹涌波涛
16	main	大海

King Richard III Act 1 Scene 4
理查三世

SECOND MURDERER	Tut, tut, my lord, we will not stand to prate¹;	350
	Talkers are no good doers. Be assured	
	We go to use our hands and not our tongues.	
RICHARD	Your eyes drop millstones² when fools' eyes fall³ tears.	
	I like you, lads. About your business straight⁴.	
	Go, go, dispatch⁵.	
MURDERERS	We will, my noble lord.	355

Exeunt

Act 1 Scene 4
A room in the Tower of London

Enter CLARENCE *and* KEEPER

KEEPER	Why looks your grace so heavily⁶ today?	
CLARENCE	Oh, I have passed a miserable night,	
	So full of fearful dreams, of ugly sights,	
	That as I am a Christian faithful man⁷,	
	I would not spend another such a night	5
	Though 'twere to buy a world of happy days,	
	So full of dismal⁸ terror was the time.	
KEEPER	What was your dream, my lord? I pray you, tell me.	
CLARENCE	Methoughts that I had broken from the Tower,	
	And was embarked to cross to Burgundy,	10
	And in my company my brother Gloucester,	
	Who from my cabin tempted⁹ me to walk	
	Upon the hatches¹⁰. There we looked toward England	
	And cited up¹¹ a thousand heavy¹² times	
	During the wars of York and Lancaster	15
	That had befall'n us. As we paced along	
	Upon the giddy¹³ footing of the hatches,	
	Methought that Gloucester stumbled, and in falling	
	Struck me, that thought to stay¹⁴ him, overboard	
	Into the tumbling billows¹⁵ of the main¹⁶.	20

Clarence tells the Keeper of the agony of drowning. He recounts how his soul goes to hell, where Warwick accuses him of betrayal. Prince Edward, whom he killed, adds another accusation.

剧情简介：克莱润向看守讲述溺水的痛苦，讲述自己的灵魂怎么去了地狱，怎么在地狱被瓦瑞克骂作叛徒。他杀死的爱德华王子也加入控诉。

1 Dreams of drowning (in pairs)

Clarence's dream of drowning can be divided into four sections. Lines 21–5 tell of the physical pain of drowning; lines 26–8 describe the wealth on the sea bed; lines 29–33 mock the worthlessness of that wealth; and lines 36–41 return to the pain Clarence feels as he wishes to die but cannot.

- One person speaks the lines while the other echoes the key words for each section – for example, words signifying pain in the first section, wealth in the second and so on. Swap roles between sections.

2 Dreams of hell (in pairs or small groups)

Hell was a real and terrifying place for the Elizabethans, and the shrieking of the 'foul fiends' convinces Clarence he is still in hell even after he awakes. The series of vivid images provides one of the most poetic moments in the play.

a Collect images from magazines or the Internet to create a collage that illustrates Clarence's fearful journey through hell. You might get some ideas by looking at paintings by Hieronymus Bosch and Pieter Bruegel.

b In writing, describe your own imagined nightmare in which you journey to hell. Start with the same words:

Oh, I have passed a miserable night,
So full of fearful dreams, of ugly sights …

Write about it 写作练习

Self-realisation (by yourself)

The dream sequence captures a moment of self-revelation as Clarence begins to realise the terrifying consequences of his actions. While in hell, Clarence is first accused of perjury by his father-in-law Warwick (Clarence betrayed Warwick when he switched allegiance in the Wars of the Roses). His second accuser is Edward, Prince of Wales. This ghostly figure, murdered by Richard and Clarence after the Battle of Tewkesbury, is still covered in his own blood.

- Imagine that Clarence had time between his nightmare and his death to write to his family. What might he confess or explain to them? Write two or three paragraphs in a letter to capture his thoughts and emotions as he feels death drawing closer.

1 wracks 沉船
2 gnawed 啃咬
3 Wedges 锭，条，块
4 Inestimable stones 无数宝石
5 unvalued 无价
6 inhabit 长在
7 in scorn of 嘲笑
8 wooed 讨好
9 yield the ghost 交出灵魂（指死亡）
10 envious flood 恶毒的海水
11 Stopped 阻拦
12 panting bulk 大口喘气的躯体
13 belch （大量）喷出
14 melancholy flood 冥河（古代神话里冥河通向阴间）
15 sour ferryman 阴着脸的摆渡人（把灵魂运过冥河去往冥府的渡夫）
16 perpetual night 永无止境的长夜（冥府）
17 stranger-soul 新死的魂灵
18 scourge 酷刑，刑罚（字面意思是"鞭刑"）
19 afford 落在……身上
20 shadow 影子（爱德华王子的鬼魂）
21 Dabbled 浸湿
22 fleeting 反复无常
23 furies 复仇女神
24 torment 地狱（受刑的地方）

O Lord, methought what pain it was to drown,
What dreadful noise of water in mine ears,
What sights of ugly death within mine eyes.
Methoughts I saw a thousand fearful wracks[1],
A thousand men that fishes gnawed[2] upon,
Wedges[3] of gold, great anchors, heaps of pearl,
Inestimable stones[4], unvalued[5] jewels,
All scattered in the bottom of the sea.
Some lay in dead men's skulls, and in the holes
Where eyes did once inhabit[6] there were crept,
As 'twere in scorn of[7] eyes, reflecting gems,
That wooed[8] the slimy bottom of the deep
And mocked the dead bones that lay scattered by.

KEEPER Had you such leisure in the time of death
To gaze upon these secrets of the deep?

CLARENCE Methought I had, and often did I strive
To yield the ghost[9]; but still the envious flood[10]
Stopped[11] in my soul and would not let it forth
To find the empty, vast, and wandering air,
But smothered it within my panting bulk[12],
Who almost burst to belch[13] it in the sea.

KEEPER Awaked you not in this sore agony?

CLARENCE No, no, my dream was lengthened after life.
Oh, then began the tempest to my soul.
I passed, methought, the melancholy flood[14],
With that sour ferryman[15] which poets write of,
Unto the kingdom of perpetual night[16].
The first that there did greet my stranger-soul[17]
Was my great father-in-law, renownèd Warwick,
Who spake aloud, 'What scourge[18] for perjury
Can this dark monarchy afford[19] false Clarence?'
And so he vanished. Then came wandering by
A shadow[20] like an angel, with bright hair
Dabbled[21] in blood, and he shrieked out aloud,
'Clarence is come: false, fleeting[22], perjured Clarence,
That stabbed me in the field by Tewkesbury.
Seize on him, furies[23], take him unto torment[24].'

Clarence, recalling his dream, confesses his misdeeds. He prays for mercy from God for his family, then sleeps. Brakenbury reflects on how outward appearance often hides inner turmoil. The Murderers bring Richard's warrant.

剧情简介：克莱润一边回忆自己的梦境，一边坦白自己的过错。他祈求上帝宽恕他的家族，然后就睡了。布莱肯布瑞感慨镇静的外表下常隐藏着汹涌的内心。杀手带着理查给的通行证来了。

1 After the dream (in threes)

Clarence admits committing horrific acts during the civil war, and his conversation with the Keeper reveals his troubled state of mind.

a Talk together about how far (if at all) Clarence's dream journey of self-exploration and confession has changed your opinion of him.

b Take parts as Clarence and the Keeper to prepare a dramatic reading of lines 64–75. The third person, in role as director, advises on the tone and the actions to express:

- the fear both men feel
- Clarence's confessional and religious tone
- the Keeper's sympathy for Clarence.

Stagecraft 导演技巧

The cares of high office (in pairs)

The actor playing Brakenbury asks you for help. He finds some of lines 76–83 unclear and is unsure what he should do as he speaks. He points out that 'unfelt imaginations' could mean 'things imagined but not experienced', or 'ordinary people imagine a happiness that princes have never felt'. He is confident in his interpretation of the first four lines (that sorrow destroys the borders between the seasons, sleep, day and night; and that even the title 'prince' cannot prevent the consequences of sorrow).

- In role as the director of a new production of the play, consider how to advise the actor. What help would you give him and what is your understanding of these lines?
- Write notes for the actor, giving your interpretation of the meaning of the second part of Brakenbury's speech (lines 80–3), and suggesting how this will affect his behaviour towards the sleeping Clarence. Remember to make reference to your interpretation of specific words and phrases from the speech in the script opposite.
- Add to your notes to describe how Brakenbury should react when his thoughts are interrupted at the stage direction '*Enter two* MURDERERS'.

1 legion 一大群
2 Environed 围困
3 hideous 可怕
4 season 很久
5 impression 形象
6 though = that
7 methinkes 我觉得
8 requites 报答
9 appease 抚慰
10 spare 饶恕
11 fain 想要
12 *Lieutenant* 副官
13 breaks seasons 打乱劳作时间
14 reposing hours 休息时间
15 inward toil 内心的不安
16 unfelt imaginations 感觉不到的荣光
17 restless 永无停歇
18 low name 白丁俗客
19 outward fame 街谈巷议
20 hither = here
21 brief 简短
22 tedious 啰唆
23 commission 通行证

	With that, methought, a legion[1] of foul fiends	
	Environed[2] me, and howlèd in mine ears	
	Such hideous[3] cries that with the very noise	60
	I trembling waked, and for a season[4] after	
	Could not believe but that I was in hell,	
	Such terrible impression[5] made my dream.	
KEEPER	No marvel, lord, though[6] it affrighted you.	
	I am afraid, methinks[7], to hear you tell it.	65
CLARENCE	Ah keeper, keeper, I have done these things	
	That now give evidence against my soul	
	For Edward's sake, and see how he requites[8] me.	
	O God, if my deep prayers cannot appease[9] thee,	
	But thou wilt be avenged on my misdeeds,	70
	Yet execute thy wrath in me alone.	
	Oh, spare[10] my guiltless wife and my poor children.	
	Keeper, I prithee sit by me awhile.	
	My soul is heavy, and I fain[11] would sleep.	
KEEPER	I will, my lord. God give your grace good rest.	75

Enter BRAKENBURY, *the Lieutenant*[12]

BRAKENBURY Sorrow breaks seasons[13] and reposing hours[14],
Makes the night morning and the noontide night.
Princes have but their titles for their glories,
An outward honour for an inward toil[15],
And for unfelt imaginations[16]   80
They often feel a world of restless[17] cares;
So that between their titles and low name[18]
There's nothing differs but the outward fame[19].

Enter two MURDERERS

FIRST MURDERER Ho, who's here?
BRAKENBURY What wouldst thou, fellow? And how cam'st thou hither[20]?   85
SECOND MURDERER I would speak with Clarence, and I came hither on my legs.
BRAKENBURY What, so brief[21]?
FIRST MURDERER 'Tis better, sir, than to be tedious[22].   90
Let him see our commission[23], and talk no more.

Brakenbury leaves the Murderers alone with Clarence. They discuss whether to kill Clarence immediately. The Second Murderer fears that he will be damned for killing Clarence, but is tempted by the thought of reward.

剧情简介：布莱肯布瑞让杀手们和克莱润单独在一起。他们商量要不要马上动手杀了克莱润。杀手乙担心自己会因为杀了他下地狱，但又不愿放弃报酬。

Write about it 写作练习

Brakenbury's motives (in pairs)

Brakenbury has received Richard's warrant. In contrast to the ambiguity of his first speech, he is now very clear about what he must do to protect himself from blame.

a   In preparation for the writing activity, take turns to speak lines 92–8. Afterwards, talk together about Brakenbury's reaction to the warrant. Why might he want to tell King Edward how he has acted? What would *you* do?

b   Write Brakenbury's diary entry at the end of the day to show his motives for behaving the way he did and his responses to the events that have taken place.

1   deliver   移交
2   reason   询问
3   will be = want to be
4   signify   禀告
5   urging   再三提及
6   bred   造成
7   remorse   怜悯
8   resolute   决心
9   passionate   慈悲，怜悯
10 wont   经常
11 tells twenty   数到二十
12 dregs   残渣
13 entertain   待见，欢迎

Themes 主题分析

The pangs (剧痛) of conscience (I) (in pairs)

Conscience is a major theme of the play. Characters delight in, or are tortured by, thoughts of their misdeeds. Both Clarence and Brakenbury have listened anxiously to their consciences, and now Shakespeare presents the Murderers wrestling with their sense of right and wrong in a witty and clever way, as they balance conscience and payment. The Second Murderer is worried that Clarence's murder could damn his soul, but is persuaded by the reward Richard will give him. Even the First Murderer seems to feel the pangs of conscience briefly.

a   To gain a first impression of this 'wrestling with conscience' episode, take parts as the two Murderers. Stand opposite each other as you read through lines 100–44. Take steps forward or backward according to how forceful or persuasive your Murderer is at any given line. Which Murderer is most dominant by the end of this section?

b   Create a table with two columns. In one column list what stops the Murderers from killing Clarence, and in the second column list the advantages of murdering him.

[Brakenbury] reads

BRAKENBURY I am in this commanded to deliver[1]
The noble Duke of Clarence to your hands.
I will not reason[2] what is meant hereby,
Because I will be[3] guiltless from the meaning. 95
There lies the duke asleep, and there the keys.
I'll to the king and signify[4] to him
That thus I have resigned to you my charge.

Exeunt [Brakenbury and Keeper]

FIRST MURDERER You may, sir, 'tis a point of wisdom. Fare you well.
SECOND MURDERER What, shall we stab him as he sleeps? 100
FIRST MURDERER No. He'll say 'twas done cowardly, when he wakes.
SECOND MURDERER Why, he shall never wake until the great judgement day.
FIRST MURDERER Why, then he'll say we stabbed him sleeping.
SECOND MURDERER The urging[5] of that word judgement hath bred[6] a 105
kind of remorse[7] in me.
FIRST MURDERER What? Art thou afraid?
SECOND MURDERER Not to kill him, having a warrant,
But to be damned for killing him, from the which
No warrant can defend me. 110
FIRST MURDERER I thought thou hadst been resolute[8].
SECOND MURDERER So I am, to let him live.
FIRST MURDERER I'll back to the Duke of Gloucester and tell him so.
SECOND MURDERER Nay, I prithee stay a little.
I hope this passionate[9] humour of mine will change. 115
It was wont[10] to hold me but while one tells twenty[11].
FIRST MURDERER How dost thou feel thyself now?
SECOND MURDERER Some certain dregs[12] of conscience are yet within me.
FIRST MURDERER Remember our reward when the deed's done. 120
SECOND MURDERER Come, he dies. I had forgot the reward.
FIRST MURDERER Where's thy conscience now?
SECOND MURDERER Oh, in the Duke of Gloucester's purse.
FIRST MURDERER When he opens his purse to give us our reward, thy
conscience flies out. 125
SECOND MURDERER 'Tis no matter; let it go. There's few or none will
entertain[13] it.
FIRST MURDERER What if it come to thee again?

The Murderers reject the claims of conscience. They decide to strike Clarence on the head and throw his body in a barrel of wine. Clarence wakes and guesses correctly that they have come to murder him.

剧情简介：两个杀手拒绝听命于良心。他们决定猛击克莱润的脑袋，然后把他扔进酒桶。克莱润醒来，猜出他们是来杀他的。

Themes 主题分析

The pangs of conscience (II) (in pairs)

Lines 129–37 are the Second Murderer's catalogue of how conscience constrains human behaviour. Stealing, swearing and adultery are three of the fundamental sins prohibited in the Bible.

a One person speaks the lines and pauses at the end of each sentence. The other person explains in their own words what conscience makes humans do.

b What else does conscience make people do? List the ideas given in the script opposite. Then come up with some ideas and add them to the list. Try to capture the same kind of comic tone by describing why conscience is such a hindrance (妨碍) to someone who has evil intentions.

1 Get on with it! (in threes)

Some critics argue that the Murderers' lines 100–44 are irrelevant to the plot. Imagine the director wants to cut the lines to reduce the play's running time. The actors playing the Murderers disagree, arguing that the episode expresses major themes of the play.

- Make notes from both perspectives, then improvise the discussion that takes place, developing each argument as you do so. Remember to quote directly from the play to illustrate your points.

Stagecraft 导演技巧

On stage or off stage? (in pairs)

Some stage designers have wanted to cut the words 'in the next room' from line 146 because they want 'the malmsey butt' to be visible to the audience as a symbol of Clarence's fear of drowning.

- In role as stage designer, write out the advice you would give to the director about the set design, props and lighting for this scene. Then give the director's response to the stage designer's ideas in the form of footnotes at the bottom of the page in your Director's Journal.

1 it （指良心）
2 checks 制止
3 detects 发现
4 shamefaced 害羞
5 mutinies 作乱
6 bosom 心里
7 beggars 让……变得贫穷
8 Take the devil 拒绝那个恶魔
9 insinuate with thee 拉拢你
10 tall 勇敢
11 Take him on the costard 击他的脑袋
12 hilts 柄
13 malmsey butt 马尔慕悉酒（一种甜葡萄酒）桶
14 sop 浸过酒的面包
15 reason 说说话
16 anon 马上
17 humble 卑微
18 darkly 隐晦；藏着煞气
19 Wherefore = Why

SECOND MURDERER   I'll not meddle with it[1]; it makes a man a coward. A man cannot steal but it accuseth him. A man cannot swear but it checks[2] him. A man cannot lie with his neighbour's wife, but it detects[3] him. 'Tis a blushing, shamefaced[4] spirit that mutinies[5] in a man's bosom[6]. It fills a man full of obstacles. It made me once restore a purse of gold that by chance I found. It beggars[7] any man that keeps it. It is turned out of towns and cities for a dangerous thing, and every man that means to live well endeavours to trust to himself and live without it.

FIRST MURDERER   'Tis even now at my elbow, persuading me not to kill the duke.

SECOND MURDERER   Take the devil[8] in thy mind, and believe him not. He would insinuate with thee[9] but to make thee sigh.

FIRST MURDERER   I am strong framed, he cannot prevail with me.

SECOND MURDERER   Spoke like a tall[10] man that respects thy reputation. Come, shall we fall to work?

FIRST MURDERER   Take him on the costard[11] with the hilts[12] of thy sword, and then throw him into the malmsey butt[13] in the next room.

SECOND MURDERER   Oh, excellent device. And make a sop[14] of him.

FIRST MURDERER   Soft, he wakes.

SECOND MURDERER   Strike!

FIRST MURDERER   No, we'll reason[15] with him.

CLARENCE   Where art thou, keeper? Give me a cup of wine.

SECOND MURDERER   You shall have wine enough, my lord, anon[16].

CLARENCE   In God's name, what art thou?

FIRST MURDERER   A man, as you are.

CLARENCE   But not, as I am, royal.

FIRST MURDERER   Nor you, as we are, loyal.

CLARENCE   Thy voice is thunder, but thy looks are humble[17].

FIRST MURDERER   My voice is now the king's, my looks mine own.

CLARENCE   How darkly[18] and how deadly dost thou speak! Your eyes do menace me. Why look you pale? Who sent you hither? Wherefore[19] do you come?

SECOND MURDERER   To, to, to –

CLARENCE   To murder me?

BOTH   Ay, ay.

CLARENCE   You scarcely have the hearts to tell me so, And therefore cannot have the hearts to do it. Wherein, my friends, have I offended you?

FIRST MURDERER   Offended us you have not, but the king.

Clarence argues that he has not been convicted of any crime, and that only God has the right to punish him. He claims that he murdered Prince Edward for the sake of his brother, King Edward.

 剧情简介： 克莱润辩解说自己并未被认定犯了任何罪行，只有上帝有权审判他。他还说杀掉爱德华王子都是为了他哥哥，即爱德华王。

Themes 主题分析
A damnable deed

To save his life, Clarence cites the supreme authority of God's law against murder. He argues that the law of God ('The great King of kings') is above the secular (世俗) power of the earthly king. In response, the Murderers remind Clarence of the murders he himself has committed in battle and tell him he has no right to tell them to keep God's law.

a   Read through the script opposite. Then condense the conversation into main points so that you capture the essence of the argument (try to limit yourself to fewer than seven points).

b   In groups, share your main points and discuss which you think carries the most weight. List them in order to show how convincing each point is, with the most convincing point at the top of the list.

c   In a paragraph, explain why you think Shakespeare extended this murder scene with such detailed discussion about God's authority versus kingly authority.

1 quest 裁决团
2 verdict 判决
3 convìct 定罪
4 as … goodness 如果你们还希望得到救赎
5 is damnable 受诅咒
6 Erroneous vassals 误入歧途的奴才
7 King of kings 诸王之王（即上帝）
8 table of his law 十诫
9 Spurn at his edict 背弃他的法令
10 receive the sacrament 向上帝发誓
11 Unripped'st 劈开，剖开
12 thy sovereign's son 君王之子（即亨利六世的儿子爱德华）
13 dear 骇人
14 yet 还要
15 he doth it publicly 他公然自己动手
16 indirect 见不得人

CLARENCE	I shall be reconciled to him again.	
SECOND MURDERER	Never, my lord. Therefore prepare to die.	170
CLARENCE	Are you drawn forth among a world of men	
	To slay the innocent? What is my offence?	
	Where is the evidence that doth accuse me?	
	What lawful quest[1] have given their verdict[2] up	
	Unto the frowning judge? Or who pronounced	175
	The bitter sentence of poor Clarence' death	
	Before I be convìct[3] by course of law?	
	To threaten me with death is most unlawful.	
	I charge you, as you hope for any goodness[4],	
	That you depart and lay no hands on me.	180
	The deed you undertake is damnable[5].	
FIRST MURDERER	What we will do, we do upon command.	
SECOND MURDERER	And he that hath commanded is our king.	
CLARENCE	Erroneous vassals[6]! The great King of kings[7]	
	Hath in the table of his law[8] commanded	185
	That thou shalt do no murder. Will you then	
	Spurn at his edict[9] and fulfil a man's?	
	Take heed, for he holds vengeance in his hand	
	To hurl upon their heads that break his law.	
SECOND MURDERER	And that same vengeance doth he hurl on thee	190
	For false forswearing and for murder, too.	
	Thou didst receive the sacrament[10] to fight	
	In quarrel of the house of Lancaster.	
FIRST MURDERER	And, like a traitor to the name of God,	
	Didst break that vow, and with thy treacherous blade	195
	Unripped'st[11] the bowels of thy sovereign's son[12].	
SECOND MURDERER	Whom thou wast sworn to cherish and defend.	
FIRST MURDERER	How canst thou urge God's dreadful law to us	
	When thou hast broke it in such dear[13] degree?	
CLARENCE	Alas! For whose sake did I that ill deed?	200
	For Edward, for my brother, for his sake.	
	He sends you not to murder me for this,	
	For in that sin he is as deep as I.	
	If God will be avengèd for the deed,	
	Oh, know you yet[14], he doth it publicly[15].	205
	Take not the quarrel from his powerful arm.	
	He needs no indirect[16] or lawless course	
	To cut off those that have offended him.	

Clarence, believing King Edward seeks his death, claims Richard will reward the Murderers for letting him live. Refusing to believe Richard has ordered his murder, he argues that the Murderers will be damned for killing him.

 剧情简介：克莱润以为是爱德华国王要杀他，声称只要饶他不死，理查会重赏杀手。他不愿相信是理查下令灭他的口，坚称杀手会因为杀了他而下地狱。

1 The Plantagenets (in sixes)

Lines 209–28 are filled with references to the Plantagenet family: Prince Edward (son of Henry VI), King Edward, Richard (Duke of Gloucester), the Duke of York.

- Take parts as Clarence (himself a Plantagenet) and these four characters. The sixth person speaks all the lines slowly, and each person raises their hand as their character is mentioned. The others should point to the character they believe is referred to.

2 Two Murderers (in pairs)

In lines 224–38, the First Murderer's play on words is at once comic and cruel. His attitude towards Clarence is contrasted with that of the Second Murderer and reveals much about his character.

a Identify each instance of sarcasm or punning in which the First Murderer contradicts Clarence, and consider how Clarence might respond to him.

b How would you describe the difference between the two Murderers? Write a paragraph comparing them and explaining how you would like to see them represented on stage.

1 **gallant-springing** 血气方刚
2 **Plantagenet** 金雀花（指爱德华王子；当时英格兰是在金雀花王朝统治之下，王室成员可以称为金雀花）
3 **novice** 初出茅庐之人
4 **tidings** 消息
5 **deceived** 欺骗
6 **holds me dear** 不计成本地爱我
7 **princely** 高贵
8 **victorious** 战无不胜
9 **lessoned** 教导
10 **labour my delivery** 为救我出狱而奔走
11 **thraldom** 奴役
12 **set you on** 指使你们

Stagecraft 导演技巧

A brother's love – or hate? (in threes)

Clarence cannot believe that his brother Richard wants him dead, but the two Murderers know the truth: Richard is scheming (诡计多端) and duplicitous (两面三刀). Somewhere between lines 236 and 240, Clarence abandons his belief that Richard loves him. Shakespeare leaves it up to the actor to work out what triggers Clarence's realisation of the truth and how he responds to the news that his brother seeks his death.

a In small groups, step into the roles of Clarence and the Murderers. Discuss what each man might do to show the audience what brings about Clarence's sudden realisation that his brother has ordered his death.

b Write notes in your Director's Journal to describe how you would want this scene to be portrayed in a modern stage production.

KING RICHARD III ACT 1 SCENE 4
理查三世

FIRST MURDERER	Who made thee, then, a bloody minister	
	When gallant-springing¹ brave Plantagenet²,	210
	That princely novice³, was struck dead by thee?	
CLARENCE	My brother's love, the devil, and my rage.	
FIRST MURDERER	Thy brother's love, our duty, and thy faults	
	Provoke us hither now to slaughter thee.	
CLARENCE	If you do love my brother, hate not me.	215
	I am his brother, and I love him well.	
	If you are hired for meed, go back again,	
	And I will send you to my brother Gloucester,	
	Who shall reward you better for my life	
	Than Edward will for tidings⁴ of my death.	220
SECOND MURDERER	You are deceived⁵. Your brother Gloucester hates you.	
CLARENCE	Oh, no, he loves me, and he holds me dear⁶.	
	Go you to him from me.	
FIRST MURDERER	Ay, so we will.	
CLARENCE	Tell him, when that our princely⁷ father York	225
	Blessed his three sons with his victorious⁸ arm,	
	He little thought of this divided friendship.	
	Bid Gloucester think on this, and he will weep.	
FIRST MURDERER	Ay, millstones, as he lessoned⁹ us to weep.	
CLARENCE	Oh, do not slander him, for he is kind.	230
FIRST MURDERER	Right, as snow in harvest.	
	Come, you deceive yourself,	
	'Tis he that sends us to destroy you here.	
CLARENCE	It cannot be, for he bewept my fortune,	
	And hugged me in his arms, and swore with sobs	235
	That he would labour my delivery¹⁰.	
FIRST MURDERER	Why, so he doth, when he delivers you	
	From this earth's thraldom¹¹ to the joys of heaven.	
SECOND MURDERER	Make peace with God, for you must die, my lord.	
CLARENCE	Have you that holy feeling in your souls	240
	To counsel me to make my peace with God,	
	And are you yet to your own souls so blind	
	That you will war with God by murdering me?	
	O sirs, consider, they that set you on¹²	
	To do this deed will hate you for the deed.	245
SECOND MURDERER	What shall we do?	

63

Clarence begs the murderers to have pity, but he is stabbed by the First Murderer, who drags off the body and throws it in the malmsey butt. The Second Murderer wishes he had saved Clarence.

 剧情简介：克莱润乞求两个杀手可怜他，但还是被杀手甲刺死，尸体被他拖着扔进马尔慕悉酒桶。杀手乙后悔没能救下克莱润。

Stagecraft 导演技巧
Staging Clarence's murder (in small groups)

a The murder of Clarence is the dramatic climax of Act 1. Work out how to stage the episode for greatest dramatic effect. Some hints and suggestions are given below.

- Clarence's words 'My friend, I spy some pity in thy looks' and the following 'Look behind you, my lord' suggest that the Second Murderer tries to prevent the killing (lines 254 and 258).
- One person speaks lines 253–9; the others mime Clarence and the two Murderers. In very slow motion, devise the most dramatically effective method for the stabbing of Clarence.
- The actor playing the First Murderer wants Clarence alive after the stabbing so he can be drowned in the malmsey butt. He argues that this will make the scene even more horrific. The actor playing the Second Murderer disagrees, saying that if Clarence were still alive, his remorse would make him intervene to save Clarence from drowning. Talk together about which actor's suggestion you find the more convincing.
- The First Murderer plans to find a temporary hiding place for Clarence's body, then escape before the deed is discovered. The Second Murderer distances himself from the killing (lines 266–8), wishing he had tried to save Clarence and refusing his share of the reward.
- Work out how to stage the exits of the two Murderers, emphasising their contrasting characters. Does the First Murderer exit with Clarence's body? Or does he leave the body on stage and expect the Second Murderer to do the heavy lifting, returning to tell him off when he does not?

b When you have worked through these ideas, experiment with different ways of performing this exciting climax. Remember to include some of the main points of the discussions between Clarence and the Murderers in the lead-up to the murder.

1 Relent 发慈悲
2 pent from liberty 被幽禁
3 entreat 哀求，恳求
4 as you would beg 仿佛你们在求饶
5 womanish 妇人心肠（莎士比亚笔下的坏人经常把怜悯、同情心和女人联系在一起）
6 spy 发现
7 if … flatterer 如果你的眼睛不是个谄媚者
8 malmsey butt within 里屋的马尔慕悉酒桶
9 desperately 孤注一掷
10 Pilate 彼拉多（罗马帝国犹太行省总督，他不认为耶稣有罪，但迫于犹太宗教领袖的压力，把耶稣钉死在十字架上后就在众人面前洗手，以示耶稣的死和他无关）
11 grievous 痛苦
12 slack 偷懒
13 will out 将人尽皆知

CLARENCE   Relent[1], and save your souls.
Which of you, if you were a prince's son,
Being pent from liberty[2], as I am now,
If two such murderers as yourselves came to you,
Would not entreat[3] for life as you would beg[4],   250
Were you in my distress?
FIRST MURDERER   Relent? No. 'Tis cowardly and womanish[5].
CLARENCE   Not to relent is beastly, savage, devilish.
My friend, I spy[6] some pity in thy looks.
Oh, if thine eye be not a flatterer[7],   255
Come thou on my side and entreat for me;
A begging prince, what beggar pities not?
SECOND MURDERER   Look behind you, my lord.
FIRST MURDERER   Take that, and that.
                              (*Stabs him*)
                    If all this will not do,
I'll drown you in the malmsey butt within[8].   260
                                        Exit [*with Clarence's body*]
SECOND MURDERER   A bloody deed, and desperately[9] dispatched.
How fain, like Pilate[10], would I wash my hands
Of this most grievous[11] murder.

                    Enter FIRST MURDERER

FIRST MURDERER   How now? What mean'st thou that thou help'st me not?
By heaven, the duke shall know how slack[12] you have been.   265
SECOND MURDERER   I would he knew that I had saved his brother.
Take thou the fee, and tell him what I say,
For I repent me that the duke is slain.   *Exit*
FIRST MURDERER   So do not I. Go, coward as thou art.
Well, I'll go hide the body in some hole   270
Till that the duke give order for his burial;
And when I have my meed, I will away,
For this will out[13], and then I must not stay.   *Exit*

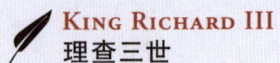

King Richard III
理查三世

Looking back at Act 1 第1幕回顾
Activities for groups or individuals

1 Setting the scene
Many productions try to establish the play's atmosphere and concerns in its opening moments through a striking dramatic image. The 1996 movie version begins with an eight-minute sequence that includes a battle followed by Yorkist celebrations. Laurence Olivier's film (made in 1955) has a five-minute portrayal of King Edward's coronation before Richard's opening soliloquy.

- Before Richard speaks, what dramatic image or brief sequence would you use to suggest an important theme of the play? Discuss with a partner, then make some notes or sketches in your Director's Journal.

2 Richard insulted
In Scenes 2 and 3, many characters insult and direct abuse at Richard.

- List as many insults directed at Richard as you can. (One example is 'hedgehog' in Scene 2, line 105, which could refer to Richard's emblem (徽章) of the hog or boar, or to his hunchback (驼背), or it could simply be a general term for a person without feelings.)
- Suggest what each of the insults you have found might mean, and identify what common themes they reveal about how others regard Richard.

3 Richard's secret agenda
Richard makes clear his secret thoughts and intentions through soliloquies or apparently innocuous (无伤大雅) remarks addressed to characters on stage. For example, in Scene 1, he openly reveals his plot against Clarence and finds ways to insult and arouse suspicions about Queen Elizabeth, the Woodville family and Jane Shore.

- Quickly read through Scenes 1, 2 and 3 and identify where Richard reveals his secret thoughts.
- Jot down the objectives he has for the future at these moments. Which of these have been achieved by the end of the act?

4 Richard's appearance
Richard's physical appearance is vital to the play. Shakespeare relied on Sir Thomas More's *History of King Richard the Third* (published in 1513) for a description of what Richard was like. More described Richard as:

Little of stature, ill featured of limbs, crook-backed, his left shoulder much higher than his right, hard favoured of visage.

In Shakespeare's play, Richard tells us that he was born 'deformed, unfinished' and so 'rudely stamped' that dogs bark at him as he limps past them. In Shakespeare's day, many people believed that Richard's 'deformity' was an outward sign of his wickedness, although in his opening speech Richard claims that he has turned to evil because he looks different and feels unloved.

Directors might choose to represent Richard as completely evil and grotesque (丑陋奇异) in appearance, or realistically as someone with a physical disability that makes him different from other people.

a In pairs, study the picture of Richard opposite and those elsewhere in this edition. Then step into role as director and the actor playing Richard and discuss some possible ways of presenting him physically.

b On your own, write a paragraph or two outlining your ideas and giving a detailed description of how you would portray Richard on stage in a new production.

King Edward attempts to reconcile the quarrelling nobles. Queen Elizabeth, Rivers and Dorset (the Woodvilles) swear love and friendship with Hastings. The King asks Buckingham to join the peace pact.

剧情简介：爱德华国王试图让争吵不休的贵族们言归于好。伊丽莎白王后、瑞沃和多塞（伍德威尔家族）起誓要与海斯廷结好。国王要求白金汉也加入和平协定。

1 Do actions speak louder than words?
(in small groups)

King Edward attempts to reconcile the Woodville family (Queen Elizabeth, her son Dorset and her brother Rivers) with those who oppose them (Hastings and Buckingham).

a As one person speaks lines 1–40, the rest of the group echoes all the words and phrases about friendship and religion.

b Draw a simple representation (such as a stick figure) of each character and write down their intentions in a thought bubble.

2 How genuine is the reconciliation? **(in sixes)**

Take parts as King Edward, Rivers, Hastings, Queen Elizabeth, Dorset and Buckingham. Act out lines 1–40, using all the actions that are mentioned or suggested – for example: 'Rivers and Hastings, take each other's hand' (line 7), 'So thrive I, as I truly swear the like' (line 11), 'There, Hastings, I will never more remember / Our former hatred, so thrive I and mine' (lines 23–24), 'Dorset, embrace him' (line 25).

- First perform the lines so that an audience would see a sincere agreement of friendship.
- Then perform the lines so that an audience would see a display of friendship that conceals hatred and suggests a lack of forgiveness.

1 peers　众位大人
2 united league　团结友爱
3 embassage　（死亡的）音讯
4 my … hence　我的救世主将我从此地救走（爱德华盼死）
5 Dissemble not　不要伪装
6 purged　净化
7 seal　印证
8 So … like　我的誓言有多真，老天就保佑我有多顺利
9 dally　弄虚作假
10 Confound　摧毁
11 award　确保
12 exempt　免除
13 factious　拉帮结派
14 unfeignedly　心怀真诚
15 protest　发誓
16 inviolable　坚不可摧

Stagecraft 导演技巧

Dramatic irony (in pairs)

King Edward warns Rivers and Hastings not to be insincere in front of him, because God will see through their deceit and their hypocrisy will be revealed. He is unaware that Clarence has just been murdered, and he uses the language of piety, love and peace.

- As the director of a modern performance, how would you use sound effects, lighting, stage space and actors' gestures to increase the dramatic tension in the script opposite? Remember, the dramatic irony is that the audience understands the King's request for peace and his threats of divine justice in the light of Clarence's murder. Discuss this with your partner, then write notes in your Director's Journal.

Act 2 Scene 1

London: a room in King Edward's palace

Flourish. Enter KING EDWARD (*sick*), QUEEN ELIZABETH,
LORD MARQUESS DORSET, RIVERS, HASTINGS, CATESBY,
BUCKINGHAM *and others*

KING EDWARD Why, so. Now have I done a good day's work.
You peers[1], continue this united league[2].
I every day expect an embassage[3]
From my redeemer to redeem me hence[4].
And more to peace my soul shall part to heaven, 5
Since I have made my friends at peace on earth.
Rivers and Hastings, take each other's hand.
Dissemble not[5] your hatred; swear your love.

RIVERS By heaven, my soul is purged[6] from grudging hate,
And with my hand I seal[7] my true heart's love. 10

HASTINGS So thrive I, as I truly swear the like[8].

KING EDWARD Take heed you dally[9] not before your king,
Lest he that is the supreme King of kings
Confound[10] your hidden falsehood and award[11]
Either of you to be the other's end. 15

HASTINGS So prosper I, as I swear perfect love.

RIVERS And I, as I love Hastings with my heart.

KING EDWARD Madam, yourself is not exempt[12] from this,
Nor you, son Dorset, Buckingham, nor you;
You have been factious[13] one against the other. 20
Wife, love Lord Hastings, let him kiss your hand,
And what you do, do it unfeignedly[14].

ELIZABETH There, Hastings, I will never more remember
Our former hatred, so thrive I and mine.

KING EDWARD Dorset, embrace him. Hastings, love lord marquess. 25

DORSET This interchange of love, I here protest[15],
Upon my part shall be inviolable[16].

HASTINGS And so swear I.

KING EDWARD Now, princely Buckingham, seal thou this league
With thy embracements to my wife's allies, 30
And make me happy in your unity.

Buckingham pledges his love and loyalty to King Edward. The King wishes for Richard to arrive to complete the peace process. Richard enters and expresses peace and goodwill to everyone present.

 剧情简介：白金汉向爱德华国王宣誓效忠。国王希望理查也加入和平进程，以使之圆满。理查登场，向在场所有人表示和平与友好。

1 Enter Ratcliffe and Richard (in pairs)

In some productions, Richard and Ratcliffe are already on stage and hear King Edward's wish that his brother Richard was present (line 43).

- Suggest what dramatic effects might be achieved by having Richard and Ratcliffe enter unobserved by the others before this point in the scene.

Characters 人物分析

Sincere friendship? (in pairs)

Richard asks to be reconciled with those he might have offended. But he suggests that people's hostility arises from wrong information ('fasle intelligence') and incorrect conclusions ('wrong surmise'). He suggests that if he did anything to cause resentment, it was done 'unwillingly, or in my rage'.

a How might an actor playing Richard make it clear to an audience that his words are not sincere?

b 'Lord Woodville' and 'Lord Scales' (line 68) are other titles of Lord Rivers. How might Richard make a joke of line 68?

c Suggest how each character reacts to Richard's offer of friendship.

1 but 除……外
2 Deep 神秘，不为人知
3 cordial 舒心药
4 wanteth 缺少
5 period 圆满
6 Good morrow = Good morning
7 charity 善事
8 swelling 怒气冲冲
9 wrong-incensèd 发错了火
10 princely heap 出身高贵的伙伴们
11 aught committed 做出任何事
12 is hardly borne 造成伤害
13 at enmity 与人为敌
14 cousin 兄弟（既可称呼近亲，也可称呼远亲）
15 lodged 存在
16 all without desert 毫无缘由

KING RICHARD III ACT 2 SCENE 1
理查三世

BUCKINGHAM Whenever Buckingham doth turn his hate
Upon your grace, but¹ with all duteous love
Doth cherish you and yours, God punish me
With hate in those where I expect most love. 35
When I have most need to employ a friend,
And most assurèd that he is a friend,
Deep², hollow, treacherous, and full of guile
Be he unto me. This do I beg of heaven,
When I am cold in love to you or yours. 40

Embrace

KING EDWARD A pleasing cordial³, princely Buckingham,
Is this thy vow unto my sickly heart.
There wanteth⁴ now our brother Gloucester here
To make the blessèd period⁵ of this peace.

BUCKINGHAM And in good time, 45
Here comes Sir Richard Ratcliffe and the duke.

Enter RATCLIFFE *and* RICHARD

RICHARD Good morrow⁶ to my sovereign king and queen;
And princely peers, a happy time of day.

KING EDWARD Happy indeed, as we have spent the day.
Gloucester, we have done deeds of charity⁷, 50
Made peace of enmity, fair love of hate,
Between these swelling⁸ wrong-incensèd⁹ peers.

RICHARD A blessèd labour, my most sovereign lord.
Among this princely heap¹⁰, if any here
By false intelligence or wrong surmise 55
Hold me a foe; if I unwillingly or in my rage
Have aught committed¹¹ that is hardly borne¹²
To any in this presence, I desire
To reconcile me to his friendly peace.
'Tis death to me to be at enmity¹³; 60
I hate it and desire all good men's love.
First, madam, I entreat true peace of you,
Which I will purchase with my duteous service;
Of you, my noble cousin¹⁴ Buckingham,
If ever any grudge were lodged¹⁵ between us; 65
Of you and you, Lord Rivers, and of Dorset,
That all without desert¹⁶ have frowned on me;
Of you, Lord Woodville, and Lord Scales, of you;
Dukes, earls, lords, gentlemen, indeed of all.

Richard claims to be free of all thoughts of enmity. Elizabeth requests a pardon for Clarence. Richard announces Clarence's death and casts suspicion on the Woodvilles. Derby asks a favour of Edward.

 剧情简介：理查声称自己没有任何敌意。伊丽莎白请求国王宽恕克莱润。理查宣布克莱润已死讯，把怀疑指向伍德威尔家族。达比请求爱德华开恩。

Stagecraft 导演技巧

'They all start' (in pairs)

Amid words of peace and reconciliation – and as Queen Elizabeth anticipates future celebrations of this new unity in the court – Richard suddenly announces the shocking news that his brother Clarence is dead.

a Discuss how you would stage lines 70–88 to make the shift in mood as dramatic as possible. How would you heighten the impact of the series of questions that follows?

b After this revelation, Richard seizes the opportunity to cast suspicion on the Woodvilles. One person speaks lines 89–96 very slowly, pausing at the end of each line. In the pause, the other suggests how Richard can use actions and expressions to throw suspicion on others.

1 Shakespeare's stage

Shakespeare's stage was bare, with none of the lavish sets, stage mechanics or special lighting and sound effects that we are familiar with today. As a result, Shakespeare included many verbal cues so that the audience could imagine rather than actually see what was happening on stage. Buckingham's line 85 ('Look I so pale, Lord Dorset, as the rest?') is an example of one of these visual clues.

- What might be the significance of Buckingham's comment, if Shakespeare is drawing the audience's attention to it in this way?

Write about it 写作练习

Stanley's awkward moment (by yourself)

Stanley, Earl of Derby, makes an unfortunate entrance at a tense and emotional moment. He asks for his servant's life to be spared as a favour, in return for the services he has rendered to his lord. Stanley does not realise that he is intruding on the King's grief and shock at the discovery of Clarence's death. Stanley is in the wrong place at the wrong time, and his request prompts an emotional outburst from the King from line 104.

- Write Stanley's diary entry, describing the treatment he receives and noting his observations of the scene he walks into. (You might like to read ahead to the end of the scene before you start writing).

1 jot 一丁点儿
2 at odds 冲突
3 be kept hereafter 被人铭记
4 compounded 平息
5 grace 宽恕
6 flouted 蔑视，辱骂
7 in this royal presence 在国王面前
8 forsook 离弃
9 reversed 撤销
10 wingèd Mercury 穿戴着翅膀的墨丘利（罗马神话里诸神的使者，头戴飞翼帽，脚穿飞翼鞋，来去如风）
11 tardy cripple 拖拖拉拉的跛子
12 lag = late
13 Nearer ... blood 血统上离得远，血腥念头上离得近
14 go current from 逍遥法外
15 boon 恩典
16 forfeit 饶恕
17 riotous 桀骜不驯
18 Lately attendant on 最近投靠

King Richard III Act 2 Scene 1
理查三世

	I do not know that Englishman alive	70
	With whom my soul is any jot¹ at odds²	
	More than the infant that is born tonight.	
	I thank my God for my humility.	
ELIZABETH	A holy day shall this be kept hereafter³.	
	I would to God all strifes were well compounded⁴.	75
	My sovereign lord, I do beseech your highness	
	To take our brother Clarence to your grace⁵.	
RICHARD	Why, madam, have I offered love for this,	
	To be so flouted⁶ in this royal presence⁷?	
	Who knows not that the gentle duke is dead?	80

They all start

You do him injury to scorn his corpse.
KING EDWARD   Who knows not he is dead?
            Who knows he is?
ELIZABETH   All-seeing heaven, what a world is this?
BUCKINGHAM   Look I so pale, Lord Dorset, as the rest?   85
DORSET   Ay, my good lord, and no man in the presence
         But his red colour hath forsook⁸ his cheeks.
KING EDWARD   Is Clarence dead? The order was reversed⁹.
RICHARD   But he (poor man) by your first order died,
          And that a wingèd Mercury¹⁰ did bear;   90
          Some tardy cripple¹¹ bare the countermand,
          That came too lag¹² to see him burièd.
          God grant that some, less noble and less loyal,
          Nearer in bloody thoughts and not in blood¹³,
          Deserve not worse than wretched Clarence did,   95
          And yet go current from¹⁴ suspicion.

Enter [STANLEY] EARL OF DERBY

STANLEY   A boon¹⁵, my sovereign, for my service done.
KING EDWARD   I prithee, peace, my soul is full of sorrow.
STANLEY   I will not rise unless your highness hear me.
KING EDWARD   Then say at once what is it thou requests.   100
STANLEY   The forfeit¹⁶, sovereign, of my servant's life,
          Who slew today a riotous¹⁷ gentleman
          Lately attendant on¹⁸ the Duke of Norfolk.

King Edward contrasts Stanley's plea with the lack of pleas for mercy for Clarence. Edward remembers Clarence's many favours to him. He grants pardon, but fears God's revenge. Richard blames the Woodvilles for Clarence's death.

剧情简介：爱德华王对比了斯坦雷的求情与无人为克莱润求情。他想起克莱润对他的许多恩情。他准许了宽恕但担心上帝报复。理查将克莱润的死归罪于伍德威尔家族。

1 Why didn't you all plead for Clarence? (in pairs)

a Put the following summary in order and match it to the King's lines in the script opposite.

1 Why should I pardon a slave, when I ordered my own brother's death?
2 Clarence killed no one, yet he was killed.
3 Why didn't anyone plead for him or remind me of all he did for me?
4 In my anger, I forgot Clarence's good deeds and none of you reminded me.
5 But when one of your servants offends, you immediately plead for mercy for them.
6 I have to grant the plea for a servant though neither I nor you pleaded for Clarence.
7 We and our children will be punished for his death.

b How convinced are you by Edward's explanation of his behaviour? Take it in turns to read his lines 104–35 aloud as meaningfully and sincerely as you can.

Stagecraft 导演技巧

Richard's friends?

Look back through this scene and note the characters who appear on stage. Then look at the stage direction at line 136: *Exeunt some with K[ing] and Queen*.

- Write a list of characters who you think are left on stage after the exit of the King and Queen. Sketch a bird's-eye view of the stage and mark on it where you would place these characters (blocking) to show their relationships.

Themes 主题分析

Manipulation and insinuations (旁敲侧击) **(in pairs)**

Richard's half-truths and insinuations allow him to manipulate the people around him. In the script opposite, Richard points out that the Queen's family looked guilty and pale (lines 138–9).

- What is the truth in his comment and what is only a half-truth? Write out what you think Richard's intentions are at this point in the play.

1 to doom   为……负责
2 slave   下人
3 killed no man   （除了在拥护爱德华的战斗中，克莱润没有杀过人）
4 his fault was thought   （爱德华认为克莱润预谋策反但并未实施）
5 advised   三思而行
6 forsake   倒戈
7 Oxford   （一敌对贵族）
8 lap   包裹
9 thin   衣着单薄
10 carters   车夫
11 waiting vassals   侍应生
12 defaced … redeemer   杀了人（人是救世主 [redeemer] 按自己的样子造的）
13 straight   毫不迟疑
14 ungracious   不仁不义
15 beholding   欠人情债
16 closet   卧室
17 the fruits of rashness   鲁莽行事的后果
18 still = always

KING EDWARD   Have I a tongue to doom[1] my brother's death,
              And shall that tongue give pardon to a slave[2]?   105
              My brother killed no man[3]; his fault was thought[4],
              And yet his punishment was bitter death.
              Who sued to me for him? Who (in my wrath)
              Kneeled at my feet and bid me be advised[5]?
              Who spoke of brotherhood? Who spoke of love?   110
              Who told me how the poor soul did forsake[6]
              The mighty Warwick and did fight for me?
              Who told me, in the field at Tewkesbury,
              When Oxford[7] had me down, he rescued me
              And said 'Dear brother, live, and be a king'?   115
              Who told me, when we both lay in the field,
              Frozen almost to death, how he did lap[8] me
              Even in his garments and did give himself
              (All thin[9] and naked) to the numb cold night?
              All this from my remembrance brutish wrath   120
              Sinfully plucked, and not a man of you
              Had so much grace to put it in my mind.
              But when your carters[10] or your waiting vassals[11]
              Have done a drunken slaughter and defaced
              The precious image of our dear redeemer[12],   125
              You straight[13] are on your knees for pardon, pardon,
              And I, unjustly too, must grant it you.
              But for my brother not a man would speak,
              Nor I, ungracious[14], speak unto myself
              For him, poor soul. The proudest of you all   130
              Have been beholding[15] to him in his life,
              Yet none of you would once beg for his life.
              O God, I fear thy justice will take hold
              On me and you, and mine and yours, for this.
              Come, Hastings, help me to my closet[16].   135
              Ah, poor Clarence!
                                    Exeunt some with K[ing] and Queen

RICHARD   This is the fruits of rashness[17]. Marked you not
              How that the guilty kindred of the queen
              Looked pale when they did hear of Clarence' death?
              Oh, they did urge it still[18] unto the king.   140
              God will revenge it. Come, lords, will you go
              To comfort Edward with our company?

BUCKINGHAM   We wait upon your grace.   *Exeunt*

Clarence's children suspect their father is dead, but the Duchess of York, their grandmother, says she grieves for King Edward's illness. She admits that Clarence is dead and warns the children not to be fooled by Richard.

剧情简介：克莱润的孩子们疑心父亲已死，但是祖母约克公爵夫人说她是为病重的爱德华王难过。她承认克莱润已死，提醒孩子们不要被理查蒙蔽。

1 The language of deceit (in threes)

The Duchess of York begins with a lie, and Clarence's son has difficulty in working out what she really means.

- Take parts as the Duchess, the Boy and the Girl. Speak lines 1–33, pausing at the end of each sentence. In each pause, talk together about whether the sentence is true, false or unproven (impossible to judge).

Write about it 写作练习

The dissembling (伪装) uncle (by yourself)

The Duchess of York is in no doubt about Richard's ability to 'dissemble' and deceive (demonstrated by the way he behaved towards Clarence's son).

- Read lines 20–6 and imagine how this brief scene might have occurred from Richard's perspective. Then write Richard's diary entry for that day, describing his meeting with Clarence's son (Edward Plantagenet) and revealing his motives and future intentions. Try to capture Richard's witty yet outrageous tone and the extent of his cunning manipulation.

Themes 主题分析

Richard's vice (in pairs)

In lines 27–30, Richard's mother, the Duchess of York, gives her unflattering (贬损) view of her son's character. The word 'vice' is significant. Not only does it refer to the way Richard hides his sins under a mask of goodness, it also reminds the audience that he is related to the Vice figure in medieval religious drama. Vice was a personification of evil and represented the devil's temptations and manipulation as he schemed against humanity.

- Talk together about the deep vices that you know Richard is hiding under his mask of goodness.
- Prepare two tableaux – one representing Richard's mask of goodness and the other depicting his hidden evil intentions.

1 *Clarence's two children* (指12岁的玛格蕊和10岁的爱德华)
2 **unhappy** 不幸
3 **castaways** 没人疼的
4 **cousins** 孙子（女）
5 **lament** 为……哭泣
6 **loath** 不愿意
7 **wail** 哀号
8 **lost … lost** 人没了，再难过也是徒劳
9 **importune** 乞求
10 **Incapable and shallow innocents** 没有能力、不知深浅的傻孩子
11 **impeachments** 罪名，指控
12 **kindly** 心疼地
13 **gentle shape** 仁慈的外表
14 **visor** 面具
15 **vice** 恶魔（中世纪戏剧中的罪恶角色）
16 **dugs** 乳房

Act 2 Scene 2
London: a room in King Edward's palace

Enter the old DUCHESS OF YORK *with Clarence's two children*[1]
[BOY *and* GIRL]

BOY	Good grandam, tell us, is our father dead?	
DUCHESS	No, boy.	
GIRL	Why do you weep so oft, and beat your breast,	
	And cry, 'O Clarence, my unhappy[2] son'?	
BOY	Why do you look on us, and shake your head,	5
	And call us orphans, wretches, castaways[3],	
	If that our noble father were alive?	
DUCHESS	My pretty cousins[4], you mistake me both.	
	I do lament[5] the sickness of the king,	
	As loath[6] to lose him, not your father's death.	10
	It were lost sorrow to wail[7] one that's lost[8].	
BOY	Then you conclude, my grandam, he is dead.	
	The king mine uncle is to blame for it.	
	God will revenge it, whom I will importune[9]	
	With earnest prayers all to that effect.	15
GIRL	And so will I.	
DUCHESS	Peace, children, peace. The king doth love you well.	
	Incapable and shallow innocents[10],	
	You cannot guess who caused your father's death.	
BOY	Grandam, we can, for my good uncle Gloucester	20
	Told me the king, provoked to it by the queen,	
	Devised impeachments[11] to imprison him.	
	And when my uncle told me so, he wept,	
	And pitied me, and kindly[12] kissed my cheek;	
	Bade me rely on him as on my father,	25
	And he would love me dearly as a child.	
DUCHESS	Ah, that deceit should steal such gentle shape[13]	
	And with a virtuous visor[14] hide deep vice[15].	
	He is my son, ay, and therein my shame,	
	Yet from my dugs[16] he drew not this deceit.	30
BOY	Think you my uncle did dissemble, grandam?	
DUCHESS	Ay, boy.	

The grieving Queen Elizabeth brings news of King Edward's death. The Duchess laments the loss of two sons and Richard's false character. She and Clarence's children seem to lack sympathy for Elizabeth.

剧情简介：悲伤的伊丽莎白王后带来了爱德华王的死讯。公爵夫人为两个儿子的死以及理查的虚伪哀怨不止。她和克莱润的孩子似乎并不同情伊丽莎白。

1 Elizabeth's grief (in pairs)

Queen Elizabeth enters, knowing her husband, King Edward, is dead. Her grief is emphasised by the stage direction: '*with her hair about her ears*'. Loose and dishevelled (蓬乱) hair was a conventional sign of distress in women.

a How would you advise the actor playing Elizabeth to make a dramatic and emotional entrance? One of you take the role of director, and instruct the other in how to read lines 35–40. Afterwards, swap roles so the other person performs Elizabeth's lines.

b List the ways in which the death of Elizabeth's husband has made her vulnerable.

Language in the play 剧中语言

Imagery of grief and loss (in pairs)

Lines 1–88 are full of references to death, loss and grief. Two children are left fatherless, Queen Elizabeth is widowed and the Duchess of York has lost two sons. Elizabeth and the Duchess use a great deal of imagery.

- The 'branches' and 'root' (line 41) are images of the family tree of King Edward – a tree that will now die.
- In lines 50–4, the 'two mirrors' are the Duchess of York's sons, Edward and Clarence, and the 'false glass' is Richard.
- In lines 66–70, Queen Elizabeth asks for her eyes to be like the ocean so she can flood the world with her tears.

a Create a visual representation of the imagery of grief and loss, using images from magazines or the Internet. Annotate your representation with words and phrases from the script opposite.

b Write a paragraph to explore how this imagery adds to your understanding of the characters' grief and the dramatic tension of the scene.

1 chide 痛斥
2 to myself become an enemy 争取把自己毁掉
3 rude 野蛮，粗鲁
4 act 表演（自杀）或戏剧演出
5 want 失去
6 brief 麻利
7 ne'er-changing night 永无尽头的黑夜
8 interest 关切
9 title 名分（作为一个母亲）
10 his images 他的遗子
11 semblance 样子
12 malignant 恶毒，邪恶
13 false glass 变形的镜像（指理查）
14 my shame in him 我为他而羞耻
15 two crutches 两根拐棍（两个儿子）
16 moiety 小半
17 moan 悲伤
18 overgo 超过
19 kindred tears 一家人的眼泪
20 widow-dolour 丧夫之痛
21 reduce 汇聚

King Richard III Act 2 Scene 2

BOY I cannot think it. Hark, what noise is this?

Enter the QUEEN [ELIZABETH] *with her hair about her ears,*
RIVERS and DORSET after her

ELIZABETH Ah, who shall hinder me to wail and weep,
To chide[1] my fortune and torment myself?
I'll join with black despair against my soul,
And to myself become an enemy[2].

DUCHESS What means this scene of rude[3] impatience?

ELIZABETH To make an act[4] of tragic violence.
Edward, my lord, thy son, our king, is dead.
Why grow the branches when the root is gone?
Why wither not the leaves that want[5] their sap?
If you will live, lament; if die, be brief[6],
That our swift-wingèd souls may catch the king's,
Or, like obedient subjects, follow him
To his new kingdom of ne'er-changing night[7].

DUCHESS Ah, so much interest[8] have I in thy sorrow
As I had title[9] in thy noble husband.
I have bewept a worthy husband's death
And lived with looking on his images[10],
But now two mirrors of his princely semblance[11]
Are cracked in pieces by malignant[12] death,
And I for comfort have but one false glass[13],
That grieves me when I see my shame in him[14].
Thou art a widow, yet thou art a mother
And hast the comfort of thy children left.
But death hath snatched my husband from mine arms
And plucked two crutches[15] from my feeble hands,
Clarence and Edward. Oh, what cause have I,
Thine being but a moiety[16] of my moan[17],
To overgo[18] thy woes and drown thy cries.

BOY Ah, aunt, you wept not for our father's death.
How can we aid you with our kindred tears[19]?

GIRL Our fatherless distress was left unmoaned.
Your widow-dolour[20] likewise be unwept.

ELIZABETH Give me no help in lamentation.
I am not barren to bring forth complaints.
All springs reduce[21] their currents to mine eyes,

35

40

45

50

55

60

65

The women and children echo each other's grief. Dorset attempts to comfort his mother. Rivers urges Queen Elizabeth to arrange that young Prince Edward is crowned King immediately. Richard says weeping is unhelpful.

剧情简介：两个妇人和两个孩子各自发出自己的悲伤。多塞努力安慰母亲。瑞沃力劝伊丽莎白王后安排年轻的爱德华王子即刻登基。理查说哭泣无益。

Language in the play 剧中语言
The rhetoric of grief and loss (in small groups)

The use of rhetorical figures and patterns in the language of the script opposite can focus attention on two aspects of grief and loss:

- the formality of the public grief of the solemn and noble royal family
- the emotional intensity of their personal sorrow and their pitiful vulnerability.

a Take parts as the children, the Duchess of York and Queen Elizabeth. Speak lines 71–85, emphasising the exact repetition and pattern of the words.

b Identify the following rhetorical figures from the script opposite:
- **Anaphora** (首语叠用) – the repetition of the same word at the beginning of successive sentences. (例如：The voice of the people is powerful, the voice of the people cannot be silenced, the voice of the people shakes the world.)
- **Epistrophe** (尾词重复) – the repetition of a word or phrase at the end of a series of sentences or clauses. (例如：We are born to sorrow, pass our time in sorrow, end our days in sorrow.)
- Rhetorical questions.

c Write a detailed stage direction at line 71 to help the actors. What tone of voice, gestures and movement would you want them to use to highlight different aspects of their grief and loss? How would you want them to emphasise the repetition and language patterns?

1 governed 受制于
2 stay 支撑，支柱
3 dear 惨痛
4 parcelled 各自（的悲伤）
5 general 所有人（的悲伤）
6 threefold distressed 三重悲伤（丈夫和两个孩子）
7 pamper 纵容
8 Comfort 想开点儿，请节哀
9 opposite with 与……作对
10 For 因为
11 requires 要求偿还
12 royal debt （指国王的命）
13 plant 安放
14 living Edward 活着的爱德华（爱德华四世的儿子）
15 Sister 王嫂
16 cry you mercy 请您原谅

1 Criticism or comfort? (in pairs)

a Read what Dorset and Rivers say to Elizabeth in lines 89–95 and 96–100. Whose advice is most fitting for this moment? Discuss the following questions, then explain why their advice is helpful or not, well timed or not.

- How does Dorset's advice affect the Queen? Is he rebuking or comforting his mother?
- How is Rivers' practical advice and understanding of political implications received by the Queen?

b What comfort or advice would you give the Queen at this point? Write your own lines of verse in **iambic pentameter** (抑扬五音步) (see p. 249), using similarly striking words as Dorset and Rivers.

King Richard III Act 2 Scene 2
理查三世

	That I, being governed¹ by the watery moon,	
	May send forth plenteous tears to drown the world.	70
	Ah, for my husband, for my dear lord Edward.	
CHILDREN	Ah, for our father, for our dear lord Clarence.	
DUCHESS	Alas for both, both mine Edward and Clarence.	
ELIZABETH	What stay² had I but Edward? And he's gone.	
CHILDREN	What stay had we but Clarence? And he's gone.	75
DUCHESS	What stays had I but they? And they are gone.	
ELIZABETH	Was never widow had so dear³ a loss.	
CHILDREN	Were never orphans had so dear a loss.	
DUCHESS	Was never mother had so dear a loss.	
	Alas, I am the mother of these griefs;	80
	Their woes are parcelled⁴, mine is general⁵.	
	She for an Edward weeps, and so do I;	
	I for a Clarence weep, so doth not she.	
	These babes for Clarence weep, and so do I;	
	I for an Edward weep, so do not they.	85
	Alas, you three, on me, threefold distressed⁶,	
	Pour all your tears; I am your sorrow's nurse,	
	And I will pamper⁷ it with lamentation.	
DORSET	Comfort⁸, dear mother. God is much displeased	
	That you take with unthankfulness his doing.	90
	In common worldly things 'tis called ungrateful	
	With dull unwillingness to repay a debt	
	Which with a bounteous hand was kindly lent;	
	Much more to be thus opposite with⁹ heaven,	
	For¹⁰ it requires¹¹ the royal debt¹² it lent you.	95
RIVERS	Madam, bethink you like a careful mother	
	Of the young prince your son. Send straight for him.	
	Let him be crowned. In him your comfort lives.	
	Drown desperate sorrow in dead Edward's grave	
	And plant¹³ your joys in living Edward's¹⁴ throne.	100

Enter RICHARD, BUCKINGHAM, [STANLEY EARL OF]
DERBY, HASTINGS, *and* RATCLIFFE

RICHARD	Sister¹⁵, have comfort. All of us have cause
	To wail the dimming of our shining star,
	But none can help our harms by wailing them.
	Madam, my mother, I do cry you mercy¹⁶;

Richard comments ironically on his mother's blessing. Buckingham argues that a small escort should bring Prince Edward to London for his coronation because a large one might provoke unrest. His advice is accepted.

剧情简介：理查冷嘲热讽地评论母亲对自己的祝福。白金汉主张派小队人马护送爱德华王子来伦敦加冕，因为大队人马可能引发骚乱。他的建议被采纳了。

1 Mother and son

The Duchess blesses Richard, but his aside shows that he does not take her words seriously. He says that the 'butt-end' (110) of her blessing would be that he would die naturally in old age, a reformed character.

- Invent an aside for the Duchess to speak to the audience before line 107. Remember that her earlier comments, including her description of Richard as a 'false glass', demonstrate what she really thinks of him (see lines 27–8 and 53).

Language in the play 剧中语言

Buckingham's imagery (in pairs)

Buckingham takes the initiative and puts forward a plan of action. To strengthen his argument, he uses a series of **metaphors** (隐喻) (see p. 250) to describe the fragility of the power structure in the kingdom:

- reaping a future harvest (lines 115–16)
- healing fractured bones (lines 117–19)
- training a horse to submit to its rider (lines 129–30).

a Talk together about how these metaphors add to Buckingham's persuasive powers and how his imagery increases the strength of his argument.

b In writing, describe each metaphor in your own words. Explore what Buckingham means by each one and the effect it might have on each of the characters present.

2 A small escort

Buckingham's proposal is accepted: only a small escort will fetch Prince Edward from Ludlow and accompany him on the journey to London for his coronation. At first Dorset questions the wisdom of this, but he is soon persuaded to change his mind.

- Write a sentence for each character that reveals either their suspicions or their true intentions regarding this 'small escort'. This should take the form of an aside that each character could deliver to the audience without any of the other characters hearing.

1 crave 乞求
2 meekness 谦顺
3 butt-end 一桶酒最后剩下的残渣；结语
4 cloudy 愁眉苦脸
5 spent 失去
6 broken rancour 中断的冤仇
7 Me seemeth 我觉得
8 train 护从
9 Forthwith 立刻
10 Ludlow 拉德洛（英格兰靠近威尔士边界处的一城堡）
11 fet 接来
12 green 青涩；羸弱
13 compact 友谊的盟约
14 apparent likelihood 明显的可能性
15 breach 破裂
16 haply 可能
17 urged 酿成
18 meet 合适
19 straight shall post 立刻（骑马）赶往

	I did not see your grace. Humbly on my knee	105
	I crave¹ your blessing.
DUCHESS	God bless thee and put meekness² in thy breast,
	Love, charity, obedience, and true duty.
RICHARD	Amen. [*Aside*] And make me die a good old man,
	That is the butt-end³ of a mother's blessing;	110
	I marvel that her grace did leave it out.
BUCKINGHAM	You cloudy⁴ princes and heart-sorrowing peers
	That bear this heavy mutual load of moan,
	Now cheer each other in each other's love.
	Though we have spent⁵ our harvest of this king,	115
	We are to reap the harvest of his son.
	The broken rancour⁶ of your high-swoll'n hates,
	But lately splintered, knit, and joined together,
	Must gently be preserved, cherished, and kept.
	Me seemeth⁷ good that with some little train⁸	120
	Forthwith⁹ from Ludlow¹⁰ the young prince be fet¹¹
	Hither to London, to be crowned our king.
RIVERS	Why with some little train,
	My lord of Buckingham?
BUCKINGHAM	Marry, my lord, lest by a multitude	125
	The new-healed wound of malice should break out,
	Which would be so much the more dangerous
	By how much the estate is green¹² and yet ungoverned.
	Where every horse bears his commanding rein
	And may direct his course as please himself,	130
	As well the fear of harm, as harm apparent,
	In my opinion, ought to be prevented.
RICHARD	I hope the king made peace with all of us,
	And the compact¹³ is firm and true in me.
RIVERS	And so in me, and so, I think, in all.	135
	Yet since it is but green, it should be put
	To no apparent likelihood¹⁴ of breach¹⁵,
	Which haply¹⁶ by much company might be urged¹⁷.
	Therefore I say with noble Buckingham
	That it is meet¹⁸ so few should fetch the prince.	140
HASTINGS	And so say I.
RICHARD	Then be it so, and go we to determine
	Who they shall be that straight shall post¹⁹ to Ludlow.

Buckingham promises to separate the Woodvilles from Prince Edward. Richard applauds his aims, which are exactly his own. Three citizens discussing King Edward's death see trouble ahead for England.

 剧情简介：白金汉允诺把伍德威尔家的人和爱德华王子隔离开。理查鼓掌赞同，因为这正合他意。三市民讨论爱德华王的死，认为英格兰前景堪忧。

1 Showing the power struggle

Richard appears to be empowering Queen Elizabeth and the Duchess of York by asking them to give their opinions on who should escort Edward, Prince of Wales, to London for his coronation. Lines 151–4 reveal that he has quite different plans in mind. The exit of the Queen's 'proud kindred', leaving Richard and Buckingham alone on stage, is a great opportunity for actors to show the struggle for power between the Woodvilles and Richard and Buckingham.

- Write notes on how to perform the stage direction at line 145, so that the audience can appreciate this power struggle.

Characters 人物分析

'My other self' (in pairs)

In lines 151–3, Richard's flattering description of Buckingham would be recognised by an Elizabethan audience as characteristic language of the Vice figure, who would flatter people in order to deceive them. Take parts as Buckingham and Richard, and enact the lines in the ways listed below. In each case, show Buckingham's response.

- Richard really means what he says.
- Richard is quite insincere.
- Richard speaks the lines as an aside to the audience as Buckingham strides away.

Themes 主题分析

'a giddy world' (in threes)

The social insecurity and political instability of England on the death of King Edward is the focus of this scene's discussion between three citizens of London. Their concern is that, with no strong leadership, the country and its people will be troubled and fearful.

a Assign parts and read through Scene 3 to bring out the differing viewpoints of the citizens.

b Pick out all the adjectives and descriptive phrases used to describe England and the world after the death of King Edward.

c What is it exactly that makes the three citizens so fearful? Discuss this in your groups.

---

1 censures 意见
2 journeys 赶赴
3 by the way 去拉德洛的路上
4 sort occasion 寻找机会
5 index 序幕
6 story 计划
7 my counsel's consistory 我心智的议事厅
8 oracle 神谕
9 as a child 孩子一样听话
10 Whither away 你去哪里
11 promise 说实话
12 abroad 流传
13 by'r Lady 圣母玛利亚在上
14 seldom comes the better 好消息难得登门
15 giddy 疯狂；动荡
16 God speed 上帝保你平安（通常作为告别语）
17 Give you = God give you
18 hold = hold true
19 while 当下
20 masters 先生们
21 troublous 混乱

	Madam, and you my sister, will you go	
	To give your censures[1] in this business?	145

Exeunt [all but] Buckingham and Richard

BUCKINGHAM My lord, whoever journeys[2] to the prince,
For God's sake let not us two stay at home,
For by the way[3] I'll sort occasion[4],
As index[5] to the story[6] we late talked of,
To part the queen's proud kindred from the prince.   150
RICHARD My other self, my counsel's consistory[7],
My oracle[8], my prophet, my dear cousin,
I, as a child[9], will go by thy direction.
Toward Ludlow then, for we'll not stay behind.

Exeunt

Act 2 Scene 3
London: a street

Enter FIRST CITIZEN *and* SECOND CITIZEN

FIRST CITIZEN Good morrow, neighbour. Whither away[10] so fast?
SECOND CITIZEN I promise[11] you, I scarcely know myself.
Hear you the news abroad[12]?
FIRST CITIZEN Yes, that the king is dead.
SECOND CITIZEN Ill news, by'r Lady[13]; seldom comes the better[14].   5
I fear, I fear, 'twill prove a giddy[15] world.

Enter another [THIRD] CITIZEN

THIRD CITIZEN Neighbours, God speed[16].
FIRST CITIZEN Give you[17] good morrow, sir.
THIRD CITIZEN Doth the news hold[18] of good King Edward's death?
SECOND CITIZEN Ay, sir, it is too true, God help the while[19].   10
THIRD CITIZEN Then, masters[20], look to see a troublous[21] world.
FIRST CITIZEN No, no, by God's good grace his son shall reign.
THIRD CITIZEN Woe to that land that's governed by a child.

The citizens hope for a peaceful future under the new young King. The Third Citizen fears that rivalry between Richard and the Woodvilles will bring harsh and dangerous times.

 剧情简介：市民们希望在新任年幼国王治下有一个安定的未来。市民丙担心理查和伍德威尔家族之争会带来艰苦、危险的日子。

1 The voice of the people (in threes)

The Second and Third Citizens have a very pessimistic view of a future England under the rule of the young Prince Edward ('Woe to that land that's governed by a child', line 13). This is the only scene in the play in which the ordinary people of England – unattended by the aristocracy – express their hopes and fears for England's future.

- Take roles as the citizens and write an aside for each of them at a suitable point in the script opposite. Your aim is to allow the characters to think aloud and to express their concerns and anxieties more fully. This scene only hints at some of the problems they may face and their expectations for the future. This is your chance to express their thoughts in more detail.

2 Formal verse (in pairs)

The citizens speak in stylised and formal language. The Third Citizen uses a lot of imagery in lines 34–7 and 44–6, and foresees dangerous rivalry between Prince Edward's uncles.

a Identify these images and discuss how effective you find them in conveying the Third Citizen's meaning.

b If you were directing a new production, how would you present the Citizens on stage? Write a set of director's notes, giving your reasons for how the Citizens dress and speak. Would you want to signal to an audience that their words are prophetic (as Shakespeare seems to do through his use of verse)?

1	nonage	童年
2	council	议事会（国王的内阁，通常在国王治下，但在国王未成年时可代其执政）
3	wot	= knows
4	politic grave counsel	忠臣良谋
5	emulation	争宠
6	touch us all too near	对我们大家伤害太甚
7	queen's sons	（指多塞和格瑞）
8	haught	傲慢
9	sickly	孱弱
10	solace	享太平
11	dearth	饥荒
12	sort	安排
13	heavily	心事重重
14	mistrust	预感到
15	Ensuing danger	即将到来的灾难
16	proof	经验
17	boisterous	狂暴

Themes 主题分析

National instability

The three citizens have been called to the justices and it is unclear whether they will be fined or reprimanded. They are more concerned about their own immediate future than that of the kingdom.

- What can you decipher (or discover through research) about beliefs in Shakespeare's day about personal distress, national chaos and unlawful kingship? Use resources in your library or the Internet, and summarise your findings as a poster, using images as well as writing.

SECOND CITIZEN   In him there is a hope of government,
    Which in his nonage[1], council[2] under him,
    And in his full and ripened years, himself
    No doubt shall then, and till then, govern well.
FIRST CITIZEN   So stood the state when Henry the Sixth
    Was crowned in Paris but at nine months old.
THIRD CITIZEN   Stood the state so? No, no, good friends, God wot[3],
    For then this land was famously enriched
    With politic grave counsel[4]. Then the king
    Had virtuous uncles to protect his grace.
FIRST CITIZEN   Why, so hath this, both by his father and mother.
THIRD CITIZEN   Better it were they all came by his father,
    Or by his father there were none at all.
    For emulation[5] who shall now be nearest
    Will touch us all too near[6], if God prevent not.
    Oh, full of danger is the Duke of Gloucester,
    And the queen's sons[7] and brothers haught[8] and proud.
    And were they to be ruled, and not to rule,
    This sickly[9] land might solace[10] as before.
FIRST CITIZEN   Come, come, we fear the worst; all will be well.
THIRD CITIZEN   When clouds are seen, wise men put on their cloaks;
    When great leaves fall, then winter is at hand;
    When the sun sets, who doth not look for night?
    Untimely storms makes men expect a dearth[11].
    All may be well, but if God sort[12] it so,
    'Tis more than we deserve or I expect.
SECOND CITIZEN   Truly, the hearts of men are full of fear.
    You cannot reason almost with a man
    That looks not heavily[13] and full of dread.
THIRD CITIZEN   Before the days of change, still is it so.
    By a divine instinct, men's minds mistrust[14]
    Ensuing danger[15], as by proof[16], we see
    The water swell before a boisterous[17] storm.
    But leave it all to God. Whither away?
SECOND CITIZEN   Marry, we were sent for to the justices.
THIRD CITIZEN   And so was I. I'll bear you company.

               Exeunt

The Archbishop reports the progress to London of Prince Edward and his escort. The Duchess of York recalls Richard's slow growth in childhood and her doubts about his character.

剧情简介：大主教报告爱德华王子和护从前来伦敦的行程。约克公爵夫人回忆理查个头矮小的童年时期，对他的品行有所疑虑。

1 Waiting for the new king (in pairs)

This scene opens with the new young King's family waiting for his arrival from Ludlow. Some productions start with a reminder of the death of his father and focus on the grief of the two royal widows. Others emphasise the youthful liveliness of the Duke of York.

a How would you want to stage this scene to contrast the grief of Queen Elizabeth and the Duchess of York with the liveliness of the young Duke of York?

b Write notes to advise the young actor on how to understand his role in this scene. Include some analysis of his character as well as considerations of how to move and speak on stage. Remember, the Duke of York is insightful, lively and observant. He understands what his uncle Richard means in line 13, but does he notice the effect of his own words on his mother and grandmother?

1 lay 过夜
2 Stony Stratford （白金汉郡一村庄）
3 my son of York （小王子，新王之弟）
4 overta'en = overtaken （超过）
5 quoth 说道
6 my uncle Gloucester （指理查）
7 herbs 花草
8 have grace 有德行
9 apace 快
10 Good faith 说实话
11 did not hold 没有道理
12 object 形容
13 leisurely 缓慢
14 rule 规矩；格言
15 gracious 有德
16 by my troth 说真的
17 had been remembered = had remembered （当时想得起来）
18 my uncle's grace 我叔叔的德行
19 flout 反唇相讥
20 touch 挖苦

Act 2 Scene 4
London: a room in King Edward's palace

Enter the ARCHBISHOP OF YORK, *the young* DUKE OF YORK, QUEEN ELIZABETH, *and the* DUCHESS OF YORK

ARCHBISHOP	Last night, I heard, they lay[1] at Stony Stratford[2],	
	And at Northampton they do rest tonight.	
	Tomorrow, or next day, they will be here.	
DUCHESS	I long with all my heart to see the prince.	
	I hope he is much grown since last I saw him.	5
ELIZABETH	But I hear no. They say my son of York[3]	
	Has almost overta'en[4] him in his growth.	
YORK	Ay, mother, but I would not have it so.	
DUCHESS	Why, my good cousin? It is good to grow.	
YORK	Grandam, one night as we did sit at supper,	10
	My uncle Rivers talked how I did grow	
	More than my brother. 'Ay', quoth[5] my uncle Gloucester[6],	
	'Small herbs[7] have grace[8]; great weeds do grow apace[9].'	
	And since, methinks, I would not grow so fast,	
	Because sweet flowers are slow, and weeds make haste.	15
DUCHESS	Good faith[10], good faith, the saying did not hold[11]	
	In him that did object[12] the same to thee.	
	He was the wretched'st thing when he was young,	
	So long a-growing, and so leisurely[13],	
	That if his rule[14] were true, he should be gracious[15].	20
YORK	And so no doubt he is, my gracious madam.	
DUCHESS	I hope he is, but yet let mothers doubt.	
YORK	Now, by my troth[16], if I had been remembered[17],	
	I could have given my uncle's grace[18] a flout[19]	
	To touch[20] his growth nearer than he touched mine.	25
DUCHESS	How, my young York? I prithee, let me hear it.	

York says that Richard was born with teeth. A messenger brings news of the imprisonment of Rivers, Grey and Vaughan. Elizabeth foresees the end of the Woodvilles under the tyranny of Richard.

剧情简介：约克说理查生来就有牙齿。信使报告瑞沃、格雷和沃恩入狱的消息。伊丽莎白预言了在理查的暴政下伍德威尔家族的末日。

Characters 人物分析

An unnatural childhood (in pairs)

Many rumours were spread about Richard of Gloucester's growth and development in childhood. In this scene, Richard's mother does not deny that he grew unusually quickly as a child or that he was born with teeth.

a When the Duke of York repeats some of these stories, his mother rebukes him and says he is mischievous and sharp-tongued. Where do you think he heard this gossip about his uncle (line 37 gives you a clue)?

b What other details of Richard's childhood have you picked up from the play so far? Do you think these stories are true or are they meant to reflect his evil nature?

c Prepare a character growth chart for Richard to describe what he was like from birth to the age of twenty. Include as many details about his character and physical appearance as you can gather from the script. You can include your own ideas, but make sure they are in keeping with the portrayal of Richard in the play.

1 crust 面包屑
2 biting jest 伤人的笑话
3 thou wast = you were
4 parlous 聪明过头的
5 go to 得了，别说了（表示批评）
6 shrewd 嘴巴不饶人
7 Pitchers 水罐（"水罐有耳"是英国谚语，此处意为孩子听到了不该听的）
8 Pomfret 断桥城（现在写作 Pontefract，是西约克郡一城堡，类似于伦敦塔，因处决政治犯而闻名）
9 committed 逮捕
10 sum 全部
11 disclosed 禀告
12 house 家族
13 gentle hind 毫无抵抗力的雌鹿
14 Insulting 暴虐
15 jut 侵犯
16 aweless throne 羽翼未丰的国王
17 massacre 屠杀
18 map 图

1 Bad news (in fours)

a Take parts as the Archbishop, the Messenger, Queen Elizabeth and the Duchess of York and prepare a dramatic reading of lines 38–51. As you do so, consider the effect of the sharp, short phrases and volley (一连串) of questions on the way you speak the lines.

b Write a stage direction at line 38 to describe how you would want the actors to perform these lines. Give them detailed advice about the mood of this part of the script. Include some reflection on the implications of the news for each character.

2 The hunter and the prey

Elizabeth foresees the destruction of the Woodvilles.

a Identify who is the 'tiger' and who 'the gentle hind' in line 53.

b Read again both Elizabeth's sudden vision of the 'end of all' and Clarence's nightmare in Act 1 Scene 4. Compare and contrast these two visions of destruction and chaos. What do you think the future holds for the Woodvilles?

YORK	Marry, they say my uncle grew so fast	
	That he could gnaw a crust[1] at two hours old.	
	'Twas full two years ere I could get a tooth.	
	Grandam, this would have been a biting jest[2].	30
DUCHESS	I prithee, pretty York, who told thee this?	
YORK	Grandam, his nurse.	
DUCHESS	His nurse? Why, she was dead ere thou wast[3] born.	
YORK	If 'twere not she, I cannot tell who told me.	
ELIZABETH	A parlous[4] boy; go to[5], you are too shrewd[6].	35
DUCHESS	Good madam, be not angry with the child.	
ELIZABETH	Pitchers[7] have ears.	

Enter a MESSENGER

ARCHBISHOP	Here comes a messenger. What news?	
MESSENGER	Such news, my lord, as grieves me to report.	
ELIZABETH	How doth the prince?	40
MESSENGER	Well, madam, and in health.	
DUCHESS	What is thy news?	
MESSENGER	Lord Rivers and Lord Grey	
	Are sent to Pomfret[8], and with them	
	Sir Thomas Vaughan, prisoners.	45
DUCHESS	Who hath committed[9] them?	
MESSENGER	The mighty dukes, Gloucester and Buckingham.	
ARCHBISHOP	For what offence?	
MESSENGER	The sum[10] of all I can, I have disclosed[11].	
	Why or for what the nobles were committed	50
	Is all unknown to me, my gracious lord.	
ELIZABETH	Aye me! I see the ruin of my house[12].	
	The tiger now hath seized the gentle hind[13];	
	Insulting[14] tyranny begins to jut[15]	
	Upon the innocent and aweless throne[16].	55
	Welcome, destruction, blood, and massacre[17].	
	I see, as in a map[18], the end of all.	

The Duchess of York remembers past battles and how, in peacetime, her sons quarrelled. Elizabeth decides to seek sanctuary for herself and York. The Archbishop pledges his loyalty and vows to share the Queen's fate.

剧情简介：约克公爵夫人回想起过去的战斗，想起他的儿子如何在和平时期争吵。伊丽莎白决定为自己和约克寻求庇护。大主教宣誓效忠并发誓和王后共命运。

1 The Wars of the Roses: a woman's view (in pairs, then whole class)

The Duchess of York bemoans the constant fighting she has witnessed in the battle for the throne (see p. 1). She describes her conflicting emotions at her husband's death and her sons' defeats and victories. Even after their success, when enthroned ('being seated') and the civil war over, they continue to fight within the family.

- Compose between three and five questions that you would want to ask the Duchess about her experience of the Wars of the Roses and her prediction of future events.
- Then, as a whole class, take turns to sit in the hot-seat* and answer questions from everyone while in role as the Duchess.

Write about it 写作练习

Sanctuary – a safe place

Queen Elizabeth wants to go with the Duke of York to the safety of Westminster Abbey (西敏寺). In medieval times, Church law guaranteed that a fugitive (逃犯) from justice or debt was immune from arrest if they sought sanctuary in a church or other sacred place.

- Script the conversation between Queen Elizabeth and the Duke of York when they leave, as she explains why they have to seek sanctuary in the church. Try to include some of the insightful observations and witty comments that Shakespeare gives to the young prince, as well as some sense of the hopes and fears that both characters have for the future.

2 The Archbishop (in pairs)

The Archbishop's lines 73–8 are open to a range of interpretations. Whom is he addressing as 'gracious lady' and 'your grace'? Does he, the keeper of the 'seal' of England – the symbol of sovereignty (line 76) – actually hand it over?

- Step into role as director and advise the actor playing the Archbishop how he should deliver his speech, line by line.

---

1 Accursèd 可憎
2 tossed 扔，抛
3 being seated 一朝登基
4 domestic broils 内乱
5 Clean over-blown 烟消云散
6 Make war upon themselves 同室操戈
7 preposterous 荒谬
8 spleen 怒火
9 sanctuary 庇护所（根据英国当时的传统，教堂和教堂周围的墓地可作为免受法律惩戒的避难所）
10 goods 财物
11 seal 国玺（英格兰大印由国王使用，并由大主教以英格兰大法官的身份保管）
12 so beticle to me 愿我也有如此好运
13 tender 敬重

* hot-seat 热座位，一种课堂游戏，玩法是请位同学坐到讲台上的一把椅子上，其他同学轮番给他/她出难题，哪个问题他/她答不出就算输。

King Richard III Act 2 Scene 4
理查三世

DUCHESS	Accursèd¹ and unquiet wrangling days,
	How many of you have mine eyes beheld?
	My husband lost his life to get the crown, 60
	And often up and down my sons were tossed²
	For me to joy and weep their gain and loss.
	And being seated³, and domestic broils⁴
	Clean over-blown⁵, themselves the conquerors
	Make war upon themselves⁶, brother to brother, 65
	Blood to blood, self against self. Oh, preposterous⁷
	And frantic outrage, end thy damnèd spleen⁸,
	Or let me die, to look on earth no more.
ELIZABETH	Come, come, my boy, we will to sanctuary⁹.
	Madam, farewell. 70
DUCHESS	Stay, I will go with you.
ELIZABETH	You have no cause.
ARCHBISHOP	My gracious lady, go,
	And thither bear your treasure and your goods¹⁰.
	For my part, I'll resign unto your grace 75
	The seal¹¹ I keep, and so betide to me¹²
	As well I tender¹³ you and all of yours.
	Go, I'll conduct you to the sanctuary.

Exeunt

King Richard III
理查三世

Looking back at Act 2 第2幕回顾
Activities for groups or individuals

1 Two scenes with children

Look again at the two scenes in which children play an important role. In Scene 2, the Duchess of York unsuccessfully attempts to hide from Clarence's children their father's murder. In Scene 4, the young Duke of York makes witty comments about his uncle, Richard.

a How would you cast the children? Make notes on their age and appearance, and find images from magazines or the Internet that suit your ideas about how they should be portrayed.

b Do they talk and act like children? Make notes on their effect on the adults around them. Are they cute and humorous, sharp and intelligent, or uncanny and unnerving (让人不安)?

c Suggest how the children affect the mood and atmosphere of the play, and how they might be played to create different moods.

2 Women in danger

In this act, there are two women who have changed from queens to widows: the Duchess lost her husband before the play started and has now lost two of her sons (Clarence and Edward). Elizabeth has just lost her husband, the King, and now fears for the life of her two young sons. Elizabeth resolves to escape danger, but comments that the Duchess of York has 'no cause' (Scene 3, line 72) to join her in seeking sanctuary.

a Step into role as the Duchess of York. Describe your feelings as you begin to understand the significance of your present situation and then give your reply to Elizabeth's comment.

b Consider how the memory of Margaret (the Lancastrian queen whose husband and sons were killed by the Duchess of York's sons before this play started) might haunt the Duchess. Do you think she would be a reminder of how these two queens might end their lives?

3 Increasing tyranny

Buckingham's decision to assist Richard begins a relationship that brings with it increasing tyranny and menace for all those who oppose them.

- Look back at the exchanges between Richard and Buckingham. Chart the growth of their relationship during the act by writing down how their affinity (密切关系) is established and how it develops. List the characters who seem to be or feel threatened by this alliance.

4 Appearance and reality

An important theme in the play is whether outside appearance is a true guide to a person's inner nature. Some characters see Richard's true nature and others are fooled by him.

- List those characters who see Richard for what he is, and make a second list of those who are fooled by him. When you have completed your lists, write down a quotation from the play for each of these characters that encompasses their thoughts about Richard.

5 Revenge

In Scene 2, line 14, Clarence's son says 'God will revenge it' and echoes Richard's words three lines from the end of the previous scene.

a Look back through Act 2 and record the motivations of different characters. Who is motivated by revenge, and who lives by the belief that God will avenge the innocent who suffer at the hands of evil people?

b Write a few paragraphs discussing how revenge becomes an increasingly important theme in the play. How does it link with other themes that have been explored so far? Use quotations and examples from the play to back up your points.

95

Arriving in London, Prince Edward is saddened by the arrest of Rivers and Grey, disagreeing with Richard that they were disloyal. He seems puzzled that his mother and brother have not yet arrived.

剧情简介：到达伦敦后，爱德华王子为瑞沃和格雷的入狱难过，不同意理查说他们不忠。他对母亲和弟弟的尚未到达感到疑惑。

1 Royal entrance (in large groups)

Richard has plotted with Buckingham and intends to proclaim himself King. There is no hint of this intention as Richard and Buckingham welcome Prince Edward, the heir to the throne, to London.

- Try out ways in which the entrance could be staged to show Edward's importance. (The stage directions list the others who enter with the Prince.) He is now, in all but name, King of England.
- Work out a running commentary from Richard, in which he reveals his thoughts about the young heir and the other characters. Present your version of the royal entrance to the rest of the class as a mime, with Richard's running commentary as a voiceover (画外音).

1 chamber 王宫
2 crosses 烦心事
3 tedious 漫长
4 want 缺少
5 more uncles 其他叔叔舅舅
　（瑞沃是爱德华的舅舅，格瑞与他是同母异父的兄弟）
6 untainted 纯洁
7 jumpeth 一致
8 heart 品质
9 sugared 好听
10 Fie 呸
11 slug 懒虫

Characters 人物分析

More duplicity (in pairs)

Richard welcomes Prince Edward with superficial courtesy, but once again his words have sinister (不祥；险恶) double meanings. 'My thoughts' sovereign' could mean both 'king of my thoughts' and 'my overriding (最重要) thought of your death'. Richard adopts the tactics he accuses Rivers and Grey of using on Edward: he tells the young Prince they are untrustworthy.

a Talk together about ways in which Richard's tone and actions could bring out the dramatic irony of his own 'sugared words'.

b Write down ways in which the young Prince Edward's unease – and consequently his vulnerability – could be made obvious on stage.

2 Prince Edward's troubles (in pairs)

Prince Edward blames problems he encountered on his journey ('crosses on the way') as the reason for his sadness. He is also unhappy at the arrest of his uncles and does not believe they are traitors. He seems further troubled by the absence of his mother and brother, and by Hastings's late arrival. The Prince does not speak between lines 26 and 59.

- Write his diary entry at the end of this eventful day. Who does he trust and who does he not trust? How does he feel about his new role and responsibilities?

Act 3 Scene 1
London: a street

The Trumpets sound. Enter young PRINCE EDWARD, RICHARD DUKE OF GLOUCESTER, BUCKINGHAM, LORD CARDINAL BOURCHIER, CATESBY, *with others*

BUCKINGHAM	Welcome, sweet prince, to London, to your chamber[1].	
RICHARD	Welcome, dear cousin, my thoughts' sovereign.	
	The weary way hath made you melancholy.	
PRINCE EDWARD	No, uncle, but our crosses[2] on the way	
	Have made it tedious[3], wearisome, and heavy.	5
	I want[4] more uncles[5] here to welcome me.	
RICHARD	Sweet prince, the untainted[6] virtue of your years	
	Hath not yet dived into the world's deceit.	
	No more can you distinguish of a man	
	Than of his outward show, which God he knows,	10
	Seldom or never jumpeth[7] with the heart[8].	
	Those uncles which you want were dangerous.	
	Your grace attended to their sugared[9] words	
	But looked not on the poison of their hearts.	
	God keep you from them and from such false friends.	15
PRINCE EDWARD	God keep me from false friends, but they were none.	
RICHARD	My lord, the Mayor of London comes to greet you.	

Enter LORD MAYOR

MAYOR	God bless your grace with health and happy days.	
PRINCE EDWARD	I thank you, good my lord, and thank you all.	
	I thought my mother and my brother York	20
	Would long ere this have met us on the way.	
	Fie[10], what a slug[11] is Hastings, that he comes not	
	To tell us whether they will come or no.	

Enter LORD HASTINGS

BUCKINGHAM	And in good time, here comes the sweating lord.	
PRINCE EDWARD	Welcome, my lord. What, will our mother come?	25

Hastings explains that the Queen has taken sanctuary, so preventing the Duke of York from meeting his brother. Buckingham recommends bringing the boy by force. The Cardinal disagrees, but is persuaded to fetch the Prince.

 剧情简介：海斯廷解释说王后已经去了避难所，以避免约克公爵与他王兄见面。白金汉主张强行将孩子带来。红衣主教起初不赞成，但最终被劝服去接王子。

Themes 主题分析

Church and state (in pairs)

Act 3 emphasises the conflict between Church and state, and this theme is obvious in the script opposite. The Cardinal, a man of the Church, says he will try to persuade the Queen to come out of hiding, but he refuses to break the 'holy privilege / Of blessèd sanctuary'. But Buckingham is a statesman and a man of action, whose humour (such as in lines 55–6) sometimes disguises his determined persuasiveness. Buckingham accuses the Cardinal of being old-fashioned, and asserts that the Duke of York neither deserved nor claimed sanctuary – he was forced into it by his mother.

a Take parts as Buckingham and the Cardinal and speak lines 31–57 to express their different attitudes. How would you advise actors playing these two men to portray their disagreement?

b Write a paragraph exploring how the conflict between Church and state in the script opposite is used by Richard and Buckingham for their own ends. Who wins the argument – the Cardinal or Buckingham? Why is this significant? Use embedded quotations and examples from the script in your writing.

1. On what occasion 因为什么
2. tender 年幼
3. Would fain have 很想
4. indirect 不诚实，不直率
5. peevish 冥顽不灵，固执
6. oratory 请求；劝说
7. mild entreaties 好言恳求
8. infringe 侵犯
9. obstinate 迂腐
10. Weigh it but with 仅靠……来衡量
11. grossness 粗俗，粗鄙
12. charter 特许状
13. sojourn 暂住

1 Can York claim sanctuary? (in pairs)

The argument between the Cardinal and Buckingham is prompted by Hastings's statement that the Duke of York wanted to meet his brother but was prevented by his mother. Buckingham's reaction to Hastings's message is to say that either the Queen must be persuaded to send the Duke of York, or Hastings must take him by force. The Cardinal finally agrees to carry out Buckingham's instructions.

- Script the scene that might have occurred when the Cardinal and Hastings arrived at Westminster Abbey to take the Duke of York away from his mother and bring him to his brother.

HASTINGS	On what occasion[1] God he knows, not I,	
	The queen your mother and your brother York	
	Have taken sanctuary. The tender[2] prince	
	Would fain have[3] come with me to meet your grace,	
	But by his mother was perforce withheld.	30
BUCKINGHAM	Fie, what an indirect[4] and peevish[5] course	
	Is this of hers. Lord Cardinal, will your grace	
	Persuade the queen to send the Duke of York	
	Unto his princely brother presently?	
	If she deny, Lord Hastings, go with him,	35
	And from her jealous arms pluck him perforce.	
CARDINAL	My lord of Buckingham, if my weak oratory[6]	
	Can from his mother win the Duke of York,	
	Anon expect him here; but if she be obdurate	
	To mild entreaties[7], God forbid	40
	We should infringe[8] the holy privilege	
	Of blessèd sanctuary. Not for all this land	
	Would I be guilty of so great a sin.	
BUCKINGHAM	You are too senseless obstinate[9], my lord,	
	Too ceremonious and traditional.	45
	Weigh it but with[10] the grossness[11] of this age:	
	You break not sanctuary in seizing him.	
	The benefit thereof is always granted	
	To those whose dealings have deserved the place	
	And those who have the wit to claim the place.	50
	This prince hath neither claimed it nor deserved it,	
	And therefore, in mine opinion, cannot have it.	
	Then taking him from thence that is not there,	
	You break no privilege nor charter[12] there.	
	Oft have I heard of sanctuary men,	55
	But sanctuary children ne'er till now.	
CARDINAL	My lord, you shall o'er-rule my mind for once.	
	Come on, Lord Hastings, will you go with me?	
HASTINGS	I go, my lord.	

[Exeunt] Cardinal and Hastings

PRINCE EDWARD	Good lords, make all the speedy haste you may.	60
	Say, uncle Gloucester, if our brother come,	
	Where shall we sojourn[13] till our coronation?	

Richard's suggestion that Prince Edward should stay in the Tower dismays the Prince. As Edward reflects on the nature of fame and reputation, Richard hints that the young Prince has not long to live.

剧情简介：理查建议爱德华王子下榻伦敦塔，这让王子忧心忡忡。爱德华思考声望和名誉的本质，理查暗示这位年轻王子将不久于世。

1 Richard's asides: to whom? (in small groups)

Prince Edward's words in line 68 may remind a modern audience of the Tower's sinister reputation: it was both a royal castle and a state prison. The sense of impending tragedy and the vulnerability of the young Prince are reinforced by Richard's three asides (lines 79, 82–3 and 94), which remind the audience that he intends Prince Edward's death.

- The theatrical convention of asides is that they are made to the audience, and not heard by the other characters on stage. Might Richard speak all three asides to Buckingham? Or are they directed at the audience? Experiment with different ways of performing these asides.
- Afterwards, talk together about the dramatic consequences of delivering them in each way. Which do you think might be most effective on stage?

2 History repeats itself

Buckingham tells Prince Edward two untruths about the Tower of London (it was not built by Julius Caesar and there is no written record that it was). Edward's reflection on Julius Caesar heightens the sense of irony in the episode, as it unwittingly forecasts his own fate. Julius Caesar was a brave man, but was murdered by the men he trusted.

- What do you think are Shakespeare's dramatic purposes in this episode? Give your reply in a written paragraph with justified reasons for your thoughts.

Stagecraft 导演技巧

The two young princes

How do the two brothers greet each other at lines 96–7? Do they embrace in an emotional reunion, or do they meet with great formality and solemnity? Take note of their formal language and the fact that the two brothers are observed by the rest of the court. Then write a stage direction at line 96 to show how you would stage the meeting of the royal brothers.

1 repose 休息
2 Julius Caesar 儒略·恺撒（伦敦塔最初部分的建造始于威廉一世，但传说恺撒也在同一地址建造了一座堡垒）
3 re-edified 修缮
4 reported 口头相传
5 registered 记载下来
6 retailed 不断地讲述
7 posterity 子孙，后代
8 the general ending day 审判日（末日）
9 characters 文字记载
10 formal Vice 老套的恶人（英格兰中世纪道德剧中一愚蠢的坏人形象，通常命名为某一具体的罪恶如"不公"[Iniquity]或"虚荣"[Vanity]）
11 Iniquity 不公
12 moralise 得出道德含义
13 wit 心智
14 lightly 轻易；常常
15 forward 早，早熟
16 how fares 怎么样，好吗（问候语）
17 my dear lord 我尊敬的国王
18 Too late 不久前

RICHARD	Where it think'st best unto your royal self.
	If I may counsel you, some day or two
	Your highness shall repose[1] you at the Tower,	65
	Then where you please and shall be thought most fit
	For your best health and recreation.
PRINCE EDWARD	I do not like the Tower, of any place.
	Did Julius Caesar[2] build that place, my lord?
BUCKINGHAM	He did, my gracious lord, begin that place,	70
	Which since, succeeding ages have re-edified[3].
PRINCE EDWARD	Is it upon recòrd, or else reported[4]
	Successively from age to age, he built it?
BUCKINGHAM	Upon recòrd, my gracious lord.
PRINCE EDWARD	But say, my lord, it were not registered[5],	75
	Methinks the truth should live from age to age,
	As 'twere retailed[6] to all posterity[7],
	Even to the general ending day[8].
RICHARD	[*Aside*] So wise so young, they say, do never live long.
PRINCE EDWARD	What say you, uncle?	80
RICHARD	I say, without characters[9] fame lives long.
	[*Aside*] Thus, like the formal Vice[10], Iniquity[11],
	I moralise[12] two meanings in one word.
PRINCE EDWARD	That Julius Caesar was a famous man.
	With what his valour did enrich his wit[13],	85
	His wit set down to make his valour live.
	Death makes no conquest of his conqueror,
	For now he lives in fame, though not in life.
	I'll tell you what, my cousin Buckingham.
BUCKINGHAM	What, my gracious lord?	90
PRINCE EDWARD	And if I live until I be a man,
	I'll win our ancient right in France again
	Or die a soldier, as I lived a king.
RICHARD	[*Aside*] Short summers lightly[14] have a forward[15] spring.

Enter young YORK, HASTINGS, *and* CARDINAL

BUCKINGHAM	Now in good time, here comes the Duke of York.	95
PRINCE EDWARD	Richard of York, how fares[16] our noble brother?
YORK	Well, my dear lord[17], so must I call you now.
PRINCE EDWARD	Ay, brother, to our grief, as it is yours.
	Too late[18] he died that might have kept that title,
	Which by his death hath lost much majesty.	100

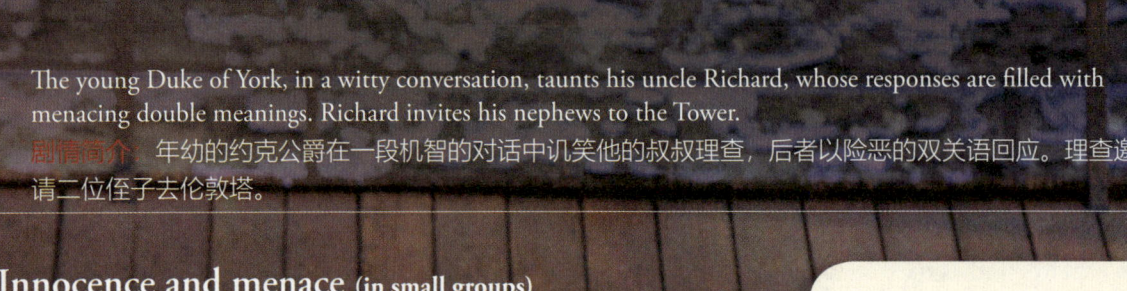

The young Duke of York, in a witty conversation, taunts his uncle Richard, whose responses are filled with menacing double meanings. Richard invites his nephews to the Tower.

剧情简介 年幼的约克公爵在一段机智的对话中讥笑他的叔叔理查，后者以险恶的双关语回应。理查邀请二位侄子去伦敦塔。

1 Innocence and menace (in small groups)

The Duke of York is reunited with his brother, Prince Edward. York seems a more exuberant (精力充沛) child, and engages in witty exchanges with his uncle, Richard, based on punning and veiled (disguised) insults. Take parts and work out a performance of lines 95–151. Use the following to help you:

- Identify lines where Richard acts like a kindly uncle, hiding his sinister intentions.
- Find some of the puns in the script opposite and suggest how Richard reacts to a young boy outsmarting him at his own verbal game.
- Is Buckingham genuine in his admiration of York in lines 133–6? Explore ways of speaking the lines – for example, sincerely, sarcastically, menacingly, or in some other way.

1 idle 无用
2 beholding 念……的好
3 kinsman 亲属，家人
4 With all my heart （可作两种解释，一为理查同意把短刀给他，一为理查想用刀刺他）
5 toy 小玩意儿
6 light 轻；不值钱
7 part 送人
8 say a beggar nay = say no to a beggar
9 cross 恼人
10 bear 担待
11 sharp-provided 机敏
12 mitigate 缓和
13 wonderful 让人赞叹
14 pass 出发

▶ In many productions, York leaps on Richard's back at line 132. What do you think of the dramatic effect of this action? How might Richard react?

RICHARD	How fares our cousin, noble lord of York?	
YORK	I thank you, gentle uncle. O my lord,	
	You said that idle[1] weeds are fast in growth;	
	The prince my brother hath outgrown me far.	
RICHARD	He hath, my lord.	105
YORK	And therefore is he idle?	
RICHARD	O my fair cousin, I must not say so.	
YORK	Then he is more beholding[2] to you than I.	
RICHARD	He may command me as my sovereign,	
	But you have power in me as in a kinsman[3].	110
YORK	I pray you, uncle, give me this dagger.	
RICHARD	My dagger, little cousin? With all my heart[4].	
PRINCE EDWARD	A beggar, brother?	
YORK	Of my kind uncle, that I know will give,	
	And being but a toy[5], which is no grief to give.	115
RICHARD	A greater gift than that I'll give my cousin.	
YORK	A greater gift? Oh, that's the sword to it.	
RICHARD	Ay, gentle cousin, were it light[6] enough.	
YORK	Oh, then I see you will part[7] but with light gifts.	
	In weightier things you'll say a beggar nay[8].	120
RICHARD	It is too weighty for your grace to wear.	
YORK	I weigh it lightly, were it heavier.	
RICHARD	What, would you have my weapon, little lord?	
YORK	I would, that I might thank you as you call me.	
RICHARD	How?	125
YORK	Little.	
PRINCE EDWARD	My lord of York will still be cross[9] in talk.	
	Uncle, your grace knows how to bear[10] with him.	
YORK	You mean to bear me, not to bear with me.	
	Uncle, my brother mocks both you and me:	130
	Because that I am little, like an ape,	
	He thinks that you should bear me on your shoulders.	
BUCKINGHAM	With what a sharp-provided[11] wit he reasons.	
	To mitigate[12] the scorn he gives his uncle,	
	He prettily and aptly taunts himself.	135
	So cunning and so young is wonderful[13].	
RICHARD	My lord, will't please you pass[14] along?	
	Myself and my good cousin Buckingham	
	Will to your mother, to entreat of her	
	To meet you at the Tower and welcome you.	140

The two princes go reluctantly to the Tower. Buckingham and Richard criticise young York. Catesby is instructed to find out whether Hastings will support Richard's bid to be crowned King.

剧情简介：两位王子不情愿地去了伦敦塔。白金汉和理查批评小约克。凯茨贝领命前去试探海斯廷，看他是否支持理查加冕为王。

1 Changes of mood (in pairs)

The mood of foreboding is heightened in the repeated references to the Tower (lines 140, 141, 143 and 151), York's fear of Clarence's ghost, and Edward's thoughts about the fate of Grey and Rivers.

a Talk together about whether Edward suspects his uncle's intentions at this point. Does he fear or respect his uncle?

b In your Director's Journal, write notes to advise the actor playing Edward how to speak all his lines opposite to reveal his true feelings about Richard.

Stagecraft 导演技巧

Stage the princes' exit (in small groups)

The departure of the princes for the Tower is the last time they appear alive in the play.

- Stage their exit with Hastings. In particular, think about what York might do to prompt Richard's descriptions of him in lines 155–6.

2 Queen Elizabeth's influence (in pairs)

Did Queen Elizabeth really incense her son against Richard, as Buckingham suggests? Or is this another of Buckingham's slanderous comments?

- Talk together about the influence the Queen may have had on how the Duke of York relates to his uncle. Then improvise an imaginary conversation between Queen Elizabeth and the young Duke of York prior to this scene.

Write about it 写作练习

Instructions to Catesby

Catesby first appears in Act 1 Scene 3. He assumes a growing importance in the play as he becomes involved in Richard's plots. Buckingham has told him of the scheme to make Richard King. He now sends Catesby to discover what Hastings thinks of the plan.

- Imagine Buckingham has also written a letter of instructions for Catesby. Write the letter, basing it on lines 158–82, and provide more details about how to sound out Lord Hastings.

---

1 **in quiet** 安稳
2 **them** （指那些故去的先人）
3 **sennet** 仪仗号（一队人到来或离去时的号声）
4 **prating** 话匣子似的
5 **incensèd** 挑唆
6 **opprobriously** 以诋毁诽谤的形式
7 **perilous** 危险
8 **ingenious** 聪明
9 **forward** 积极
10 **capable** 聪明
11 **deeply** 信誓旦旦
12 **effect** 取得
13 **of our mind** 与我们一条心
14 **instalment** 就位
15 **as it were far off** 委婉；微妙
16 **Sound** 试探
17 **doth stand affected to** 对……感觉如何
18 **sit about** 参加一个关于……的会议
19 **tractable to** 与……一致

YORK	What, will you go unto the Tower, my lord?	
PRINCE EDWARD	My Lord Protector will have it so.	
YORK	I shall not sleep in quiet[1] at the Tower.	
RICHARD	Why, what should you fear?	
YORK	Marry, my uncle Clarence' angry ghost.	145
	My grandam told me he was murdered there.	
PRINCE EDWARD	I fear no uncles dead.	
RICHARD	Nor none that live, I hope.	
PRINCE EDWARD	And if they live, I hope I need not fear.	
	But come, my lord, and with a heavy heart,	150
	Thinking on them[2], go I unto the Tower.	

A sennet[3]. Exeunt Prince, York, Hastings, [and others, except] Richard, Buckingham, and Catesby

BUCKINGHAM	Think you, my lord, this little prating[4] York	
	Was not incensèd[5] by his subtle mother	
	To taunt and scorn you thus opprobriously[6]?	
RICHARD	No doubt, no doubt. Oh, 'tis a perilous[7] boy,	155
	Bold, quick, ingenious[8], forward[9], capable[10].	
	He is all the mother's, from the top to toe.	
BUCKINGHAM	Well, let them rest. Come hither, Catesby.	
	Thou art sworn as deeply[11] to effect[12] what we intend	
	As closely to conceal what we impart.	160
	Thou know'st our reasons urged upon the way.	
	What think'st thou? Is it not an easy matter	
	To make William Lord Hastings of our mind[13]	
	For the instalment[14] of this noble duke	
	In the seat royal of this famous isle?	165
CATESBY	He for his father's sake so loves the prince	
	That he will not be won to aught against him.	
BUCKINGHAM	What think'st thou, then, of Stanley? Will not he?	
CATESBY	He will do all in all as Hastings doth.	
BUCKINGHAM	Well then, no more but this:	170
	Go, gentle Catesby, and as it were far off[15],	
	Sound[16] thou Lord Hastings	
	How he doth stand affected to[17] our purpose,	
	And summon him tomorrow to the Tower	
	To sit about[18] the coronation.	175
	If thou dost find him tractable to[19] us,	
	Encourage him, and tell him all our reasons.	

Buckingham tells Catesby to bring news of Hastings's intentions. Richard threatens to behead Hastings if he refuses his support. He promises Buckingham the earldom of Hereford. Hastings receives a messenger from Stanley.

 剧情简介： 白金汉吩咐凯茨贝通报海斯廷的意图。理查威胁说如果海斯廷不配合就砍下他的脑袋。他许诺白金汉赏他赫里福伯爵爵位。海斯廷见了斯坦雷派来的信使。

1 'Divided councils'

The two 'divided councils' refer to the two councils that Richard will summon. The first will meet at Crosby Place (Richard's London home) to offer him the crown. The second council, mainly the supporters of Edward IV, will meet at the Tower to plan Prince Edward's coronation.

- In role as Richard, write a soliloquy for the end of this scene, in which you relate your thoughts, feelings and plans for what will happen at these two councils. Try to capture Richard's ability to engage the audience as well as to make outrageous plans that allow him to move closer to the throne. Remind yourself of Richard's other soliloquies (Act 1 Scene 1 and Act 1 Scene 2) to prompt your own writing.

2 Richard takes the initiative (in pairs)

Richard's greeting to Hastings ('Lord William') seems clear and favourable. But is there a threatening meaning behind the good news that his enemies are to be killed?

- Speak lines 183–7 in two ways: first, as a friendly greeting with 'good news'; and second, in a tone of menace that hints at future trouble for Hastings.
- Decide which one you prefer, or whether you would recommend a quite different delivery.

Characters 人物分析

Richard's manipulations

What do we learn about Richard's character and schemes in lines 196–205?

- Compile a list of all the techniques he has used so far in the play to manipulate his way to the throne. You could start your list with bribery, murder and feigned friendship. Try to give a specific example of each technique by quoting or referring to the script as you add to this list.

---

1 divided councils 两个不同的会议
2 highly （地位）至关重要
3 knot 团伙
4 are let blood 将被放血
5 Mistress Shore 肖夫人（国王死后姬嫣·肖做了海斯廷的情人）
6 soundly 妥帖
7 heed 小心
8 complots 谋划
9 determine 安排
10 movables 动产（不包括土地和房屋）
11 look 期盼
12 betimes 及早
13 digest 实施
14 form 顺序

	If he be leaden, icy, cold, unwilling,
	Be thou so too, and so break off the talk,
	And give us notice of his inclination. 180
	For we tomorrow hold divided councils[1],
	Wherein thyself shalt highly[2] be employed.
RICHARD	Commend me to Lord William. Tell him, Catesby,
	His ancient knot[3] of dangerous adversaries
	Tomorrow are let blood[4] at Pomfret Castle; 185
	And bid my lord, for joy of this good news,
	Give Mistress Shore[5] one gentle kiss the more.
BUCKINGHAM	Good Catesby, go, effect this business soundly[6].
CATESBY	My good lords both, with all the heed[7] I can.
RICHARD	Shall we hear from you, Catesby, ere we sleep? 190
CATESBY	You shall, my lord.
RICHARD	At Crosby House, there shall you find us both.

Exit Catesby

BUCKINGHAM Now, my lord,
What shall we do if we perceive
Lord Hastings will not yield to our complots[8]? 195

RICHARD Chop off his head.
Something we will determine[9].
And look when I am king, claim thou of me
The earldom of Hereford and all the movables[10]
Whereof the king my brother was possessed. 200

BUCKINGHAM I'll claim that promise at your grace's hand.

RICHARD And look[11] to have it yielded with all kindness.
Come, let us sup betimes[12], that afterwards
We may digest[13] our complots in some form[14].

Exeunt

Act 3 Scene 2
Outside the house of Lord Hastings

Enter a MESSENGER *who knocks on the door of Hastings*

MESSENGER My lord! My lord!
HASTINGS [*Within*] Who knocks?
MESSENGER One from the Lord Stanley.

> The Messenger warns Hastings that Stanley has dreamt that Richard revealed his cruel nature, and danger threatens at tomorrow's councils. He urges Hastings to flee. Hastings mocks his fears and says Richard is friendly.
>
> 剧情简介：信使提醒海斯廷，说斯坦雷梦见理查暴露了残忍的本性，明天的会议将危机重重。他催促海斯廷逃亡。海斯廷嘲笑他自寻烦恼，说理查很友好。

▲ The boar was Richard's emblem, as seen in his crest at the Bosworth Battlefield Heritage Centre near Market Bosworth in Leicestershire. How could the actors make it clear that the 'boar' refers to Richard?

1 **Upon the stroke of four** 4 点了
2 **commends him** 送来他的问候
3 **certifies** 保证，发誓
4 **boar** 野猪（理查的徽章上有野猪的图案）
5 **razèd** 撞破
6 **helm** 头盔
7 **rue** 后悔
8 **post** 快马赶往
9 **the north** （指斯坦雷的大本营）
10 **divines** 预卜
11 **toucheth** 波及
12 **intelligence** 消息
13 **shallow** 无根据
14 **instance** 理由
15 **simple** 愚蠢
16 **mockery** 嘲弄
17 **slumbers** 睡眠
18 **use us kindly** 客气地对待我们
19 **stirring** 起床
20 **tott'ring** = tottering（摇摇晃晃）

1 Naive Hastings (in pairs)

Shakespeare builds a good deal of dramatic irony into Hastings's lines 19–33. Only a few minutes earlier, the audience has heard Richard's intention towards Hastings: 'Chop off his head' (Scene 1, line 196). Now Shakespeare makes Hastings appear naive and trusting by giving him language that stands in ironic contrast to what the play has revealed.

a Hastings speaks of his 'good friend Catesby' (line 22) and his confidence that 'the boar will use us kindly' (line 33). How is this ironic?

b Stanley's dream reveals his fear that Richard will turn on Hastings and himself. Hastings dismisses Stanley's dream and the fear it has provoked in him. Given what you know of the significance of other dreams in the play so far, why is this foolish?

c Take parts as Hastings and the Messenger and speak lines 4–33 to bring out Hastings's confident but ill-founded trust.

King Richard III Act 3 Scene 2
理查三世

HASTINGS [*Within*] What is't o'clock?
MESSENGER Upon the stroke of four[1].

Enter LORD HASTINGS

HASTINGS Cannot my Lord Stanley sleep these tedious nights?
MESSENGER So it appears by that I have to say.
First, he commends him[2] to your noble self.
HASTINGS What then?
MESSENGER Then certifies[3] your lordship that this night
He dreamt the boar[4] had razèd[5] off his helm[6].
Besides, he says there are two councils kept,
And that may be determined at the one
Which may make you and him to rue[7] at th'other.
Therefore he sends to know your lordship's pleasure,
If you will presently take horse with him
And with all speed post[8] with him toward the north[9],
To shun the danger that his soul divines[10].
HASTINGS Go, fellow, go, return unto thy lord;
Bid him not fear the separated council.
His honour and myself are at the one,
And at the other is my good friend Catesby,
Where nothing can proceed that toucheth[11] us
Whereof I shall not have intelligence[12].
Tell him his fears are shallow[13], without instance[14].
And for his dreams, I wonder he's so simple[15]
To trust the mockery[16] of unquiet slumbers[17].
To fly the boar before the boar pursues
Were to incense the boar to follow us
And make pursuit where he did mean no chase.
Go, bid thy master rise and come to me,
And we will both together to the Tower,
Where he shall see the boar will use us kindly[18].
MESSENGER I'll go, my lord, and tell him what you say. *Exit*

Enter CATESBY

CATESBY Many good morrows to my noble lord.
HASTINGS Good morrow, Catesby. You are early stirring[19].
What news, what news, in this our tott'ring[20] state?

Hastings refuses to support Richard's bid for the crown, but welcomes news of the fate of Rivers, Grey and Vaughan. He feels confident of Richard's friendship, but Catesby's words have an ominous meaning.

剧情简介：海斯廷拒绝支持理查争夺王位，但他乐见瑞沃、格雷和沃恩的结局。他对理查的友谊信心十足，但觉得凯茨贝的话不怀好意。

1 Hastings's fatal mistakes (in pairs)

Catesby probes Hastings's intentions and Hastings is unaware that his words are sealing his own fate. Take parts as Hastings and Catesby and speak lines 35–71 to emphasise the menace and dramatic irony of the situation. Use the following points to help you:

- Hastings constantly refers to death, both his own and his enemies'. Emphasise these in your performance.
- Catesby's replies are full of double meanings. Explore ways of showing how Catesby's sinister implications are hidden from the self-confident Hastings, but not the audience.

1	reeling 旋转；踉跄
2	crown of mine 我的脑袋
3	forward / Upon 支持
4	adversaries 敌人
5	my … descent 我先王的子嗣继承王位
6	to the death 宁死不为
7	send some packing 打发一些人去阴间
8	vile 不幸
9	monstrous 可怕极了
10	The princes （指理查和白金汉）
11	make high account of 器重
12	account 打算
13	the bridge 伦敦桥（叛徒首级悬挂于此示众）
14	unprovided 毫无准备

Themes 主题分析

False confidence (in pairs)

Because of his false confidence in his supposed friendship with Richard, Hastings fails to see that he has fallen on the wrong side of this ambitious man. He disagrees with Catesby's conclusion that Richard should be King, arguing that he would rather first lose his own head ('this crown').

- In line 70, Catesby's aside refers to the custom of displaying the heads of traitors on poles at London Bridge. If Catesby addresses line 70 directly to the audience, what gestures and expressions might he use to draw attention to Hastings's false confidence?

Language in the play 剧中语言

Personification

Catesby develops the metaphor of 'our tott'ring state' (line 37) to convey the impression of a country that is drunk and out of control, and to support the idea that the only solution is to crown Richard as King. This is an example of **personification** (giving human attributes to non-human things, see p. 250).

- What other images could be used to personify the political instability of England at this point in the play? Develop your ideas as an extended metaphor in writing, or assemble a collection of images from magazines to represent this instability and insecurity.

CATESBY	It is a reeling¹ world indeed, my lord,	
	And I believe will never stand upright	
	Till Richard wear the garland of the realm.	40
HASTINGS	How, wear the garland? Dost thou mean the crown?	
CATESBY	Ay, my good lord.	
HASTINGS	I'll have this crown of mine² cut from my shoulders	
	Before I'll see the crown so foul misplaced.	
	But canst thou guess that he doth aim at it?	45
CATESBY	Ay, on my life, and hopes to find you forward	
	Upon³ his party for the gain thereof.	
	And thereupon he sends you this good news,	
	That this same very day your enemies,	
	The kindred of the queen, must die at Pomfret.	50
HASTINGS	Indeed, I am no mourner for that news,	
	Because they have been still my adversaries⁴.	
	But that I'll give my voice on Richard's side	
	To bar my master's heirs in true descent⁵,	
	God knows I will not do it, to the death⁶.	55
CATESBY	God keep your lordship in that gracious mind.	
HASTINGS	But I shall laugh at this a twelvemonth hence,	
	That they which brought me in my master's hate,	
	I live to look upon their tragedy.	
	Well, Catesby, ere a fortnight make me older,	60
	I'll send some packing⁷ that yet think not on't.	
CATESBY	'Tis a vile⁸ thing to die, my gracious lord,	
	When men are unprepared and look not for it.	
HASTINGS	Oh, monstrous⁹, monstrous! And so falls it out	
	With Rivers, Vaughan, Grey; and so 'twill do	65
	With some men else that think themselves as safe	
	As thou and I, who, as thou know'st, are dear	
	To princely Richard and to Buckingham.	
CATESBY	The princes¹⁰ both make high account of¹¹ you.	
	[*Aside*] For they account¹² his head upon the bridge¹³.	70
HASTINGS	I know they do, and I have well deserved it.	

Enter LORD STANLEY [EARL OF DERBY]

Come on, come on, where is your boar spear, man?
Fear you the boar and go so unprovided¹⁴?

Stanley is troubled by the separate meetings of the two councils and the executions at Pomfret. He agrees to go with Hastings to the Tower. Hastings recalls his own former imprisonment there.

 剧情简介：斯坦雷对两派势力各自开会和在断桥城处决犯人感到不安。他同意和海斯廷一起去伦敦塔。海斯廷想起自己也曾经被囚禁在那里。

1 Changing fortunes (in pairs)

Both Stanley and Hastings are aware of the dramatic changes in fortune experienced by those close to the throne. Hastings was himself imprisoned in the Tower. He now feels 'triumphant' (line 81) because he believes his future is secure. Stanley's warning that Rivers, Grey and Vaughan were happy when they rode to London to meet Prince Edward fails to shake Hastings's confidence.

a Take parts and speak lines 72–95. Work out how, in speech and action, you might express Hastings's feelings of triumph, in contrast to Stanley's concern about the rapid executions at Pomfret in line 86.

b Make a list of the contrasting views of Stanley and Hastings by copying and completing the table below.

Stanley	Hastings
Concerned that the councils are a bad sign	Certain that the councils pose no threat

Characters 人物分析

Hastings's visitors

In this scene, Hastings receives visits from the Messenger, Catesby and Stanley. Each brings messages and news that Hastings ignores.

- Consider each 'visitor' in turn, suggesting how each adds to the dramatic effect of the scene (e.g. what they reveal of Hastings's character and how they deepen the dramatic irony).

1 rood 十字架
2 several 分开，分头
3 state 位置；处境
4 jocund 高兴，快活
5 o'ercast 变暗
6 rancour 仇视
7 spent 不早了
8 have with you 和您一起走
9 truth 忠心
10 wear their hats 在职
11 PURSUIVANT 缉拿使（有逮捕权的王家信使）
12 sirrah 伙计（对地位较低者的称呼）
13 suggestion 挑唆
14 then = than
15 hold it 让它永久
16 Gramercy 多谢

STANLEY	My lord, good morrow. Good morrow, Catesby.	
	You may jest on, but by the holy rood[1],	75
	I do not like these several[2] councils, I.	
HASTINGS	My lord, I hold my life as dear as yours,	
	And never in my days, I do protest,	
	Was it so precious to me as 'tis now.	
	Think you, but that I know our state[3] secure,	80
	I would be so triumphant as I am?	
STANLEY	The lords at Pomfret, when they rode from London,	
	Were jocund[4] and supposed their states were sure,	
	And they indeed had no cause to mistrust.	
	But yet you see how soon the day o'ercast[5].	85
	This sudden stab of rancour[6] I misdoubt.	
	Pray God, I say, I prove a needless coward.	
	What, shall we toward the Tower? The day is spent[7].	
HASTINGS	Come, come, have with you[8].	
	Wot you what, my lord?	90
	Today the lords you talk of are beheaded.	
STANLEY	They, for their truth[9], might better wear their heads	
	Than some that have accused them wear their hats[10].	
	But come, my lord, let's away.	

Enter a PURSUIVANT[11]

HASTINGS	Go on before, I'll talk with this good fellow.	95

Exeunt Lord Stanley and Catesby

	How now, sirrah[12]? How goes the world with thee?	
PURSUIVANT	The better that your lordship please to ask.	
HASTINGS	I tell thee, man, 'tis better with me now	
	Than when thou met'st me last where now we meet.	
	Then was I going prisoner to the Tower	100
	By the suggestion[13] of the queen's allies.	
	But now I tell thee (keep it to thyself)	
	This day those enemies are put to death,	
	And I in better state then[14] e'er I was.	
PURSUIVANT	God hold it[15] to your honour's good content.	105
HASTINGS	Gramercy[16], fellow. There, drink that for me.	

Throws him his purse

PURSUIVANT	I thank your honour.	*Exit Pursuivant*

Hastings promises to pay the Priest on the following Sunday. Buckingham's aside reminds the audience that Hastings will die. Rivers, Grey and Vaughan show defiance as they face death.

 剧情简介：海斯廷答应下个星期天付酬劳给牧师。白金汉的旁白提醒观众海斯廷将死。瑞沃、格雷和沃恩面对死亡显得大义凛然。

1 Pursuivant and Priest

Hastings's meeting with the Pursuivant (line 94) and Priest (line 108) appear to be chance encounters.

- What do you think is Shakespeare's dramatic purpose in introducing them at this point in the play? When you have recorded your ideas, look at Act 3 Scene 4, lines 86–90 to see how Hastings reflects on this meeting.

2 More dramatic irony

The dramatic irony of Hastings's situation continues to the end of the scene. If Richard's plan succeeds, Hastings will not be alive to pay the Priest. The phrase 'no shriving work' is Buckingham's cruel joke and is dramatically ironic. 'Shriving', as Buckingham uses it, is the blessing for confessing his sins to a priest that a condemned person receives shortly before his execution. The confession and blessing signified that the executed person would not suffer in hell. Buckingham's surface meaning is that Hastings is in no need of shriving, but his aside at line 122 reminds the audience that Hastings is doomed (he will stay for 'supper', but he will be dead).

- Look back over Scene 2 to remind yourself of examples of irony and dramatic irony. Choose one example of each that you think is particularly effective on stage and write down how you would perform it.

1 Sir （对神职人员的尊称）
2 exercise 布道
3 sabbath 安息日（星期日为基督教安息日）
4 content you 给您酬劳
5 no shriving work 无须忏悔
6 thence 离开那里
7 dinner 午饭
8 supper 晚饭
9 pack 一帮人
10 Dispatch 行动
11 The … out 你们活到头了

Stagecraft 导演技巧

Executions at Pontefract Castle (by yourself)

The opening stage direction of Scene 3 describes the soldiers ('*Halberds*') taking the three men to their deaths. How would you stage an effective dramatic entrance for Rivers, Grey and Vaughan? Would they be treated as royal prisoners, with sympathy, cruelly, violently or with cold formality?

- Write notes in your Director's Journal outlining how you would stage their entrance and how you would want to influence the feelings of the audience towards the men as they face execution.

Enter a PRIEST

PRIEST   Well met, my lord. I am glad to see your honour.
HASTINGS   I thank thee, good Sir¹ John, with all my heart.
                I am in your debt for your last exercise². 110
                Come the next sabbath³, and I will content you⁴.
PRIEST   I'll wait upon your lordship.

Enter BUCKINGHAM

BUCKINGHAM   What, talking with a priest, Lord Chamberlain?
                Your friends at Pomfret, they do need the priest.
                Your honour hath no shriving work⁵ in hand. 115
HASTINGS   Good faith, and when I met this holy man,
                The men you talk of came into my mind.
                What, go you toward the Tower?
BUCKINGHAM   I do, my lord, but long I cannot stay there.
                I shall return before your lordship thence⁶. 120
HASTINGS   Nay, like enough, for I stay dinner⁷ there.
BUCKINGHAM   [*Aside*] And supper⁸ too, although thou know'st it not. –
                Come, will you go?
HASTINGS   I'll wait upon your lordship.

Exeunt

Act 3 Scene 3
Yorkshire: Pontefract Castle

Enter SIR RICHARD RATCLIFFE *with Halberds, taking* RIVERS, GREY, *and* VAUGHAN *to their deaths*

RIVERS   Sir Richard Ratcliffe, let me tell thee this:
                Today shalt thou behold a subject die
                For truth, for duty, and for loyalty.
GREY   God bless the prince from all the pack⁹ of you.
                A knot you are of damnèd bloodsuckers. 5
VAUGHAN   You live that shall cry woe for this hereafter.
RATCLIFFE   Dispatch¹⁰. The limit of your lives is out¹¹.

The Woodvilles recall past murders at Pontefract Castle. They remember Margaret's curses and hope that Richard, Buckingham and Hastings will also suffer. The council begins planning Prince Edward's coronation.

剧情简介：伍德威尔成员回忆起断桥城堡发生过的谋杀。他们想起玛格蕊的诅咒，希望理查、白金汉和海斯廷也不得善终。会议开始筹划爱德华王子的加冕事宜。

1 Triple executions: on or off stage? (in pairs)

The stage direction clearly indicates that the Woodvilles are executed off stage. However, some productions show their deaths in front of the theatre audience.

a In your own production, would you show the executions or not? Explain your choice to your partner.

b How would you advise Rivers and Grey to speak their lines as they remember Margaret's curses? Vaughan has no lines. What might he be doing?

c Feed back your ideas to the rest of the class and discuss what is lost and gained by the different approaches to staging (or not staging) the execution.

1 ominous 不祥
2 slander 恶名
3 dismal seat 悲伤之所
4 exclaimed on 痛心斥责
5 is expiate 已经到来
6 determine of 对……做决定
7 wants but nomination 只欠择选良辰吉日
8 Lord Protector 摄政大臣（指理查）
9 inward 亲密

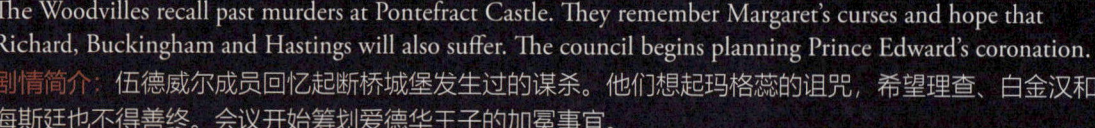

King Richard III Act 3 Scene 4
理查三世

RIVERS	O Pomfret, Pomfret! O thou bloody prison,	
	Fatal and ominous[1] to noble peers.	
	Within the guilty closure of thy walls	10
	Richard the Second here was hacked to death,	
	And, for more slander[2] to thy dismal seat[3],	
	We give to thee our guiltless blood to drink.	
GREY	Now Margaret's curse is fall'n upon our heads,	
	When she exclaimed on[4] Hastings, you, and I	15
	For standing by when Richard stabbed her son.	
RIVERS	Then cursed she Richard,	
	Then cursed she Buckingham,	
	Then cursed she Hastings. O remember God,	
	To hear her prayer for them, as now for us.	20
	And for my sister and her princely sons,	
	Be satisfied, dear God, with our true blood,	
	Which, as thou know'st, unjustly must be spilt.	
RATCLIFFE	Make haste. The hour of death is expiate[5].	
RIVERS	Come, Grey, come, Vaughan, let us here embrace.	25
	Farewell, until we meet again in heaven.	

Exeunt

Act 3 Scene 4
A room in the Tower of London

Enter BUCKINGHAM, STANLEY EARL OF DERBY, HASTINGS, BISHOP OF ELY, NORFOLK, RATCLIFFE, LOVELL, *with others*

HASTINGS	Now, noble peers, the cause why we are met	
	Is to determine of[6] the coronation.	
	In God's name, speak. When is the royal day?	
BUCKINGHAM	Is all things ready for the royal time?	
STANLEY	It is, and wants but nomination[7].	5
ELY	Tomorrow, then, I judge a happy day.	
BUCKINGHAM	Who knows the Lord Protector's[8] mind herein?	
	Who is most inward[9] with the noble duke?	
ELY	Your grace, we think, should soonest know his mind.	

Buckingham denies his close association with Richard. Hastings assumes that Richard will vote as he does. Richard sends Ely for strawberries, then tells Buckingham of Hastings's opposition to his plans.

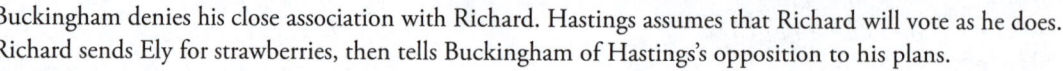

剧情简介： 白金汉否认和理查过从密切。海斯廷以为理查会和他做出相同的表决。理查让伊利摘些草莓来，然后把海斯廷反对其计划的事情告诉了白金汉。

Write about it 写作练习

Faces and hearts

Buckingham's lines 10–13 give dramatic force to the theme of appearance and reality and the ability to judge a person correctly by external signs. Buckingham says he knows Richard's outward appearance ('faces') but not his inward thoughts ('hearts').

In sharp contrast, Hastings claims a close relationship with Richard, and assumes that Richard will willingly accept Hastings's view as his own.

- The play has already shown many examples of the differences between 'faces' and 'hearts'. Write out a few of these and accompany each with a quotation. Then write two or three paragraphs describing the meaning and significance of these examples in relation to the general theme of appearance and reality.

1. purpose 意图
2. sounded 询问
3. take in gentle part 欣然接受
4. neglect 错过
5. design 计划
6. voice 允许，赞成
7. strawberries （理查突然讨要草莓乃故意表现出他心情好）
8. testy 一触即跳
9. hot 愤怒
10. His master's child （指爱德华王子）
11. sudden 仓促
12. provided 准备停当
13. prolonged 延缓

1 Hastings's downfall (I) (in large groups)

Lines 21–78 trace the downfall of Hastings – a man who has proved unable to distinguish between 'faces' and 'hearts'. Take parts as Buckingham, Ely, Stanley, Hastings and Richard, and work out a performance of the lines. Use the following questions to help you:

- In what tone does Richard speak lines 22–5?
- How might you give special emphasis to Buckingham's use of theatrical metaphors (such as 'cue', 'pronounced', 'part', 'your voice' in lines 26–8)?
- In what style does Richard speak to Buckingham in lines 35–40?
- How do Richard and Buckingham make their exit? Are they obviously plotting or pretending normality?

BUCKINGHAM	We know each other's faces. For our hearts,	10
	He knows no more of mine than I of yours,	
	Or I of his, my lord, than you of mine.	
	Lord Hastings, you and he are near in love.	
HASTINGS	I thank his grace, I know he loves me well.	
	But for his purpose¹ in the coronation,	15
	I have not sounded² him, nor he delivered	
	His gracious pleasure any way therein.	
	But you, my honourable lords, may name the time,	
	And in the duke's behalf I'll give my voice,	
	Which I presume he'll take in gentle part³.	20

Enter [RICHARD DUKE OF] GLOUCESTER

ELY	In happy time, here comes the duke himself.	
RICHARD	My noble lords and cousins all, good morrow.	
	I have been long a sleeper, but I trust	
	My absence doth neglect⁴ no great design⁵	
	Which by my presence might have been concluded.	25
BUCKINGHAM	Had you not come upon your cue, my lord,	
	William Lord Hastings had pronounced your part,	
	I mean your voice⁶ for crowning of the king.	
RICHARD	Than my Lord Hastings no man might be bolder.	
	His lordship knows me well and loves me well. –	30
	My lord of Ely, when I was last in Holborn,	
	I saw good strawberries⁷ in your garden there.	
	I do beseech you, send for some of them.	
ELY	Marry, and will, my lord, with all my heart. *Exit Bishop*	
RICHARD	Cousin of Buckingham, a word with you.	35
	Catesby hath sounded Hastings in our business,	
	And finds the testy⁸ gentleman so hot⁹	
	That he will lose his head ere give consent	
	His master's child¹⁰, as worshipfully he terms it,	
	Shall lose the royalty of England's throne.	40
BUCKINGHAM	Withdraw yourself a while; I'll go with you.	
	Exeunt [*Richard and Buckingham*]	
STANLEY	We have not yet set down this day of triumph.	
	Tomorrow, in my judgement, is too sudden¹¹,	
	For I myself am not so well provided¹²	
	As else I would be, were the day prolonged¹³.	45

Hastings claims that Richard's face is filled with good will. Richard accuses Queen Elizabeth and Jane Shore of using witchcraft to wither his arm. He condemns Hastings to death as Jane Shore's protector.

剧情简介：海斯廷声称理查面相和善。理查指控伊丽莎白王后和姬嫣·肖使用巫术让他的胳膊萎缩。他以姬嫣·肖保护人的罪名要处死海斯廷。

1 Hastings's downfall (II) (in large groups)

The dramatic irony intensifies as Hastings continues to assume that 'faces' equal 'hearts'. He claims that Richard is unable to conceal his feelings and intentions ('I think there's never a man in Christendom / Can lesser hide his love or hate, than he'). Continue to work on your performance by thinking about the following:

- How does Stanley speak lines 54–5? Does his tone reveal that he suspects Richard of false appearance?
- At what point does Hastings realise his faith in recognising 'hearts' and 'faces' is mistaken, and how does he react to his death sentence?
- How does Richard perform the internal stage direction in lines 66–8?
- Richard's command 'rise and follow me' (line 78) is an important part of his power-play. How do the nobles obey his order to desert Hastings and follow Richard? Identify how each character shows their allegiance to Richard.
- How do Lovell and Ratcliffe respond to Richard's order in line 77?

1	smooth	平和
2	conceit	想法
3	Christendom	基督教国家
4	livelihood	脸色
5	prevailed / Upon	控制
6	doom	审判，判处死刑
7	blasted	被雷劈
8	sapling	树苗
9	Consorted	伙同
10	harlot, strumpet	娼妇，妓女
11	markèd	伤害

▼ Richard (on the table in the middle) accuses Hastings (far left) of treachery.

Enter the BISHOP OF ELY

ELY | Where is my lord the Duke of Gloucester?
I have sent for these strawberries.
HASTINGS | His grace looks cheerfully and smooth¹ this morning.
There's some conceit² or other likes him well
When that he bids good morrow with such spirit. 50
I think there's never a man in Christendom³
Can lesser hide his love or hate, than he,
For by his face straight shall you know his heart.
STANLEY | What of his heart perceive you in his face
By any livelihood⁴ he showed today? 55
HASTINGS | Marry, that with no man here he is offended,
For were he, he had shown it in his looks.

Enter RICHARD *and* BUCKINGHAM

RICHARD | I pray you all, tell me what they deserve
That do conspire my death with devilish plots
Of damnèd witchcraft and that have prevailed 60
Upon⁵ my body with their hellish charms.
HASTINGS | The tender love I bear your grace, my lord,
Makes me most forward in this princely presence
To doom⁶ th'offenders, whosoe'er they be.
I say, my lord, they have deservèd death. 65
RICHARD | Then be your eyes the witness of their evil.
Look how I am bewitched. Behold, mine arm
Is like a blasted⁷ sapling⁸, withered up.
And this is Edward's wife, that monstrous witch,
Consorted⁹ with that harlot, strumpet¹⁰ Shore, 70
That by their witchcraft thus have markèd¹¹ me.
HASTINGS | If they have done this deed, my noble lord –
RICHARD | If? Thou protector of this damnèd strumpet,
Talk'st thou to me of ifs? Thou art a traitor.
Off with his head! Now by Saint Paul I swear, 75
I will not dine until I see the same.
Lovell and Ratcliffe, look that it be done.
The rest that love me, rise and follow me.

Exeunt [all but] Lovell and Ratcliffe, with the Lord Hastings

Hastings regrets ignoring Stanley's warning, the omen of his horse's stumbling and his earlier overconfidence. He recalls Margaret's curse, reflects on the nature of fame, and prophesies a bleak future for England under Richard.

剧情简介：海斯廷后悔没有理睬斯坦雷的警告，忽视了自己坐骑失蹄这一恶兆，还过于自信。他想起玛格蕊的诅咒，反思名声的本质，预言在理查治下英格兰会暗无天日。

1 What warnings did Hastings ignore? (in pairs)

As Hastings reflects on his actions and decisions, he blames his own foolishness for his fate. He now realises he has ignored or misinterpreted events and has failed to respond to ominous signs.

- Identify each event or sign he mentions in lines 79–92 (there are four of them). Copy and complete the table below to remind yourself of the particular moment when each occurred and how Hastings responded.

Event	Significance	Hastings's response
Stanley's dream of the violent boar.	It was a premonition (不祥预感) of Richard's intent.	He joked about it and refused to take it seriously.

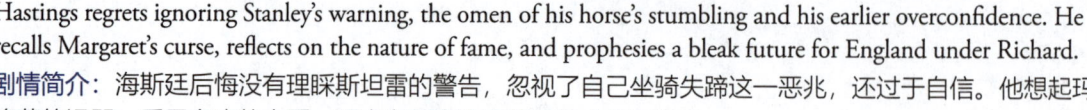

1 whit　一丁点儿
2 fond　愚蠢
3 rouse our helms　挑翻我们的头盔
4 distain　鄙视
5 fly　逃跑
6 footcloth horse　盛装的马（财富的象征）
7 lighted　降临
8 short shrift　简短的忏悔
9 grace　好运
10 in air of　于虚幻之上
11 the deep　海
12 bootless　徒劳
13 exclaim　哀叹
14 block　断头台

Characters 人物分析

Does Hastings gain self-knowledge?

Hastings realises too late that in pursuing earthly fame ('momentary grace of mortal men') he has ignored the blessing of God. In an extended **simile** (明喻) (see p. 250), he compares the fragility of human success to a drunken sailor on the mast (桅杆) of a sailing ship.

- How convincing do you find Hastings's discovery of self-knowledge as he is about to be executed?
- How would you advise the actor playing Hastings to deliver his final rhyming couplet (押韵二行连句；对偶句)?

2 Who? Us?

Lovell and Ratcliffe take Hastings away for execution.

- How would you direct the actors playing Lovell and Ratcliffe? Should they be brutal, mechanical, officious (爱摆官架子), embarrassed, or display some other emotion? How do they react to Hastings's final line (which appears to be directed at them)?

King Richard III Act 3 Scene 4
理查三世

HASTINGS Woe, woe for England, not a whit[1] for me,
For I, too fond[2], might have prevented this. 80
Stanley did dream the boar did rouse our helms[3],
And I did scorn it and disdain[4] to fly[5].
Three times today my footcloth horse[6] did stumble,
And started when he looked upon the Tower,
As loath to bear me to the slaughterhouse. 85
Oh, now I need the priest that spake to me.
I now repent I told the pursuivant,
As too triumphing, how mine enemies
Today at Pomfret bloodily were butchered,
And I myself secure in grace and favour. 90
O Margaret, Margaret, now thy heavy curse
Is lighted[7] on poor Hastings' wretched head.

RATCLIFFE Come, come, dispatch. The duke would be at dinner.
Make a short shrift[8]; he longs to see your head.

HASTINGS O momentary grace[9] of mortal men, 95
Which we more hunt for than the grace of God,
Who builds his hope in air of[10] your good looks
Lives like a drunken sailor on a mast,
Ready with every nod to tumble down
Into the fatal bowels of the deep[11]. 100

LOVELL Come, come, dispatch; 'tis bootless[12] to exclaim[13].

HASTINGS O bloody Richard, miserable England,
I prophesy the fearful'st time to thee
That ever wretched age hath looked upon.
Come, lead me to the block[14]; bear him my head. 105
They smile at me who shortly shall be dead.

Exeunt

Buckingham claims that he can act terror convincingly. He and Richard pretend an attack is imminent. Richard pretends to mourn Hastings's death, saying he loved him and thought him a great friend.

剧情简介：白金汉声称自己可以把恐怖表演得惟妙惟肖。他和理查假装政变将至。理查假惺惺地悼念海斯廷，说他爱海斯廷，认为他是一个伟大的朋友。

1 Enjoying the performance (in pairs)

Richard and Buckingham reveal the techniques they will use to act convincingly in front of the Mayor of London, then begin to put them into action.

a Lines 1–9 describe the techniques and methods of delivering lines used by actors of the great tragedies in Shakespeare's time. Practise each technique they describe, such as 'quake', 'change thy colour' and so on – there are at least twelve actions.

b Richard is a consummate (技艺高超) actor who delights in playing roles that deceive or manipulate people. Buckingham clearly relishes the same type of deception. Discuss how effective you think their performance will be and whether you think their techniques will deceive the Mayor.

Stagecraft 导演技巧

Stage-managing an enemy attack (in large groups)

In the script opposite, Richard and Buckingham stage-manage a crisis for the benefit of the Mayor. They pretend they are being attacked by enemies.

a Take parts as Richard, Buckingham, Lovell, Ratcliffe, Catesby and the Mayor. Rehearse and perform lines 1–24, playing up Richard and Buckingham's malicious sense of fun and the panic they generate.

b The two men appear in rusty armour which is extremely ugly ('*marvellous ill-favoured*'). How might you achieve an impression of their appearance if you have no armour or costume?

c Identify the internal stage directions in the script opposite, and use them to work out your own performance to convince the Mayor that an attack is taking place. What is the Mayor doing and how is he reacting to this crisis?

d How and when might Hastings's head be revealed for greatest dramatic effect?

1 *rotten* 生锈
2 *marvellous ill-favoured* 丑陋至极
3 *distraught* 心烦意乱
4 *counterfeit the deep tragedian* 模仿高明的悲惨剧*演员
5 *pry* 四处张望
6 *wagging* 摇动
7 *Intending* 装出
8 *ghastly* 惊恐
9 *in their offices* 发挥作用
10 *stratagems* 计谋
11 *o'erlook* 查看……那边
12 *defend thee* (赶快) 自卫
13 *ignoble* 卑鄙，可耻
14 *plainest* 最诚实
15 *my book* 我的日记，我秘密的守护者

* tragedy 一般译为"悲剧"，但古典tragedy的戏剧效果是引发观众对剧中主要人物最终惨死这一命运的悲悯和恐惧，因此tragedy的意思严格来说是"悲惨剧"而不是简单的"悲剧"。

Act 3 Scene 5
The courtyard of the Tower of London

Enter RICHARD *and* BUCKINGHAM *in rotten[1] armour, marvellous ill-favoured[2]*

RICHARD	Come, cousin, canst thou quake and change thy colour,	
	Murder thy breath in middle of a word,	
	And then again begin, and stop again,	
	As if thou were distraught[3] and mad with terror?	
BUCKINGHAM	Tut, I can counterfeit the deep tragedian[4],	5
	Speak and look back, and pry[5] on every side,	
	Tremble and start at wagging[6] of a straw.	
	Intending[7] deep suspicion, ghastly[8] looks	
	Are at my service, like enforcèd smiles.	
	And both are ready in their offices[9]	10
	At any time to grace my stratagems[10].	
	But what, is Catesby gone?	
RICHARD	He is, and see, he brings the Mayor along.	

Enter the MAYOR *and* CATESBY

BUCKINGHAM	Lord Mayor –	
RICHARD	Look to the drawbridge there!	15
BUCKINGHAM	Hark, a drum!	
RICHARD	Catesby, o'erlook[11] the walls!	
BUCKINGHAM	Lord Mayor, the reason we have sent –	
RICHARD	Look back, defend thee[12], here are enemies!	
BUCKINGHAM	God and our innocency defend and guard us!	20

Enter LOVELL *and* RATCLIFFE *with Hastings's head*

RICHARD	Be patient; they are friends, Ratcliffe and Lovell.	
LOVELL	Here is the head of that ignoble[13] traitor,	
	The dangerous and unsuspected Hastings.	
RICHARD	So dear I loved the man that I must weep.	
	I took him for the plainest[14] harmless creature	25
	That breathed upon the earth a Christian,	
	Made him my book[15], wherein my soul recorded	
	The history of all her secret thoughts.	

Richard says that Hastings, apart from his affair with Jane Shore, was never suspected of evil. Buckingham claims Hastings plotted to kill him and Richard. He pretends to regret the Lord Mayor did not hear Hastings's confession.

 剧情简介：理查说尽管海斯廷和姬嫣·肖有奸情，却从没有人疑心他是个恶人。白金汉声称海斯廷曾密谋要杀掉他和理查。他假装惋惜市长大人没有听到海斯廷的忏悔。

1 Convincing the Lord Mayor (in threes)

Richard and Buckingham must convince the Lord Mayor that the seemingly innocent Hastings was a clever traitor who plotted their deaths and deserved to die. Take parts as Richard, Buckingham and the Lord Mayor and perform lines 24–71. Consider the following:

- The Lord Mayor's response (line 40) to Buckingham's lie that Hastings intended to murder both Richard and him could be spoken in different ways. How might you speak the line to express doubt, shock, disbelief, suspicion, amazement, or another emotion?
- Richard answers the Mayor with rhetorical questions (lines 41–6) invoking Christian ethics, the law, the country and the importance of his own and Buckingham's security. Speak the lines, giving each item different emphasis. What convinces the Lord Mayor? Is it one particular item or the collective argument? Or is it Richard's tone, gestures or physical movements that persuade him?

1 daubed 粉饰
2 omitted 抹去
3 conversation 发生性关系
4 from all attainder of suspects 没有让人怀疑的污点
5 covert'st sheltered 隐藏最深
6 by great preservation 上天保佑
7 subtle 狡猾
8 Turks or infidels 土耳其人或异教徒（土耳其人因不信仰基督教，被认为是异教徒）
9 our persons' safety 我们的人身安全
10 fair befall you 愿好运降临给您两位
11 determined 意图

12 meanings 本意
13 prevented 预先阻止
14 timorously 惊恐地
15 Misconster 误解
16 carping 苛刻

So smooth he daubed[1] his vice with show of virtue
That his apparent open guilt omitted[2],
I mean his conversation[3] with Shore's wife,
He lived from all attainder of suspects[4].

BUCKINGHAM Well, well, he was the covert'st sheltered[5] traitor
That ever lived.
Would you imagine, or almost believe,
Were't not that by great preservation[6]
We live to tell it, that the subtle[7] traitor
This day had plotted, in the Council House,
To murder me and my good lord of Gloucester?

MAYOR Had he done so?

RICHARD What? Think you we are Turks or infidels[8]?
Or that we would, against the form of law,
Proceed thus rashly in the villain's death,
But that the extreme peril of the case,
The peace of England, and our persons' safety[9],
Enforced us to this execution?

MAYOR Now fair befall you[10], he deserved his death,
And your good graces both have well proceeded
To warn false traitors from the like attempts.

BUCKINGHAM I never looked for better at his hands
After he once fell in with Mistress Shore.
Yet had we not determined[11] he should die
Until your lordship came to see his end,
Which now the loving haste of these our friends,
Something against our meanings[12], have prevented[13];
Because, my lord, I would have had you heard
The traitor speak and timorously[14] confess
The manner and the purpose of his treasons,
That you might well have signified the same
Unto the citizens, who haply may
Misconster[15] us in him and wail his death.

MAYOR But, my good lord, your graces' words shall serve
As well as I had seen and heard him speak.
And do not doubt, right noble princes both,
But I'll acquaint our duteous citizens
With all your just proceedings in this case.

RICHARD And to that end we wished your lordship here,
T'avoid the censures of the carping[16] world.

Richard sends Buckingham to spread rumours about Edward IV: the illegitimacy of his children, his uncontrolled lust, his injustice and his bastardy. If believed, Buckingham must bring the Lord Mayor and citizens to Baynard Castle.

 剧情简介： 理查派白金汉散播关于爱德华四世的谣言：他的孩子是私生子，他本人淫欲无度，赏罚不公，是个杂种。人们一旦相信了谣言，白金汉就把市长大人和市民们带到贝纳城堡。

1 Four rumours

Richard instructs Buckingham to spread rumours about Edward IV and his children, raising questions about their legal right to the throne. Buckingham is to make four allegations (指控) to the Lord Mayor and leading citizens at Guildhall:

- **Line 75** The illegitimacy of Edward IV's children.
- **Lines 76–9** Edward ordered the unjust execution of a merchant who had told his son he would inherit his house, named 'The Crown'. Edward misinterpreted the merchant's wishes, believing he referred to his 'crown', meaning kingdom.
- **Lines 80–4** Edward's lustful nature.
- **Lines 85–92** Edward is illegitimate because the Duchess of York conceived him while her husband was fighting in France, and there was no physical resemblance between father and son.

In Richard's time, the equivalent of a press release was a poster nailed up in public places. Use the rumours above to create the poster that Buckingham issues, casting doubt on Prince Edward's right to the throne.

Language in the play 剧中语言
Slander and suspicion (in pairs)

Explore Richard's use of language as he tells Buckingham what to say at Guildhall.

- Pick out all the words in the script opposite that are emotive and persuasive. Write brief notes on how you think Richard would say these words or use gestures on stage.
- What contrast does he develop between his brother 'that insatiate Edward' and his father 'the noble duke'? Note the language he uses to describe both. Explain how effective his words would be in creating suspicion among the crowd at Guildhall.

1 witness 见证
2 Go after 跟着
3 hies him in all post 以最快的速度去
4 meetest vantage of the time 最恰当的时机
5 Infer 暗示
6 house 店铺（他做生意的场所也叫"王冠"）
7 by the sign thereof 因为店铺的招牌
8 luxury 性欲
9 prey 猎物
10 went with child / Of 怀了……的孩子
11 insatiate 贪得无厌
12 computation 计算
13 his begot 他（约克）亲生的孩子
14 lineaments 容貌
15 sparingly 隐晦地
16 golden fee 王位
17 adieu = farewell
18 Baynard's Castle （理查在伦敦的一处住所）
19 reverend 尊贵的，尊敬的

BUCKINGHAM   Which, since you come too late of our intent,
             Yet witness¹ what you hear we did intend.
             And so, my good Lord Mayor, we bid farewell.

                                              Exit Mayor

RICHARD   Go after², after, cousin Buckingham.
             The Mayor towards Guildhall hies him in all post³.
             There, at your meetest vantage of the time⁴,
             Infer⁵ the bastardy of Edward's children.
             Tell them how Edward put to death a citizen
             Only for saying he would make his son
             Heir to the crown, meaning indeed his house⁶,
             Which, by the sign thereof⁷, was termèd so.
             Moreover, urge his hateful luxury⁸
             And bestial appetite in change of lust,
             Which stretched unto their servants, daughters, wives,
             Even where his raging eye or savage heart,
             Without control, lusted to make a prey⁹,
             Nay, for a need, thus far come near my person:
             Tell them, when that my mother went with child
             Of¹⁰ that insatiate¹¹ Edward, noble York,
             My princely father, then had wars in France,
             And by true computation¹² of the time
             Found that the issue was not his begot¹³,
             Which well appearèd in his lineaments¹⁴,
             Being nothing like the noble duke, my father.
             Yet touch this sparingly¹⁵, as 'twere far off,
             Because, my lord, you know my mother lives.

BUCKINGHAM   Doubt not, my lord, I'll play the orator
             As if the golden fee¹⁶ for which I plead
             Were for myself. And so, my lord, adieu¹⁷.

RICHARD   If you thrive well, bring them to Baynard's Castle¹⁸,
             Where you shall find me well accompanied
             With reverend¹⁹ fathers and well-learnèd bishops.

BUCKINGHAM   I go, and towards three or four o'clock
             Look for the news that the Guildhall affords.

                                         Exit Buckingham

Richard sends for two churchmen, then plans to isolate Clarence's and Edward's children. The Scrivener reflects on the deceit involved in Hastings's execution. Buckingham reports the citizens' lack of reaction to his speech.

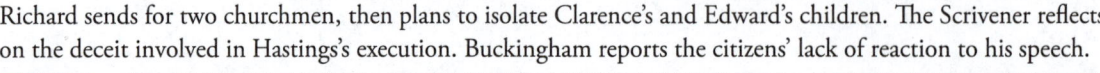

剧情简介：理查派人请来两名牧师，随后计划隔离克莱润和爱德华的孩子。抄写员回想海斯廷被处死的黑幕。白金汉通报说市民们对他的演讲反应冷淡。

1 The next steps to the throne (in pairs)

Richard sends Lovell to fetch two influential churchmen, Dr Shaw and Friar Penker, to help win the citizens' support for his plan to become King.

a How do you think Richard intends to use the two churchmen? Write down your guess and then see what he actually does in Scene 7, lines 94–6.

b Richard intends to make secret arrangements ('some privy order') to ensure Clarence's children are kept out of the public eye. He will ensure King Edward's rightful heirs, the princes in the Tower, receive no visitors. Talk together about why Richard feels these moves are necessary to his plotting.

c Add to your list of techniques that Richard uses to manipulate and manoeuvre his way to the throne.

Stagecraft 导演技巧

Tampering (篡改) with justice (in pairs)

The Scrivener, a professional writer who drafts legal documents, estimates eleven hours of work have gone into the original draft. He has worked on the draft for another eleven hours – yet only five hours previously, Hastings was a free man. The Scrivener questions whether anyone is so stupid that they cannot see such injustice. His thoughts reveal the world Richard is creating, in which people are afraid to criticise obvious injustice.

a This brief scene is often cut in performance. Write reasons for or against its inclusion, then script a conversation between the director who wants to cut it and an actor playing the Scrivener who thinks it is important.

b How else might a director demonstrate that this is a society full of oppression and repression? Write down some ideas for how to show this in a modern performance. For example, you might choose to have offstage sounds of torture, or silhouettes (暗色轮廓) showing at the back of the stage.

---

1 Doctor Shaw （历史上肖是市长的兄弟，一名专职教士，亲理查一派）
2 privy 私下
3 brats 小兔崽子
4 no manner person = nobody
5 recourse 接近
6 indictment 起诉书
7 in … engrossed 以规范的法律形式
8 Paul's 圣保罗大教堂（律师们开会的场所）
9 the sequel 下面发生的事情
10 precedent 原稿
11 Untainted 未加指控
12 unexamined 未加审查
13 the while 当下
14 gross 愚蠢
15 palpable device 显而易见的诡计
16 seen in thought 烂在肚子里
17 mum 缄默
18 Touched you 您提到……了吗

RICHARD   Go, Lovell, with all speed to Doctor Shaw[1].
          Go thou to Friar Penker. Bid them both
          Meet me within this hour at Baynard's Castle.   105

                                                    Exit [Lovell]

          Now will I go to take some privy[2] order
          To draw the brats[3] of Clarence out of sight,
          And to give order that no manner person[4]
          Have any time recourse[5] unto the princes.

                                                    Exeunt

Act 3 Scene 6
London: the scrivener's house

Enter a SCRIVENER

SCRIVENER   Here is the indictment[6] of the good Lord Hastings,
            Which in a set hand fairly is engrossed[7]
            That it may be today read o'er in Paul's[8].
            And mark how well the sequel[9] hangs together:
            Eleven hours I have spent to write it over,   5
            For yesternight by Catesby was it sent me;
            The precedent[10] was full as long a-doing.
            And yet within these five hours Hastings lived,
            Untainted[11], unexamined[12], free, at liberty.
            Here's a good world the while[13].   10
            Who is so gross[14] that cannot see this palpable device[15]?
            Yet who so bold but says he sees it not?
            Bad is the world, and all will come to naught
            When such ill dealing must be seen in thought[16].

                                                    Exit

Act 3 Scene 7
London: the courtyard of Baynard's Castle

Enter RICHARD *and* BUCKINGHAM

RICHARD   How now, how now, what say the citizens?
BUCKINGHAM   Now, by the holy mother of our Lord,
             The citizens are mum[17], say not a word.
RICHARD   Touched you[18] the bastardy of Edward's children?

Buckingham reports that the citizens remained silent as he slandered Edward and praised Richard. He explains how he used the cheers of a few of his own men to claim that all the citizens supported Richard.

剧情简介： 白金汉报告说市民对于他诋毁爱德华、赞美理查都无动于衷。他解释自己怎样利用几个手下在人群中起哄，宣称所有市民都支持理查。

1 Buckingham's evidence (in pairs)

Buckingham plays an increasingly important role as Richard's chief henchman (走狗) and mouthpiece (代言人), and he reveals a strong understanding of political double-dealing. He uses the four allegations suggested by Richard (see p. 128) and adds more ideas of his own in lines 5–6 and 15–17 in the script opposite.

- Identify the evidence Buckingham presents in favour of Richard and against the former King and his family. Then discuss how effective each example is in tarnishing (败坏) the reputation of the dead King Edward and in presenting Richard in a more favourable light.

Write about it 写作练习

Buckingham: an unsuccessful orator (演讲者)?

Buckingham has said that he will 'play the orator' (Act 3 Scene 5, line 95), but he does not seem to have been very successful.

- Imagine you are a newspaper reporter who observes Buckingham's attempts to get the citizens to support Richard. Write a report for your newspaper, describing what you heard and the citizens' reaction to it. Use quotations from the script opposite and make up some of your own from imagined interviews with the people who were there.

1	Lady Lucy	（有史料记载，爱德华在追求伊丽莎白·伍德威尔时已与伊丽莎白·露西订婚）
2	enforcement	强暴
3	got	怀胎
4	right idea	正确模样
5	Laid open	大肆宣扬
6	discipline in war	作战本领
7	bounty	慷慨
8	handled	处理
9	discourse	演说
10	reprehended	指责
11	willful silence	故意沉默
12	the Recorder	登记官
13	nothing … himself	他拒绝用自己的名义（为理查摇旗呐喊）
14	Argues	证明
15	blocks	蠢材

BUCKINGHAM	I did, with his contràct with Lady Lucy[1]	5
	And his contràct by deputy in France;	
	Th'insatiate greediness of his desire	
	And his enforcement[2] of the city wives;	
	His tyranny for trifles; his own bastardy,	
	As being got[3], your father then in France,	10
	And his resemblance being not like the duke.	
	Withal, I did infer your lineaments,	
	Being the right idea[4] of your father	
	Both in your form and nobleness of mind;	
	Laid open[5] all your victories in Scotland,	15
	Your discipline in war[6], wisdom in peace,	
	Your bounty[7], virtue, fair humility;	
	Indeed, left nothing fitting for your purpose	
	Untouched or slightly handled[8] in discourse[9].	
	And when my oratory drew toward end,	20
	I bid them that did love their country's good	
	Cry 'God save Richard, England's royal king!'	
RICHARD	And did they so?	
BUCKINGHAM	No, so God help me, they spake not a word,	
	But like dumb statuès or breathing stones	25
	Stared each on other and looked deadly pale.	
	Which when I saw, I reprehended[10] them,	
	And asked the Mayor what meant this wilful silence[11].	
	His answer was, the people were not used	
	To be spoke to but by the Recorder[12].	30
	Then he was urged to tell my tale again:	
	'Thus saith the duke, thus hath the duke inferred',	
	But nothing spoke in warrant from himself[13].	
	When he had done, some followers of mine own	
	At lower end of the hall hurled up their caps,	35
	And some ten voices cried 'God save King Richard!'	
	And thus I took the vantage of those few:	
	'Thanks, gentle citizens and friends', quoth I,	
	'This general applause and cheerful shout	
	Argues[14] your wisdom and your love to Richard.'	40
	And even here broke off and came away.	
RICHARD	What tongueless blocks[15] were they! Would they not speak?	
	Will not the Mayor, then, and his brethren, come?	

Buckingham instructs Richard to appear saintly before the Lord Mayor. Catesby reports that Richard cannot be disturbed while he is praying. Buckingham contrasts Richard's piety with Edward's dissolute ways.

剧情简介：白金汉教理查怎样在市长大人面前假装神圣。凯茨贝报告说理查在祷告，不能打扰。白金汉对比理查的虔诚和爱德华的放荡。

1 Sexism?

To fool the Lord Mayor and the citizens, Buckingham urges Richard to pretend fear and to be interrupted only by very important entreaties ('mighty suit'). The two men agree that Richard will 'Play the maid's part' and make jokes about women who say 'no' when they mean 'yes'. Richard hopes his 'nay' will bring a successful outcome.

- Imagine that someone says to you: 'I think lines 50–3 should be cut in performance. They are sexist and add nothing to the play.' Write your reply.

Themes 主题分析

'a holy descant' (in threes)

Using a musical metaphor, Buckingham describes how he will play a variety of ingenious variations on Richard's repeated theme of pretended piety. He intends to present Richard as a religious man, and both hide their ambitious intentions beneath a display of piety and gentleness. Buckingham makes a start in lines 70–9, in which he contrasts Richard with Edward.

a As one person speaks Buckingham's lines slowly, the second person echoes each example of Edward's wantonness (放纵), and the third person echoes each example of Richard's piety.

b Prepare two tableaux of Richard – the first showing how Buckingham is presenting him, and the second showing his true personality.

Write about it 写作练习

Catesby's role (by yourself)

What is the dramatic significance of Catesby acting as a mediator between Richard and Buckingham during this 'performance'?

- In role as Buckingham, write a paragraph explaining why you wanted Catesby to be involved and what you hoped to achieve.

1 **intend some fear** 装作谨小慎微的样子
2 **mighty suit** 竭力恳请
3 **descant** 高谈阔论（在一个主旋律上的各种音乐变奏）
4 **Play the maid's part** 装作姑娘般害羞、腼腆
5 **issue** 结果
6 **leads** （指用铅板覆盖的屋顶）
7 **dance attendance** 过分殷勤地伺候
8 **spoke withal** 与……交谈
9 **Divinely bent** 虔诚地进行
10 **holy exercise** 礼拜
11 **aldermen** 市参议员，市政长老
12 **deep designs** 重要的事情
13 **No less importing than** 重要性不亚于
14 **lulling** 懒洋洋地躺
15 **dallying … courtesans** 与一对妓女调情（brace：一对）
16 **deep divines** 博学的神职人员
17 **engross** 使变胖
18 **watchful** 警觉
19 **sovereignty** 王位

BUCKINGHAM	The Mayor is here at hand; intend some fear¹.	
	Be not you spoke with but by mighty suit².	45
	And look you get a prayer book in your hand	
	And stand between two churchmen, good my lord,	
	For on that ground I'll make a holy descant³.	
	And be not easily won to our requests;	
	Play the maid's part⁴: still answer nay and take it.	50
RICHARD	I go; and if you plead as well for them	
	As I can say nay to thee for myself,	
	No doubt we bring it to a happy issue⁵.	
BUCKINGHAM	Go, go, up to the leads⁶. The Lord Mayor knocks.	

Exit [Richard]

Enter the MAYOR *and Citizens*

Welcome, my lord. I dance attendance⁷ here. 55
I think the duke will not be spoke withal⁸.

Enter CATESBY

BUCKINGHAM	Now, Catesby, what says your lord to my request?	
CATESBY	He doth entreat your grace, my noble lord,	
	To visit him tomorrow or next day.	
	He is within, with two right reverend fathers,	60
	Divinely bent⁹ to meditation,	
	And in no worldly suits would he be moved	
	To draw him from his holy exercise¹⁰.	
BUCKINGHAM	Return, good Catesby, to the gracious duke.	
	Tell him myself, the Mayor, and aldermen¹¹	65
	In deep designs¹², in matter of great moment,	
	No less importing than¹³ our general good,	
	Are come to have some conference with his grace.	
CATESBY	I'll signify so much unto him straight.	*Exit*
BUCKINGHAM	Ah ha, my lord, this prince is not an Edward.	70
	He is not lulling¹⁴ on a lewd love-bed	
	But on his knees at meditation,	
	Not dallying with a brace of courtesans¹⁵	
	But meditating with two deep divines¹⁶,	
	Not sleeping to engross¹⁷ his idle body	75
	But praying to enrich his watchful¹⁸ soul.	
	Happy were England, would this virtuous prince	
	Take on his grace the sovereignty¹⁹ thereof,	
	But sure I fear we shall not win him to it.	

Catesby reports that Richard fears the citizens wish him harm. Richard appears between two churchmen. Buckingham asks him to listen to the citizens' requests, but Richard says he fears he has displeased them.

剧情简介：凯茨贝传话说理查担心市民害他。理查在两名牧师的左右陪同下上场。白金汉请他倾听市民的请求，但是理查说他担心自己已经让他们不高兴了。

1 Richard and the bishops

Richard's appearance with the two bishops has been played on stage in all kinds of ways. The bishops have been portrayed as medieval monks in cowls (大兜帽，风帽) and robes, as modern clergymen, as bishops wearing mitres and copes (elaborate gowns), and as 'holy fools' (almost naked religious prophets).

- How would you choose to present them? Why? What effect might be gained by your particular presentation of the bishops? Write down your thoughts in your Director's Journal.

▼ Richard appearing between two bishops. Compare this picture with the picture on page x. How are they similar? In what ways are they different?

1	end	目的
2	devout	虔诚
3	at their beads	祷告（通常会手捻念珠）
4	much to draw them thence	难以吸引他们的注意力
5	props	支柱
6	stay	阻止
7	know	辨别
8	right	真诚
9	Deferred the visitation	推迟了拜访
10	ungoverned	无统治者
11	disgracious	令人不悦，无法接受

136

MAYOR	Marry, God defend his grace should say us nay.	80
BUCKINGHAM	I fear he will. Here Catesby comes again.	

Enter CATESBY

Now, Catesby, what says his grace?

CATESBY   He wonders to what end[1] you have assembled
Such troops of citizens to come to him,
His grace not being warned thereof before. 85
He fears, my lord, you mean no good to him.

BUCKINGHAM   Sorry I am my noble cousin should
Suspect me that I mean no good to him.
By heaven, we come to him in perfect love,
And so once more return and tell his grace. 90

Exit [*Catesby*]

When holy and devout[2] religious men
Are at their beads[3], 'tis much to draw them thence[4],
So sweet is zealous contemplation.

Enter RICHARD *aloft, between two Bishops*

MAYOR   See where his grace stands, 'tween two clergymen.
BUCKINGHAM   Two props[5] of virtue for a Christian prince, 95
To stay[6] him from the fall of vanity.
And see, a book of prayer in his hand,
True ornaments to know[7] a holy man –
Famous Plantagenet, most gracious prince,
Lend favourable ear to our requests, 100
And pardon us the interruption
Of thy devotion and right[8] Christian zeal.

RICHARD   My lord, there needs no such apology.
I do beseech your grace to pardon me,
Who, earnest in the service of my God, 105
Deferred the visitation[9] of my friends.
But leaving this, what is your grace's pleasure?

BUCKINGHAM   Even that, I hope, which pleaseth God above
And all good men of this ungoverned[10] isle.

RICHARD   I do suspect I have done some offence 110
That seems disgracious[11] in the city's eye,
And that you come to reprehend my ignorance.

BUCKINGHAM   You have, my lord. Would it might please your grace
On our entreaties to amend your fault.

Buckingham puts forward several reasons to persuade Richard to become King. He claims it is the citizens' wish. Richard debates whether he should reply or remain silent.

剧情简介：白金汉摆出几条理由劝说理查称王。他声称这是民心所向。理查斟酌该不该回应。

1 Buckingham's rhetoric (in pairs)

The plot to fool the Lord Mayor and citizens into accepting Richard as King continues with a brilliant display of rhetoric:

- **Lines 116–21** Buckingham tells Richard that he is wrong to give up his right to the crown in favour of corrupt members of his family.
- **Lines 122–8** He urges Richard to take action because England is sick and its royal family at the point of death.
- **Lines 129–35** The people beg Richard to cure England by becoming not the agent of another, but the true King in his own right.
- **Lines 136–9** All this is the wish of the citizens; he speaks for them.

Take turns to speak Buckingham's lines 116–39, experimenting with a range of tone, volume, pitch and pace to be as persuasive as you can.

2 Mock-modest Richard (I) (in pairs)

In lines 140–72 – in which Richard responds to Buckingham's offer of the crown – his formal language masks his ambition. The first twelve lines are like an internal debate in which he attempts to balance two opposing arguments: speak or be silent.

a Write out in your own words what Richard means by this response to Buckingham's offer of the crown. Which of his two arguments do you think will carry the most weight with the Mayor and the citizens?

b Provide two (or more) asides that show what Richard is really thinking as he describes his dilemma between speaking out or remaining silent.

1	sceptered office	手持王杖的职责
2	Your state of fortune	命中注定的地位
3	lineal glory	世袭的光荣
4	blemished stock	被玷污的血统
5	proper limbs	正统的支脉
6	graft with	被嫁接上了
7	ignoble plants	卑劣的植株
8	shouldered in	推进……之中
9	recure	恢复
10	factor	代理人
11	successively	通过继承
12	empery	帝国
13	consorted	联合
14	vehement instigation	热烈的怂恿
15	move	说服
16	degree	身份
17	fondly	荒唐
18	suit	要求
19	seasoned	加了佐料
20	checked	指责

Write about it 写作练习

A citizen's perspective (by yourself)

Consider these events from the perspective of one of the citizens of London who was present at both Buckingham's addresses.

- Write a diary entry giving an account of the events described in this scene and your understanding of what is really happening. How do you feel about Richard becoming King and about Buckingham's persuasive performance? Why do you remain silent at the beginning of the scene (see lines 1–42)? What is your response when Richard speaks for himself?

| RICHARD | Else wherefore breathe I in a Christian land? | 115 |

BUCKINGHAM Know, then, it is your fault that you resign
The supreme seat, the throne majestical,
The sceptered office[1] of your ancestors,
Your state of fortune[2] and your due of birth,
The lineal glory[3] of your royal house, 120
To the corruption of a blemished stock[4];
While in the mildness of your sleepy thoughts,
Which here we waken to our country's good,
The noble isle doth want her proper limbs[5];
Her face defaced with scars of infamy, 125
Her royal stock graft with[6] ignoble plants[7],
And almost shouldered in[8] the swallowing gulf
Of dark forgetfulness and deep oblivion.
Which to recure[9], we heartily solicit
Your gracious self to take on you the charge 130
And kingly government of this your land,
Not as protector, steward, substitute,
Or lowly factor[10] for another's gain,
But as successively[11] from blood to blood,
Your right of birth, your empery[12], your own. 135
For this, consorted[13] with the citizens,
Your very worshipful and loving friends,
And by their vehement instigation[14],
In this just cause come I to move[15] your grace.

RICHARD I cannot tell if to depart in silence 140
Or bitterly to speak in your reproof
Best fitteth my degree[16] or your condition.
If not to answer, you might haply think
Tongue-tied ambition, not replying, yielded
To bear the golden yoke of sovereignty, 145
Which fondly[17] you would here impose on me.
If to reprove you for this suit[18] of yours,
So seasoned[19] with your faithful love to me,
Then on the other side I checked[20] my friends.
Therefore, to speak, and to avoid the first, 150
And then, in speaking, not to incur the last,
Definitively thus I answer you:

Richard argues that he is unworthy to be King and that young Edward will in time become a successful monarch. Buckingham reminds Richard of the Prince of Wales's suspect family history.

 剧情简介：理查提出自己不配称王，说假以时日少年爱德华会成为一位明君。白金汉提醒理查威尔士王子可疑的家族史。

1 Mock-modest Richard (II)

- In lines 155–65, Richard argues he is unfit for such a high position. He compares himself to a ship ('bark') unfit to endure a great ocean ('brook no mighty sea'), claiming that he would rather avoid kingship ('greatness') than desire it ('covet to be hid') and would be overwhelmed by such an awesome responsibility.
- In lines 166–72, he asserts that the Prince of Wales is the rightful heir who will mature ('mellowed by the stealing hours of time') into a distinguished monarch. But Richard's 'no doubt' is a sting in the tail of his praise of Edward.

a Make notes on the main points of Richard's speech, using the information above and on page 138. Use your notes to help you deliver Richard's lines 140–72. Try to bring out his hypocrisy.

b How would you advise the actor playing Richard at this point in the play? Write notes in your Director's Journal.

Characters 人物分析
Sneering at Queen Elizabeth

Buckingham repeats the accusations of Prince Edward's illegitimacy and King Edward's breaking of two marriage contracts. In highly insulting language, he turns his attention to Elizabeth Grey.

a List the words and phrases Buckingham uses to describe the Queen. Then write out his description of her in modern English. What picture is he painting of her and her son?

b Write a defence of the Queen in the form of an opinion article submitted to the national newspaper. What other perspectives can you put forward to save the Queen's reputation and that of her family?

1	desert / Unmeritable	功寡德鲜
2	shuns	拒绝
3	even	顺利，平稳
4	As … birth	我生而应得的
5	covet	热烈地渴望
6	need	缺乏
7	mellowed	使成熟
8	defend	禁止
9	nice	微小
10	a poor petitioner	一个卑微的破落户
11	beauty-waning	人老珠黄
12	the afternoon … days	中年
13	Made … eye	勾住了他一双色眼
14	pitch	高位
15	base declension	可耻的屈服
16	bigamy	重婚
17	our manners	我们出于礼节

Your love deserves my thanks, but my desert
Unmeritable¹ shuns² your high request.
First, if all obstacles were cut away, 155
And that my path were even³ to the crown
As the ripe revenue and due of birth⁴,
Yet so much is my poverty of spirit,
So mighty and so many my defects,
That I would rather hide me from my greatness, 160
Being a bark to brook no mighty sea,
Than in my greatness covet⁵ to be hid
And in the vapour of my glory smothered.
But, God be thanked, there is no need of me,
And much I need to help you, were there need⁶. 165
The royal tree hath left us royal fruit,
Which, mellowed⁷ by the stealing hours of time,
Will well become the seat of majesty
And make (no doubt) us happy by his reign,
On him I lay that you would lay on me, 170
The right and fortune of his happy stars,
Which God defend⁸ that I should wring from him.

BUCKINGHAM My lord, this argues conscience in your grace,
But the respects thereof are nice⁹ and trivial,
All circumstances well considerèd. 175
You say that Edward is your brother's son.
So say we too, but not by Edward's wife,
For first was he contràct to Lady Lucy,
Your mother lives a witness to his vow,
And afterward by substitute betrothed 180
To Bona, sister to the King of France.
These both put off, a poor petitioner¹⁰,
A care-crazed mother to a many sons,
A beauty-waning¹¹ and distressèd widow,
Even in the afternoon of her best days¹², 185
Made prize and purchase of his wanton eye¹³,
Seduced the pitch¹⁴ and height of his degree
To base declension¹⁵ and loathed bigamy¹⁶.
By her, in his unlawful bed, he got
This Edward, whom our manners¹⁷ call the prince. 190

Buckingham says he will refrain from further criticism. He begs Richard to accept the crown, echoed by the Lord Mayor on behalf of the people. Richard refuses. Buckingham threatens to enthrone another. Catesby adds his pleas.

剧情简介：白金汉说他会避免进行更多的批评。他恳求理查接受王冠，市长大人也以人民的名义附和。理查拒绝了。白金汉以拥护他人登基来要挟。凯茨贝也在一旁帮腔。

1 Richard the unwilling King? (in large groups)

The unsettling macabre (可怕) humour and dramatic irony continue to the end of the scene, as Richard and his co-conspirators act out their charade (做戏) for the Lord Mayor and citizens.

a Decide whether they really are deceived by Richard. Take parts as the Lord Mayor and citizens, Richard, Buckingham and Catesby. Work out a performance of lines 191–245 to bring out the humour and hypocrisy in the episode. Use the following to help you:

- Read through lines 191–9 to work out how Buckingham might speak as much to the Lord Mayor and citizens as he does to Richard.
- The Lord Mayor's plea at line 200 is (probably) sincere. Buckingham's and Catesby's lines 201–2 are deeply insincere. Use tones and gestures to bring out what is really in each man's mind.
- How can Richard speak or act in lines 203–4 to reveal his hypocrisy?
- How does Richard react to Buckingham's description of him in lines 209–10?

b Write notes in your Director's Journal about how you want the script opposite to be staged. Remember to include your thoughts about what the crowd is doing and thinking during this 'performance'.

1 expostulate 阐释
2 give … tongue 不愿多说爱德华国王可耻的过往
3 proffered benefit of dignity 奉上的尊荣
4 draw forth 拯救
5 amiss 见怪，错怪
6 zeal 热诚
7 gentle 有教养
8 effeminate remorse 妇人之仁，优柔寡断
9 kindred 家族
10 all estates 天下之人
11 whe'er = whether
12 Call him again 把他召回来

Themes 主题分析

Acting the part (in pairs)

Both Buckingham and Richard give convincing performances, and they work well together, with each man offering the other the opportunity to develop his part.

- In role as Richard and Buckingham, write asides at suitable points in the script opposite to allow them to comment on their own and each other's performance.
- Take turns to perform your asides to the rest of the class, while three others read out the scripted lines from the page opposite, pausing for you to give your character's comments.

KING RICHARD III ACT 3 SCENE 7
理查三世

More bitterly could I expostulate[1],
Save that for reverence to some alive,
I give a sparing limit to my tongue[2].
Then, good my lord, take to your royal self
This proffered benefit of dignity[3], 195
If not to bless us and the land withal,
Yet to draw forth[4] your noble ancestry
From the corruption of abusing times
Unto a lineal true-derivèd course.

MAYOR   Do, good my lord, your citizens entreat you. 200
BUCKINGHAM   Refuse not, mighty lord, this proffered love.
CATESBY   Oh, make them joyful. Grant their lawful suit.
RICHARD   Alas, why would you heap this care on me?
I am unfit for state and majesty.
I do beseech you, take it not amiss[5]; 205
I cannot nor I will not yield to you.
BUCKINGHAM   If you refuse it, as in love and zeal[6]
Loath to depose the child, your brother's son,
As well we know your tenderness of heart
And gentle[7], kind, effeminate remorse[8], 210
Which we have noted in you to your kindred[9]
And equally indeed to all estates[10],
Yet know, whe'er[11] you accept our suit or no,
Your brother's son shall never reign our king,
But we will plant some other in the throne 215
To the disgrace and downfall of your house.
And in this resolution here we leave you.
Come, citizens. We will entreat no more.
                                                                   Exeunt
CATESBY   Call him again[12], sweet prince; accept their suit.
If you deny them, all the land will rue it. 220

Richard orders Catesby to recall everyone. He grudgingly accepts the burden of kingship, but says that if discord follows, he is free of blame. He is proclaimed King, with the coronation to take place the following day.

剧情简介：理查命凯茨贝把大家喊回来。他勉强接受了君主的重任，但是说明一旦有反对意见，不要怪罪他。他被拥戴为王，加冕仪式将在第二天举行。

1 'Call them again' (in small groups)

The stage direction *Exeunt* at line 218 implies that only Richard, the bishops and Catesby remain on stage. In some productions, following a long pause after line 221, Richard is genuinely afraid that the citizens will not come back.

- Use that interpretation to suggest how Richard speaks his words 'Call them again' to get a laugh from the audience.

Language in the play 剧中语言
Denying responsibility

Richard's lines 225–34 reveal more of his cunning. He says he must patiently accept the burden of kingship that they are fastening like armour on his back. As this role has been imposed upon him, so those who forced him to become King must acquit him of any future blame.

- Experiment with ways of performing these lines. Are they spoken grudgingly, sorrowfully, gravely or threateningly? In your delivery, show how Richard's language shifts responsibility away from himself and reinforces his appearance of grudgingly accepting the crown (for example, in his use of 'you' and 'your' and 'I', and in the words that mean burden and faults).

Stagecraft 导演技巧
Long live King Richard (in small groups)

Many stage productions place the interval at this point, closing with a striking image, as a triumphant Richard achieves his aim and is proclaimed King. In one stage production, Richard threw away his prayer book and the bishops revealed themselves as armed soldiers. In Laurence Olivier's movie of the play, Richard's final action was to force Buckingham to kneel and kiss his hand in an act of submission.

- Work out a final, effective dramatic image of your own to close the scene.

1 penetrable 会被……打动
2 Albeit 尽管
3 sage 贤达
4 buckle 为……披上甲胄
5 Attend the sequel 因……引发
6 Your mere enforcement 你们强我所难这一事实
7 acquittance 让……免于责难
8 impure blots 污点
9 cousins 兄弟们（理查如此称呼市民以示亲密）

King Richard III Act 3 Scene 7
理查三世

RICHARD	Will you enforce me to a world of cares?
	Call them again. I am not made of stones,
	But penetrable¹ to your kind entreaties,
	Albeit² against my conscience and my soul.

Enter BUCKINGHAM *and the rest*

	Cousin of Buckingham, and sage³, grave men,	225
	Since you will buckle⁴ fortune on my back,	
	To bear her burden, whe'er I will or no,	
	I must have patience to endure the load.	
	But if black scandal or foul-faced reproach	
	Attend the sequel⁵ of your imposition,	230
	Your mere enforcement⁶ shall acquittance⁷ me	
	From all the impure blots⁸ and stains thereof;	
	For God doth know, and you may partly see,	
	How far I am from the desire of this.	
MAYOR	God bless your grace; we see it and will say it.	235
RICHARD	In saying so, you shall but say the truth.	
BUCKINGHAM	Then I salute you with this royal title:	
	Long live King Richard, England's worthy king.	
ALL	Amen.	
BUCKINGHAM	Tomorrow may it please you to be crowned?	240
RICHARD	Even when you please, for you will have it so.	
BUCKINGHAM	Tomorrow, then, we will attend your grace,	
	And so most joyfully we take our leave.	
RICHARD	[*To the Bishops*] Come, let us to our holy work again. –	
	Farewell, my cousins⁹, farewell, gentle friends.	245

Exeunt

King Richard III
理查三世

Looking back at Act 3 第3幕回顾
Activities for groups or individuals

1 Richard plays many parts

Richard takes a malicious delight in acting out a variety of parts as he plots and kills his way to the throne. Act 3 contains many examples of Richard's duplicity, from his ironic warning to Prince Edward to beware 'false friends' (Scene 1) to the full-scale production put on for the benefit of the Lord Mayor and citizens (Scene 7).

a Trace all Richard's 'performances' in the act and discuss how they compare with other examples from Acts 1 and 2 of Richard's techniques for dissembling and cynically using others.

b Analyse each performance and give a score out of ten for his acting abilities. Then write a report on his acting skills and his ability to influence the people around him.

2 The rat, the cat, the dog

Sir Richard Ratcliffe's power and influence has steadily increased through his unquestioning loyalty to Richard since his first appearance (Act 2 Scene 1). His two friends, Catesby and Lovell, have similarly flourished under Richard's patronage as they carry out his sinister commands. Catesby is entrusted to test Hastings's loyalty, and Lovell brings in Hastings's severed head. The three men featured in a contemporary verse:

> The Cat, the Rat and Lovell the dog
> Do rule all England under the Hog.

- Look back through the play and write down what other services the three have performed for Richard so far. Suggest how a director might emphasise their new-found status. As you read on, look out for what else they do.

3 Buckingham the spin-doctor (公关老手，政治顾问)

Buckingham uses a variety of methods to ensure that Richard gains the crown. The techniques he employs are similar to those used by present-day political spin-doctors, who manipulate unpleasant facts to make them appear attractive to the voting public (see the picture on p. 158).

- Look back at Buckingham's words and actions in Scenes 1, 4, 5 and 7, then step into role as Buckingham and write yourself a memo setting out your intention to make Richard King and the methods you will use to achieve this aim.

4 Depicting the two princes

The plight of the two young princes, sent off to the Tower by their scheming and murderous uncle, has been depicted in moving detail by artists since Shakespeare's play was first performed.

a Look at the representation of the princes in the Tower opposite. Is this how you imagine them to look?

b How else might the princes be represented? You might like to refer back to Act 3 Scene 1 and at the image on page 102.

c Describe in your own words the significance of the princes in developing the character of Richard III.

LOOKING BACK AT ACT 3

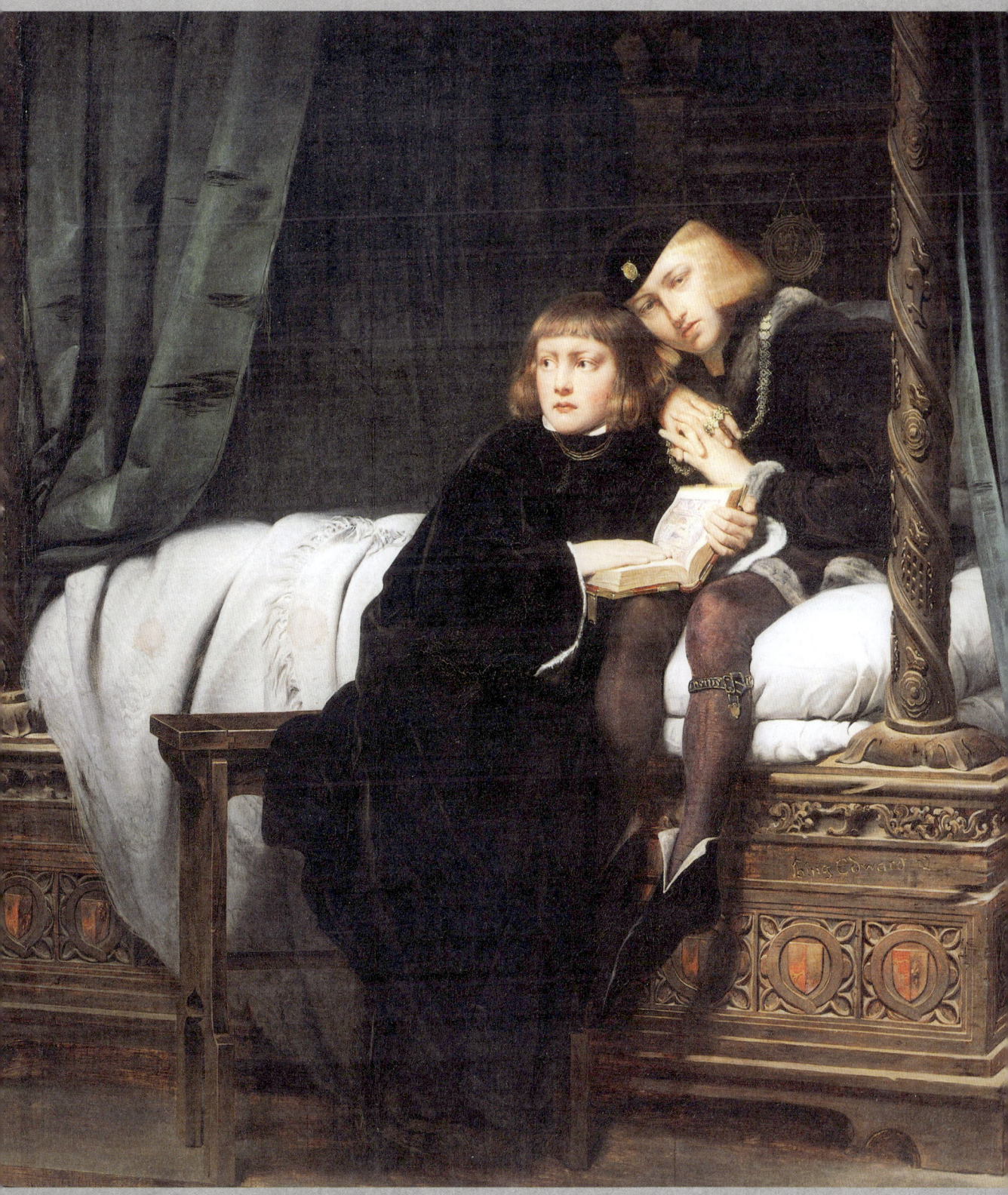

Queen Elizabeth, the Duchess of York, Dorset and Anne meet outside the Tower, where they have come to visit the princes. Brakenbury, on Richard's orders, refuses them entry.

剧情简介：伊丽莎白王后、约克公爵夫人、多塞和安娜在伦敦塔外相遇，他们是来看望两位王子的。布莱肯布瑞奉理查之命，不准他们进入。

1 Family tree: a reminder (whole class)

At the opening of Act 4, the three main female characters emphasise their close family ties, united in opposition to Richard.

- To remind yourself of their relationship to each other and to Richard, three volunteers take parts as the Duchess, Anne and Elizabeth and speak lines 1–11. Project the Plantagenet family tree (see p. 266) onto a whiteboard or screen. Everyone points to the appropriate name on the family tree as any words showing relationships are spoken.

1	niece	孙女
2	kind aunt	好婶婶
3	for my life	我以性命担保
4	sister	弟媳
5	Whither away?	您去哪儿？
6	devotion	热爱；忠诚
7	gratulate	欢迎
8	in good time	赶巧
9	suffer	允许
10	bounds	障碍
11	thy office	你的责任
12	on my peril	后果由我承担
13	leave it so	就让它这个样子

Themes 主题分析

The role of women (in fours)

Women start to play an increasingly significant role in the play. In depicting the main female characters as a group, united in adversity, Shakespeare was probably drawing on early Renaissance Resurrection (复活) plays. These popular dramas enacted stories from the Christian Bible, particularly focusing on the crucifixion (钉死在十字架上) and resurrection of Jesus. Here, Anne, Elizabeth and the Duchess of York take on a similar role to the three Biblical Marys (Mary Magdalene, Mary Salome and Mary, the mother of James). They shift attention away from the figure of Richard and focus instead on the victims of his crimes.

a The stage direction at the start suggests that Clarence's young daughter accompanies the delegation, but she is sometimes omitted in productions. What difference do you think this would make to the scene?

b Take parts as Brakenbury, Elizabeth, the Duchess and Anne, then read lines 12–28. How do you think the women react to Brakenbury's refusal to allow them to see the princes in the Tower? For example, do you think they are pleading and desperate, assertive and accustomed to giving orders, fearful, angry and dismissive, or something else?

c Is it important that all the women react in the same way, or do you think they can each behave differently? Make a decision and then explain your reasons. Write your thoughts in your Director's Journal.

Act 4 Scene 1
Outside the Tower of London

Enter QUEEN ELIZABETH, *the* DUCHESS OF YORK, *and* MARQUESS DORSET, *meeting* ANNE DUCHESS OF GLOUCESTER *and Clarence's daughter*

DUCHESS Who meets us here? My niece[1] Plantagenet
Led in the hand of her kind aunt[2] of Gloucester?
Now, for my life[3], she's wand'ring to the Tower,
On pure heart's love to greet the tender prince.
Daughter, well met.

ANNE God give your graces both 5
A happy and a joyful time of day.

ELIZABETH As much to you, good sister[4]. Whither away?[5]

ANNE No farther than the Tower, and, as I guess,
Upon the like devotion[6] as yourselves,
To gratulate[7] the gentle princes there. 10

ELIZABETH Kind sister, thanks. We'll enter all together.

Enter the Lieutenant [BRAKENBURY]

And in good time[8], here the Lieutenant comes.
Master Lieutenant, pray you, by your leave,
How doth the prince and my young son of York?

BRAKENBURY Right well, dear madam. By your patience, 15
I may not suffer[9] you to visit them.
The king hath strictly charged the contrary.

ELIZABETH The king? Who's that?

BRAKENBURY I mean the Lord Protector.

ELIZABETH The Lord protect him from that kingly title. 20
Hath he set bounds[10] between their love and me?
I am their mother. Who shall bar me from them?

DUCHESS I am their father's mother. I will see them.

ANNE Their aunt I am in law, in love their mother.
Then bring me to their sights; I'll bear thy blame 25
And take thy office[11] from thee, on my peril[12].

BRAKENBURY No, madam, no; I may not leave it so[13].
I am bound by oath, and therefore pardon me.

Exit Lieutenant

Stanley's news of Richard's intended coronation dismays the women. Elizabeth tells Dorset to flee to join Richmond. Stanley's son will help him. Anne says she would prefer to die than to be Queen.

剧情简介：斯坦雷带来理查意图加冕的消息，这让几个女人心灰意冷。伊丽莎白劝多塞投奔瑞奇蒙。斯坦雷的儿子会帮助他。安娜说自己宁愿去死也不愿做王后。

1 Events gather pace (in small groups)

The speed with which Richard's coronation takes place surprises all the characters. Realising that her son Dorset is in danger, Elizabeth shows political astuteness (机敏) in urging him to leave the country and join Richmond in France.

a Read the script opposite and write down all the words and phrases that help create the impression of speed and urgency.

b Take parts and read lines 29–63 in a way that emphasises this sense of urgency. Consider tone and pace when speaking, then experiment with appropriate movements.

2 Remembering Margaret's curse (in pairs)

In lines 46–7, Elizabeth recalls Margaret's curse.

- Turn back to Act 1 Scene 3, line 207, and compare Margaret's curse with Elizabeth's words here.

Language in the play 剧中语言
Images of outrage (in small groups)

Elizabeth, the Duchess and Anne express their emotions through a number of powerful images, including those linked with hell, death and monstrous animals.

a Choose three images from the script opposite that you find particularly striking and construct a series of tableaux. Show your tableaux to other groups and ask them to guess which images you are representing. If you have access to a digital camera, take some photographs of each of the tableaux and create a classroom display. Add to this as you progress through the rest of this act, collecting the most graphic images used to describe Richard.

b Discuss the effectiveness of this vivid language in the play. How does it affect an audience's view of Richard and of the three women?

---

1 **looker-on** 见证人，目睹人
2 **Westminster** 西敏寺（加冕礼在此举行）
3 **lace** (束腰) 绳（用来收紧紧身内衣或腰封）
4 **asunder** 成两截
5 **pent** 被囚禁的
6 **scope** 空间
7 **swoon** 晕倒
8 **Despiteful** 残酷
9 **dogs** 追踪，尾随
10 **outstrip** 跑得比……快
11 **thrall** 奴隶
12 **counted** 被承认的
13 **ta'en tardy** 后来被抓到
14 **cockatrice** 蛇怪（目光可杀人的毒蛇）
15 **inclusive verge** 紧箍圈
16 **sear** 烤焦
17 **Anointed** 涂抹
18 **deadly venom** 要命的蛇毒
19 **feed my humour** 让我心安

King Richard III Act 4 Scene 1

Enter STANLEY [EARL OF DERBY]

STANLEY	Let me but meet you ladies one hour hence,
	And I'll salute your grace of York as mother
	And reverend looker-on[1] of two fair queens.
	[*To Anne*] Come, madam, you must straight to Westminster[2],
	There to be crownèd Richard's royal queen.
ELIZABETH	Ah, cut my lace[3] asunder[4],
	That my pent[5] heart may have some scope[6] to beat,
	Or else I swoon[7] with this dead-killing news.
ANNE	Despiteful[8] tidings. Oh, unpleasing news.
DORSET	Be of good cheer, mother; how fares your grace?
ELIZABETH	O Dorset, speak not to me; get thee gone.
	Death and destruction dogs[9] thee at thy heels.
	Thy mother's name is ominous to children.
	If thou wilt outstrip[10] death, go, cross the seas
	And live with Richmond, from the reach of hell.
	Go hie thee, hie thee from this slaughterhouse,
	Lest thou increase the number of the dead
	And make me die the thrall[11] of Margaret's curse,
	Nor mother, wife, nor England's counted[12] queen.
STANLEY	Full of wise care is this your counsel, madam –
	[*To Dorset*] Take all the swift advantage of the hours.
	You shall have letters from me to my son
	In your behalf, to meet you on the way.
	Be not ta'en tardy[13] by unwise delay.
DUCHESS	O ill-dispersing wind of misery.
	O my accursèd womb, the bed of death.
	A cockatrice[14] hast thou hatched to the world,
	Whose unavoided eye is murderous.
STANLEY	Come, madam, come. I in all haste was sent.
ANNE	And I with all unwillingness will go.
	Oh, would to God that the inclusive verge[15]
	Of golden metal that must round my brow
	Were red-hot steel, to sear[16] me to the brains.
	Anointed[17] let me be with deadly venom[18]
	And die ere men can say 'God save the queen.'
ELIZABETH	Go, go, poor soul, I envy not thy glory.
	To feed my humour[19], wish thyself no harm.

Anne recalls Richard's wooing and her curse, which has become a curse upon herself. She predicts that Richard will kill her. The Duchess urges all to leave. Elizabeth pleads to the Tower to pity the princes.

剧情简介：安娜回忆理查对她的追求和她的诅咒，这个诅咒已经应验在自己身上。她预言理查会杀掉她。公爵夫人敦促大家离开。伊丽莎白乞求伦敦塔可怜两位王子。

1 Bad dreams

Line 85 suggests that Richard has nightmares that keep Anne awake. Shakespeare appears to have been fascinated by dreams and the way a guilty conscience could play on a person's subconscious mind.

- Imagine you are making a movie version of *King Richard III*. You have decided to create a scene in which Richard's nightmares are briefly visualised for the audience. Make a list of Richard's past crimes, then choose one or two that you think would work well in the shape of a nightmarish vision, and storyboard the scene. How will you highlight the disorienting (迷惑) effect that nightmares often have? Add notes to suggest suitable lighting, sound effects and music.

2 Taking leave (in fours)

Elizabeth, Anne, Dorset and the Duchess of York bid each other farewell in lines 88–94.

a As you read through the script aloud, identify which lines are addressed to which character. What actions might they use?

b Anne voices her fear that Richard will want to get rid of her, now that he has gained the throne (line 87). This is the last time that Anne will see Elizabeth and the Duchess. What advice would you give to the actor playing Anne so that the sombre finality (终结) of this farewell is communicated to the audience?

Stagecraft 导演技巧

Set the scene

Elizabeth's plea for the Tower to show pity towards the two princes contrasts the impersonal, menacing prison ('Rough cradle') with the vulnerable, innocent boys ('those tender babes'). She addresses the Tower as if it is alive: it is the only 'nurse' her children now have.

- How might a stage designer present a strong visual image of the Tower's menace to contrast with Elizabeth's pleas? Think about set design and lighting. Compile some notes and sketches in your Director's Journal.

1	accursed	受到诅咒
2	wed'st	结婚
3	Grossly	愚蠢
4	honey	甜蜜
5	hitherto	直到现在
6	still awaked	总是睁着双眼
7	complaining	怨言
8	glory	王后桂冠
9	teen	悲伤
10	Stay	等等
11	immured	囚禁
12	Rude	粗鲁
13	sullen	郁郁寡欢

King Richard III Act 4 Scene 1
理查三世

ANNE No? Why? When he that is my husband now
Came to me as I followed Henry's corpse,
When scarce the blood was well washed from his hands
Which issued from my other angel husband
And that dear saint which then I weeping followed, 70
Oh, when, I say, I looked on Richard's face,
This was my wish: 'Be thou', quoth I, 'accursed[1]
For making me, so young, so old a widow.
And when thou wed'st[2], let sorrow haunt thy bed;
And be thy wife, if any be so mad, 75
More miserable by the life of thee
Than thou hast made me by my dear lord's death.'
Lo, ere I can repeat this curse again,
Within so small a time, my woman's heart
Grossly[3] grew captive to his honey[4] words 80
And proved the subject of mine own soul's curse,
Which hitherto[5] hath held mine eyes from rest.
For never yet one hour in his bed
Did I enjoy the golden dew of sleep,
But with his timorous dreams was still awaked[6]. 85
Besides, he hates me for my father Warwick,
And will, no doubt, shortly be rid of me.
ELIZABETH Poor heart, adieu; I pity thy complaining[7].
ANNE No more than with my soul I mourn for yours.
DORSET Farewell, thou woeful welcomer of glory[8]. 90
ANNE Adieu, poor soul, that tak'st thy leave of it.
DUCHESS Go thou to Richmond, and good fortune guide thee –
Go thou to Richard, and good angels tend thee –
Go thou to sanctuary, and good thoughts possess thee;
I to my grave, where peace and rest lie with me. 95
Eighty-odd years of sorrow have I seen,
And each hour's joy wracked with a week of teen[9].
ELIZABETH Stay[10], yet look back with me unto the Tower.
Pity, you ancient stones, those tender babes
Whom envy hath immured[11] within your walls, 100
Rough cradle for such little pretty ones.
Rude[12], ragged nurse, old sullen[13] playfellow
For tender princes, use my babies well.
So foolish sorrows bids your stones farewell.

Exeunt

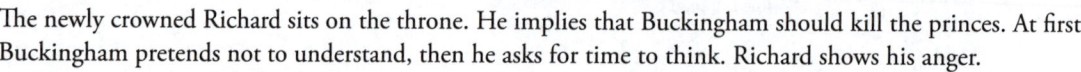

The newly crowned Richard sits on the throne. He implies that Buckingham should kill the princes. At first, Buckingham pretends not to understand, then he asks for time to think. Richard shows his anger.

剧情简介：新加冕的理查坐上了王位。他暗示白金汉应该杀掉两位王子。白金汉起初装作没听懂，随后说需要时间考虑。理查很生气。

Characters 人物分析

Richard the King (in groups of six or more)

a Richard, now the crowned King, makes a stately entrance and then seats himself on the throne. Stage these two moments, showing each as a tableau:

- Enter King Richard. Where and how is Richard standing? How might you suggest his state of anticipation? How are his courtiers positioned around him? Think carefully about body language and facial expressions. Who looks at whom?
- What is the manner of Richard's taking the throne? Is he triumphant? Gracious? Cynical and sneering? Or does he feel insecure? How will you show Buckingham's closeness to Richard?

b Share your tableaux with the rest of the class. Can they identify the participants? Be prepared to bring your character to life if asked to do so, to express his innermost thoughts at this moment.

Write about it 写作练习

Buckingham's doubts

Buckingham is reluctant to carry out Richard's orders to murder the young princes, and does not give the answer that the new King is hoping for. Imagine Buckingham's political diaries have just been published. Write the entry for this day. Consider the following questions as you write:

- What has the day of coronation been like?
- What does it feel like to have succeeded in finally getting Richard crowned? Has it all been worthwhile?
- What is your immediate reaction when you learn that Richard wants to have the princes killed?

1 *fanfare* 喇叭声
2 *in pomp* 穿着庄严华丽
3 *apart* 在旁边
4 *Sound* 另一阵喇叭声
5 *rejoice* 高兴
6 *Still* = Always
7 *touch* 试金石（用来检验黄金的纯度）
8 *current* 成色十足；真正
9 *thrice-renownèd* 尽人皆知
10 *consequence* 答复
11 *thou … dull* 你一向不这么愚笨
12 *suddenly* 立即
13 *may do your pleasure* 可以随心所欲
14 *resolve* 回答
15 *herein* 关于此事

Act 4 Scene 2
London: the throne-room of the palace

A fanfare[1] sounds. RICHARD, *newly crowned as king enters in pomp[2] with* BUCKINGHAM, CATESBY, RATCLIFFE, LOVELL, *a* PAGE, *and others*

RICHARD   Stand all apart[3]. Cousin of Buckingham.
BUCKINGHAM   My gracious sovereign.
RICHARD   Give me thy hand.
Sound[4]
Thus high, by thy advice and thy assistance,
Is King Richard seated.   5
But shall we wear these glories for a day?
Or shall they last, and we rejoice[5] in them?
BUCKINGHAM   Still[6] live they, and forever let them last.
RICHARD   Ah, Buckingham, now do I play the touch[7]
To try if thou be current[8] gold indeed.   10
Young Edward lives; think now what I would speak.
BUCKINGHAM   Say on, my loving lord.
RICHARD   Why, Buckingham, I say I would be king.
BUCKINGHAM   Why, so you are, my thrice-renownèd[9] lord.
RICHARD   Ha, am I king? 'Tis so. But Edward lives.   15
BUCKINGHAM   True, noble prince.
RICHARD   O bitter consequence[10],
That Edward still should live, true noble prince.
Cousin, thou wast not wont to be so dull[11].
Shall I be plain? I wish the bastards dead,
And I would have it suddenly[12] performed.   20
What say'st thou now? Speak suddenly, be brief.
BUCKINGHAM   Your grace may do your pleasure[13].
RICHARD   Tut, tut, thou art all ice; thy kindness freezes.
Say, have I thy consent that they shall die?
BUCKINGHAM   Give me some little breath, some pause, dear lord,   25
Before I positively speak in this.
I will resolve[14] you herein[15] presently.   *Exit Buckingham*
CATESBY   The king is angry; see, he gnaws his lip.

Richard orders Tyrrel to be brought to him. He will no longer confide in Buckingham. Stanley brings news of Dorset's escape. Richard plots against Anne and Clarence's daughter and resolves to marry Princess Elizabeth.

 剧情简介：理查命人将提若尔带来见他。他不再信任白金汉。斯坦雷带来多塞逃跑的消息。理查暗算安娜和克莱润的女儿，决心要娶伊丽莎白公主。

1 Where is Anne?

The stage direction at the start of Scene 2 leaves Anne out of the coronation. However, some directors choose to include her in this scene. In one production, Richard callously (冷酷无情) talks about her illness and imminent death right in front of her (see lines 51–8).

- If you were staging this scene, would you include Anne or not? Give reasons for your choice.
- If you would include her, what advice would you give to the actor playing Anne? Remember, she has no lines in this scene.

▼ What does this image suggest about Richard and his relationship with Anne?

1	iron-witted	浑浑噩噩
2	unrespective	有眼无珠
3	considerate	瞻前顾后
4	circumspect	谨小慎微
5	close exploit	秘密勾当
6	haughty	高傲，傲慢
7	partly	略微
8	deep-revolving	老谋深算
9	witty	聪明
10	counsels	秘密
11	abides	居住
12	Rumour it abroad	把谣言散出去
13	take order	下令
14	keeping close	禁闭
15	mean	卑贱
16	The boy	(指克莱润的儿子)
17	give out	放出消息
18	it stands me much upon	这对我有很大优势
19	Uncertain way of gain	此事颇有风险
20	pluck on	鼓动

2 Richard and Buckingham (in pairs)

At the beginning of this scene, Richard takes Buckingham's hand as he seats himself on the throne. Within the space of twenty lines, Richard is gnawing his lip with anger (according to Catesby) when Buckingham hesitates to carry out an order.

a Read lines 43–6, in which Richard reflects upon Buckingham. He ends with the ambiguous line 'Well, be it so'. How does Richard say this? Experiment with a number of different interpretations – for example, lightly dismissive, ominously, obviously intending to harm Buckingham, resigned or with a sigh. What gesture might accompany the words?

b Is anyone else on stage at this point in the play? What difference (if any) might that make?

RICHARD	I will converse with iron-witted[1] fools	
	And unrespective[2] boys. None are for me	30
	That look into me with considerate[3] eyes.	
	High-reaching Buckingham grows circumspect[4]. –	
	Boy!	
PAGE	My lord.	
RICHARD	Know'st thou not any whom corrupting gold	35
	Will tempt unto a close exploit[5] of death?	
PAGE	I know a discontented gentleman	
	Whose humble means match not his haughty[6] spirit.	
	Gold were as good as twenty orators	
	And will, no doubt, tempt him to anything.	40
RICHARD	What is his name?	
PAGE	His name, my lord, is Tyrrel.	
RICHARD	I partly[7] know the man. Go call him hither, boy.	

Exit [Page]

The deep-revolving[8], witty[9] Buckingham
No more shall be the neighbour to my counsels[10].
Hath he so long held out with me, untired, 45
And stops he now for breath? Well, be it so.

Enter STANLEY [EARL OF DERBY]

	How now, Lord Stanley, what's the news?	
STANLEY	Know, my loving lord, the Marquess Dorset,	
	As I hear, is fled to Richmond	
	In the parts where he abides[11].	50
RICHARD	Come hither, Catesby. Rumour it abroad[12]	
	That Anne my wife is very grievous sick.	
	I will take order[13] for her keeping close[14].	
	Inquire me out some mean[15] poor gentleman,	
	Whom I will marry straight to Clarence' daughter.	55
	The boy[16] is foolish, and I fear not him.	
	Look how thou dream'st! I say again, give out[17]	
	That Anne my queen is sick and like to die.	
	About it, for it stands me much upon[18]	
	To stop all hopes whose growth may damage me.	60
	I must be married to my brother's daughter,	
	Or else my kingdom stands on brittle glass.	
	Murder her brothers, and then marry her:	
	Uncertain way of gain[19]. But I am in	
	So far in blood that sin will pluck on[20] sin.	65
	Tear-falling pity dwells not in this eye.	

Richard orders Tyrrel to kill the princes and warns Stanley not to support Richmond. Richard ignores Buckingham's request for the promised earldom of Hereford and recalls Henry VI's prophecy that Richmond will become King.

剧情简介： 理查命提若尔杀死两位王子，还警告斯坦雷不许支持瑞奇蒙。理查不理睬白金汉的请求，拒绝兑现赫里福伯爵爵位，他还回忆起亨利六世预言瑞奇蒙将称王的事。

Characters 人物分析

Tyrrel: cast the part

What kind of man is Tyrrel and how should he be played?

a Re-read lines 35–40, which describe the kind of man Richard is looking for, and the Page's reply. Then summarise the characteristics that Tyrrel displays.

b Read the dialogue between Richard and Tyrrel in lines 67–83. How does Tyrrel react to Richard's proposal? Does he hesitate at all?

c If you were casting (挑选演员) a new production of the play, who would you choose to play the part of Tyrrel? Consider television and film actors you are familiar with, then go online and download a couple of photos of actors you would recommend. Give reasons for your choices.

d Write some notes to the actor playing Tyrrel.

1 Prove 考验
2 Please you = If it please you
3 deal upon 对付
4 open means 顺利无阻
5 Go by 带着……去
6 token 信物
7 prefer 赏赐
8 late 上次
9 sound me in 询问我
10 due 应得之物
11 pawned 抵押；保证
12 look to 留心
13 you shall answer it 拿您是问
14 peevish 不明事理
15 vein 心情

▼ The once-influential Buckingham is now ignored by Richard. How would you show his desperation on stage?

King Richard III Act 4 Scene 2
理查三世

Enter TYRREL

	Is thy name Tyrrel?	
TYRREL	James Tyrrel, and your most obedient subject.	
RICHARD	Art thou indeed?	
TYRREL	Prove[1] me, my gracious lord.	
RICHARD	Dar'st thou resolve to kill a friend of mine?	70
TYRREL	Please you[2].	
	But I had rather kill two enemies.	
RICHARD	Why then thou hast it: two deep enemies,	
	Foes to my rest and my sweet sleep's disturbers	
	Are they that I would have thee deal upon[3].	75
	Tyrrel, I mean those bastards in the Tower.	
TYRREL	Let me have open means[4] to come to them,	
	And soon I'll rid you from the fear of them.	
RICHARD	Thou sing'st sweet music. Hark, come hither, Tyrrel.	
	Go by[5] this token[6]. Rise, and lend thine ear. *Whispers*	80
	There is no more but so; say it is done,	
	And I will love thee and prefer[7] thee for it.	
TYRREL	I will dispatch it straight. *Exit*	

Enter BUCKINGHAM

BUCKINGHAM	My lord, I have considered in my mind	
	The late[8] request that you did sound me in[9].	85
RICHARD	Well, let that rest. Dorset is fled to Richmond.	
BUCKINGHAM	I hear the news, my lord.	
RICHARD	Stanley, he is your wife's son. Well, look unto it.	
BUCKINGHAM	My lord, I claim the gift, my due[10] by promise,	
	For which your honour and your faith is pawned[11]:	90
	Th'earldom of Hereford and the movables	
	Which you have promisèd I shall possess.	
RICHARD	Stanley, look to[12] your wife. If she convey	
	Letters to Richmond, you shall answer it[13].	
BUCKINGHAM	What says your highness to my just request?	95
RICHARD	I do remember me, Henry the Sixth	
	Did prophesy that Richmond should be king,	
	When Richmond was a little peevish[14] boy.	
	A king, perhaps.	
BUCKINGHAM	May it please you to resolve me in my suit?	100
RICHARD	Thou troublest me; I am not in the vein[15]. *Exit*	

Buckingham resolves to flee to safety in Wales. Tyrrel describes the remorse of the murderers who smothered the princes.

剧情简介：白金汉决心逃往威尔士以求保命。提若尔描述杀手捂死两位王子后的懊悔。

1 The death of the princes (in fours)

The murder of the princes in the Tower is a famous piece of English history, although historians do not know for sure whether Richard III was responsible for their deaths. Over the centuries, many artists and writers have recreated this event, but Shakespeare chooses not to show the boys' murder on stage.

- Read Tyrrel's description of the princes' murder (lines 1–22) and then mime the scene, making your actions and emotions clear through body language, facial expressions and gesture. You might like to look at the picture on this page and the one on page 147, which show how two different artists have interpreted the scene. How do they differ? What emotional impact is each artist striving for?
- Perform your mime for the rest of the class as someone reads the script aloud. What differences in interpretation emerge in the different mimes?

▼ The murder of the princes in the Tower.

1 deep 重要
2 Brecknock 布雷肯（如今写作Brecon，是白金汉在威尔士的封地）
3 most arch 最高等级
4 suborn 收买；唆使
5 ruthful 可怜
6 fleshed 铁石心肠
7 in their deaths' sad story 在讲述他们如何惨死
8 girdling 拥抱
9 alabaster 雪花石膏般（冰凉光洁）
10 stalk 茎
11 replenishèd 完美
12 prime creation 造物之初
13 she （即大自然）

BUCKINGHAM And is it thus? Repays he my deep[1] service
With such contempt? Made I him king for this?
Oh, let me think on Hastings and be gone
To Brecknock[2], while my fearful head is on.   105

Exeunt

Act 4 Scene 3
London: a room in King Richard's palace

Enter TYRREL

TYRREL   The tyrannous and bloody act is done,
The most arch[3] deed of piteous massacre
That ever yet this land was guilty of.
Dighton and Forrest, who I did suborn[4]
To do this piece of ruthful[5] butchery,   5
Albeit they were fleshed[6] villains, bloody dogs,
Melted with tenderness and mild compassion,
Wept like to children in their deaths' sad story[7].
'Oh, thus', quoth Dighton, 'lay the gentle babes.'
'Thus, thus', quoth Forrest, 'girdling[8] one another   10
Within their alabaster[9] innocent arms.
Their lips were four red roses on a stalk[10],
And in their summer beauty kissed each other.
A book of prayers on their pillow lay,
Which once', quoth Forrest, 'almost changed my mind.   15
But oh, the devil', there the villain stopped.
When Dighton thus told on: 'we smotherèd
The most replenishèd[11] sweet work of nature
That from the prime creation[12] e'er she[13] framed'.
Hence both are gone; with conscience and remorse   20
They could not speak, and so I left them both
To bear this tidings to the bloody king.

Enter RICHARD

And here he comes. All health, my sovereign lord.

Tyrrel assures Richard that the princes are dead. Richard plans marriage to Elizabeth. Ratcliffe's news is that Ely has joined Richmond and Buckingham has raised an army in Wales. Richard resolves to fight.

剧情简介：提若尔向理查保证两位王子已死。理查计划迎娶伊丽莎白。拉克利夫带来消息称伊利投靠了瑞奇蒙，白金汉也在威尔士举兵。理查决心一战。

1 Does Tyrrel show his feelings? (in pairs)

Tyrrel's soliloquy in lines 1–22 reveals his real feelings about the murder, but his words to Richard mask his emotion.

a Talk about how Tyrrel might react to Richard's entrance and decide if he would hint at his real feelings in the way he speaks the lines or in his body language. Then take parts as Richard and Tyrrel and act out lines 24–35.

b Look back at the 'Characters' box on page 158. What additional notes would you make about Tyrrel's character now? Extend your initial advice for the actor playing Tyrrel to encompass his lines in Scene 3.

2 Richard's achievements

Richard lists the successes he has rapidly achieved (lines 36–43). Remind yourself of the plans Richard made straight after his coronation (Scene 2, lines 51–63) and then copy and complete the table below, using quotations from Richard's two speeches where possible.

Richard's plan (Scene 2)	Lines	Outcome (Scene 3)
'Rumour it abroad … Anne my queen is sick and like to die'	51–8	
		'The sons of Edward sleep in Abraham's bosom'

Characters 人物分析

Richard: from 'woo-er' to soldier (in pairs)

Richard is about to play the role of 'jolly thriving wooer' (line 43), intending to claim the hand of Elizabeth's daughter and thus strengthen his power-base. However, within the space of fourteen lines he has abandoned that plan in reaction to Ratcliffe's news, and is taking up arms against his enemies.

- Choose two or three words or phrases that demonstrate the change in Richard's attitude and tone at this point in the play.

1 Kind 志同道合
2 gave in charge 交代；吩咐
3 process 情形
4 be inheritor of thy desire 让你梦想成真
5 meanly 下（嫁）
6 sleep in Abraham's bosom 在亚伯拉罕怀里睡着（即死去）
7 Breton 布列塔尼人（这一族裔的家乡过去也叫Breton，曾经是个独立的国家，1532年并入法国。现在叫Brittany，位于法国西北部。瑞奇蒙已经逃往布列塔尼）
8 by that knot 靠着那桩婚姻
9 Morton 莫顿（英国剑桥郡的伊利市）主教
10 Is in the field 已经开始兴兵作乱
11 power 军队
12 rash-levied strength 乌合之众
13 fearful commenting 惴惴不安的谈论
14 leaden servitor 呆笨的仆人
15 leads 导致
16 beggary 毁灭
17 fiery expedition 敏捷的行动
18 Jove's Mercury 乔武的墨丘利（神的信使；Jove即罗马神话中的主神Jupiter，他的信使Mercury行动迅捷，来去匆匆）
19 muster men 招募人马
20 My counsel is my shield 我的想法就是我的盾牌
21 brave the field 在战场叫嚣

RICHARD	Kind¹ Tyrrel, am I happy in thy news?	
TYRREL	If to have done the thing you gave in charge²	25
	Beget your happiness, be happy then,	
	For it is done.	
RICHARD	But did'st thou see them dead?	
TYRREL	I did, my lord.	
RICHARD	And buried, gentle Tyrrel?	
TYRREL	The chaplain of the Tower hath buried them,	
	But where, to say the truth, I do not know.	30
RICHARD	Come to me, Tyrrel, soon and after supper,	
	When thou shalt tell the process³ of their death.	
	Meantime, but think how I may do thee good,	
	And be inheritor of thy desire⁴.	
	Farewell till then.	
TYRREL	I humbly take my leave. [*Exit*]	35
RICHARD	The son of Clarence have I pent up close,	
	His daughter meanly⁵ have I matched in marriage,	
	The sons of Edward sleep in Abraham's bosom⁶,	
	And Anne my wife hath bid this world good night.	
	Now, for I know the Breton⁷ Richmond aims	40
	At young Elizabeth, my brother's daughter,	
	And by that knot⁸ looks proudly on the crown,	
	To her go I, a jolly thriving wooer.	

Enter RATCLIFFE

RATCLIFFE	My lord.	
RICHARD	Good or bad news, that thou com'st in so bluntly?	45
RATCLIFFE	Bad news, my lord. Morton⁹ is fled to Richmond,	
	And Buckingham, backed with the hardy Welshmen,	
	Is in the field¹⁰, and still his power¹¹ increaseth.	
RICHARD	Ely with Richmond troubles me more near	
	Than Buckingham and his rash-levied strength¹².	50
	Come. I have learned that fearful commenting¹³	
	Is leaden servitor¹⁴ to dull delay.	
	Delay leads¹⁵ impotent and snail-paced beggary¹⁶.	
	Then fiery expedition¹⁷ be my wing,	
	Jove's Mercury¹⁸, and herald for a king!	55
	Go muster men¹⁹. My counsel is my shield²⁰.	
	We must be brief when traitors brave the field²¹.	

Exeunt

Margaret recounts how she has secretly watched the destruction of her enemies. She hopes for further calamities. Queen Elizabeth and the Duchess mourn their dead relatives. Margaret sees the deaths as justice for her own losses.

剧情简介：玛格蕊描述她怎样在暗中注视自己的敌人毁灭。她希望有更多的灾难。伊丽莎白王后和公爵夫人为她们各自死去的亲属悲痛。玛格蕊把对方亲人的死看作是对自己的补偿。

1 United in grief (in threes)

a Lines 1–135 involve only Queen Margaret, the Duchess and Elizabeth. To gain a first impression of the whole episode, take parts and read it through without pausing. The following may help you.

- **Queen Margaret** Hiding within the walls of the court ('confines'), Margaret has watched the loss of power ('the waning') of the Yorkists and Woodvilles. Margaret's asides show how she views each death as justice or repayment for her own losses ('right for right', 'doth quit', 'pays a dying debt').
- **Elizabeth** Grieving for her two sons murdered in the Tower, Elizabeth speaks of them as flowers in bud ('unblowed', 'new-appearing') and hopes they have escaped limbo (地狱边缘) ('doom perpetual') to become angels.
- **The Duchess of York** She mourns for her son, King Edward. She feels she has lived long enough.

b Talk together how the tone changes between this and the last scene. How does Shakespeare create this change of tone?

c Look carefully at the language used by the women. Pick out any images referring to nature or infancy and motherhood. What do these images contribute to the scene? How do they convey the mood?

2 Oxymorons (矛盾修辞法)

The Duchess of York describes herself as 'Dead life', 'blind sight' and a 'poor mortal living ghost' (lines 26–8). Opposite ideas linked together in this way are called **oxymorons**.

a Choose one of the three oxymorons listed above and create a human statue that you feel illustrates the image suggested by the Duchess's words. Show your statue to the rest of the class and see if they can guess which oxymoron you are portraying.

b Write a paragraph explaining the significance of these oxymorons.

---

1 prosperity 成功
2 confines 疆界
3 induction 序幕
4 will 要去
5 consequence 结局
6 Withdraw thee 快躲起来
7 unblowed 尚未开放
8 sweets 芬芳的花朵
9 doom perpetual 永远的劫难
10 lamentation 悲痛
11 right for right 正义回报正义
12 your infant morn 您新生的黎明
13 agèd night 漫漫长夜
14 crazed 撕裂
15 gentle lambs 温顺的羊羔（指死去的两个王子）
16 entrails 肚子
17 holy Harry （指亨利六世）
18 mortal living 行尸走肉
19 grave's due by life usurped 我本应被埋葬在坟墓中，可却偏活在人间
20 abstract 缩影；概要
21 Rest 消停

Act 4 Scene 4
London: outside King Richard's palace

Enter old QUEEN MARGARET

MARGARET So now prosperity[1] begins to mellow
And drop into the rotten mouth of death.
Here in these confines[2] slyly have I lurked
To watch the waning of mine enemies.
A dire induction[3] am I witness to, 5
And will[4] to France, hoping the consequence[5]
Will prove as bitter, black, and tragical.
Withdraw thee[6], wretched Margaret. Who comes here?

Enter DUCHESS [OF YORK] *and* QUEEN [ELIZABETH]

ELIZABETH Ah, my poor princes! Ah, my tender babes!
My unblowed[7] flowers, new-appearing sweets[8]! 10
If yet your gentle souls fly in the air
And be not fixed in doom perpetual[9],
Hover about me with your airy wings
And hear your mother's lamentation[10].

MARGARET [*Aside*] Hover about her; say that right for right[11] 15
Hath dimmed your infant morn[12] to agèd night[13].

DUCHESS So many miseries have crazed[14] my voice
That my woe-wearied tongue is still and mute.
Edward Plantagenet, why art thou dead?

MARGARET [*Aside*] Plantagenet doth quit Plantagenet; 20
Edward for Edward pays a dying debt.

ELIZABETH Wilt thou, O God, fly from such gentle lambs[15]
And throw them in the entrails[16] of the wolf?
When didst thou sleep when such a deed was done?

MARGARET [*Aside*] When holy Harry[17] died, and my sweet son. 25

DUCHESS Dead life, blind sight, poor mortal living[18] ghost;
Woe's scene, world's shame, grave's due by life usurped[19];
Brief abstract[20] and recòrd of tedious days,
Rest[21] thy unrest on England's lawful earth,
Unlawfully made drunk with innocent blood. 30

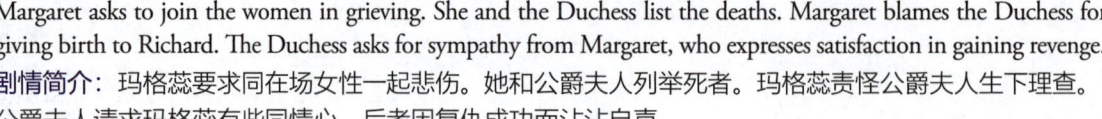

Margaret asks to join the women in grieving. She and the Duchess list the deaths. Margaret blames the Duchess for giving birth to Richard. The Duchess asks for sympathy from Margaret, who expresses satisfaction in gaining revenge.

 剧情简介：玛格蕊要求同在场女性一起悲伤。她和公爵夫人列举死者。玛格蕊责怪公爵夫人生下理查。公爵夫人请求玛格蕊有些同情心，后者因复仇成功而沾沾自喜。

1 Listing the victims

Margaret and the Duchess of York list the dead (lines 35–70). To help you sort out who is who, copy and complete the following table. The family tree on page 266 may also help you. Colour code the killers and victims according to whether they are the house of York or the house of Lancaster.

Line	Victim	Killed by	Other Information?
39	Margaret's son, Prince Edward	Edward IV, Richard and Clarence	Killed after the Battle of Tewkesbury
40	Margaret's husband, Henry VI		Murdered in the Tower
41		Dighton and Forrest (ordered by Richard)	
42		Dighton and Forrest	
43			
44			
45			
63			
64			
65			
69	Hastings, Rivers, Vaughan and Grey	Ratcliffe and Lovell	Executed on Richard's orders

Language in the play 剧中语言

A disturbing image

Margaret accuses the Duchess of York of giving birth to a dog-like creature (Richard).

- Look at exactly what she says (lines 47–58) and consider the various animal-related metaphors she uses to convey a deeply disturbing image of Richard. Create a collage of words and pictures that you think captures the image that Margaret draws in words.

---

1 thou （指英格兰的土地）
2 reverend 值得尊重
3 benefit of seniory 年长的好处
4 let … hand 让我的痛苦锁紧占上风者的双眉吧
5 society 伙伴
6 holp'st = helped
7 kennel 狗窝
8 worry 咬住……的喉咙
9 lap 吮吸
10 God's handiwork 上帝的手工品（指人类）
11 gallèd 红肿
12 carnal cur 杀人的恶狗
13 pew-fellow 教友
14 cloy me 让我腻烦
15 quit 报复
16 boot 添头（指白白搭进去的）
17 both they （两个爱德华）
18 beholders of this frantic play 这出惨剧的旁观者
19 Th'adulterate 那个与人通奸的

ELIZABETH	Ah, that thou¹ wouldst as soon afford a grave	
	As thou canst yield a melancholy seat.	
	Then would I hide my bones, not rest them here.	
	Ah, who hath any cause to mourn but we?	
MARGARET	If ancient sorrow be most reverend²,	35
	Give mine the benefit of seniory³,	
	And let my griefs frown on the upper hand⁴,	
	If sorrow can admit society⁵.	
	I had an Edward, till a Richard killed him;	
	I had a husband, till a Richard killed him.	40
	Thou hadst an Edward, till a Richard killed him;	
	Thou hadst a Richard, till a Richard killed him.	
DUCHESS	I had a Richard too, and thou didst kill him;	
	I had a Rutland too, thou holp'st⁶ to kill him.	
MARGARET	Thou hadst a Clarence, too,	45
	And Richard killed him.	
	From forth the kennel⁷ of thy womb hath crept	
	A hell-hound that doth hunt us all to death:	
	That dog, that had his teeth before his eyes	
	To worry⁸ lambs and lap⁹ their gentle blood,	50
	That foul defacer of God's handiwork¹⁰	
	That reigns in gallèd¹¹ eyes of weeping souls,	
	That excellent grand tyrant of the earth	
	Thy womb let loose to chase us to our graves.	
	O upright, just, and true-disposing God,	55
	How do I thank thee, that this carnal cur¹²	
	Preys on the issue of his mother's body	
	And makes her pew-fellow¹³ with others' moan.	
DUCHESS	O Harry's wife, triumph not in my woes.	
	God witness with me, I have wept for thine.	60
MARGARET	Bear with me. I am hungry for revenge,	
	And now I cloy me¹⁴ with beholding it.	
	Thy Edward he is dead that killed my Edward;	
	The other Edward dead to quit¹⁵ my Edward;	
	Young York he is but boot¹⁶, because both they¹⁷	65
	Matched not the high perfection of my loss.	
	Thy Clarence he is dead that stabbed my Edward,	
	And the beholders of this frantic play¹⁸,	
	Th'adulterate¹⁹ Hastings, Rivers, Vaughan, Grey,	
	Untimely smothered in their dusky graves.	70

Margaret calls Richard an agent of hell. Elizabeth remembers Margaret's prophecy that she would ask her help to curse Richard. Margaret recalls her descriptions of Elizabeth and contrasts Elizabeth's past situation with her present situation.

剧情简介：玛格蕊把理查叫作地狱代理人。伊丽莎白想起玛格蕊的预言是她将要她帮忙诅咒理查。玛格蕊回想她对伊丽莎白的描述，并把伊丽莎白过去的境况和她现在做对比。

Write about it 写作练习

Hell's agent

Margaret says that Richard is a spy operating on behalf of the Devil. Write a modern-day story of about 500 words involving a spy from hell. When planning your story, consider the following:

- What is their mission?
- What do they do and with what consequences?
- How is it resolved?

Decide whether you are going to write it from the perspective of the evil agent or that of another character. Use some characteristics of Richard in your own spy.

Language in the play 剧中语言

'Bottled spider', 'bunch-backed toad' (in pairs)

In Act 1 Scene 3, Margaret called Richard a 'bottled spider' and a 'bunch-backed toad' (lines 242 and 246). Now Elizabeth repeats the insults.

a Discuss what properties of spiders and toads are appropriate when describing Richard.

b Sketch some ideas to show ways in which spiders and/or toads might be used as a central visual motif (图案) in stage design or costumes. (For example, if you look at the picture of Richard on p. 255, you will see that he has the appearance of a spider in the way he is dressed and positioned.)

1 Where are they now? (in small groups)

In lines 92–6, Margaret asks a series of rhetorical questions designed to emphasise the extent of Elizabeth's personal losses. This is a poetic convention from classical and medieval poetry known as *ubi sunt* (Latin for 'where are they?'). Margaret then proceeds to answer her own questions, listing in order all the miseries that Elizabeth has endured (lines 97–110).

a Take it in turn to read each of Margaret's questions, then match each question with an answer.

b Divide the questions and answers between you, then devise a dramatic presentation of these lines. Use movement and your voices to emphasise the tone of grief and sense of loss contained in the words.

1 intelligencer 间谍
2 reserved 让……活着
3 factor 代理人
4 at hand 很快
5 piteous and unpitied 可怜却不值得同情
6 bond 契约
7 vain flourish 空洞的花架子
8 painted queen 画里的王后
9 presentation 复制品
10 direful pageant 蹩脚的表演
11 sign 招牌，幌子
12 fill the scene 充台面
13 sues 求情
14 bending 卑躬屈膝
15 Decline 从头到尾过一遍
16 caitiff 可怜虫
17 one （指理查）
18 whirled about 打转转
19 Having … wast 除了回忆过去，什么也没剩下

Richard yet lives, hell's black intelligencer[1],
Only reserved[2] their factor[3] to buy souls
And send them thither. But at hand[4], at hand
Ensues his piteous and unpitied[5] end.
Earth gapes, hell burns, fiends roar, saints pray, 75
To have him suddenly conveyed from hence.
Cancel his bond[6] of life, dear God, I pray,
That I may live and say the dog is dead.

ELIZABETH　Oh, thou didst prophesy the time would come
That I should wish for thee to help me curse 80
That bottled spider, that foul bunch-backed toad.

MARGARET　I called thee then vain flourish[7] of my fortune;
I called thee then poor shadow, painted queen[8],
The presentation[9] of but what I was,
The flattering index of a direful pageant[10], 85
One heaved a-high to be hurled down below,
A mother only mocked with two fair babes,
A dream of what thou wast, a garish flag
To be the aim of every dangerous shot,
A sign[11] of dignity, a breath, a bubble, 90
A queen in jest, only to fill the scene[12].
Where is thy husband now? Where be thy brothers?
Where be thy two sons? Wherein dost thou joy?
Who sues[13] and kneels and says 'God save the queen'?
Where be the bending[14] peers that flattered thee? 95
Where be the thronging troops that followed thee?
Decline[15] all this, and see what now thou art:
For happy wife, a most distressèd widow;
For joyful mother, one that wails the name;
For one being sued to, one that humbly sues; 100
For queen, a very caitiff[16] crowned with care;
For she that scorned at me, now scorned of me;
For she being feared of all, now fearing one[17];
For she commanding all, obeyed of none.
Thus hath the course of justice whirled about[18] 105
And left thee but a very prey to time,
Having no more but thought of what thou wast[19],
To torture thee the more, being what thou art.
Thou didst usurp my place, and dost thou not
Usurp the just proportion of my sorrow? 110

Elizabeth asks Margaret to teach her how to curse. Margaret offers harsh advice. The Duchess tells Elizabeth to complain bitterly and often to Richard. Richard enters and the women verbally attack him.

剧情简介：伊丽莎白要玛格蕊教她如何诅咒。玛格蕊给出恶毒的建议。公爵夫人让伊丽莎白常去向理查倒苦水。理查上场，女人们七嘴八舌攻击他。

Write about it 写作练习

How to curse successfully

a In Margaret's final appearance in the play, she gives Elizabeth a lesson in how to curse someone successfully (lines 118–25). Read Margaret's advice. List each item of advice in modern English.

b Imagine you are an 'agony aunt' working for a teenage magazine. You receive the following letter:

> Dear Marge,
> About six months ago, I fell out badly with my best friend and she is now being really nasty to me. I am in danger of dropping out of school if things carry on. She is evil; I think she might be an agent from hell (no, really!). I want to put a curse on her that will get her out of my life for ever. Can you help?
> Liz

- Write Marge's reply.

Themes 主题分析

Words as weapons (in threes)

Elizabeth and the Duchess of York realise, like Margaret, that words are the only weapons they have against Richard (lines 126–35).

a Read lines 136–146 and pick out all the insults (e.g. 'wretch') and accusations (e.g. 'all the slaughters … thou hast done').

b Two of you hurl insults and accusations, one at a time, at the third person, who repeats the words as if in shocked disbelief, contemptuous anger or in any other style you feel is appropriate. Experiment with pace and tone.

Stagecraft 导演技巧

Marching to battle

The stage direction at line 135 tells us that Richard enters with his 'train' (accompanied by soldiers, drummers, flag bearers and so on) marching to war ('expedition', line 136).

- Make notes suggesting how you might stage this entrance, firstly for a film version of the play and then for a stage production. How do your two versions differ? Why do you think this is?

1 mischance 不幸
2 Forbear 放弃
3 fast 禁食
4 Bett'ring 夸大
5 causer 凶手
6 Revolving 再三玩味
7 quicken 削尖
8 Windy attorneys 喋喋不休的律师
9 Airy succeeders of intestine joys 大肠快乐后接着排出的气体
10 scope 空间
11 Be copius in exclaims 滔滔不绝地呼号吧
12 intercepts 阻拦
13 expedition 征讨
14 owed = owned
15 Ned （爱德华的爱称）

	Now thy proud neck bears half my burdened yoke,	
	From which even here I slip my wearied head	
	And leave the burden of it all on thee.	
	Farewell, York's wife, and queen of sad mischance[1].	
	These English woes shall make me smile in France.	115
ELIZABETH	O thou well skilled in curses, stay awhile,	
	And teach me how to curse mine enemies.	
MARGARET	Forbear[2] to sleep the night, and fast[3] the day;	
	Compare dead happiness with living woe;	
	Think that thy babes were sweeter than they were	120
	And he that slew them fouler than he is.	
	Bett'ring[4] thy loss makes the bad causer[5] worse;	
	Revolving[6] this will teach thee how to curse.	
ELIZABETH	My words are dull. Oh, quicken[7] them with thine.	
MARGARET	Thy woes will make them sharp, and pierce like mine.	125

Exit Margaret

DUCHESS	Why should calamity be full of words?	
ELIZABETH	Windy attorneys[8] to their clients' woes,	
	Airy succeeders of intestine joys[9],	
	Poor breathing orators of miseries,	
	Let them have scope[10]. Though what they will impart	130
	Help nothing else, yet do they ease the heart.	
DUCHESS	If so, then be not tongue-tied. Go with me,	
	And in the breath of bitter words let's smother	
	My damnèd son that thy two sweet sons smothered.	
	The trumpet sounds. Be copious in exclaims[11].	135

Enter RICHARD and his train

RICHARD	Who intercepts[12] me in my expedition[13]?	
DUCHESS	Oh, she that might have intercepted thee,	
	By strangling thee in her accursèd womb,	
	From all the slaughters, wretch, that thou hast done.	
ELIZABETH	Hid'st thou that forehead with a golden crown	140
	Where should be branded, if that right were right,	
	The slaughter of the prince that owed[14] that crown	
	And the dire death of my poor sons and brothers?	
	Tell me, thou villain slave, where are my children?	
DUCHESS	Thou toad, thou toad, where is thy brother Clarence,	145
	And little Ned[15] Plantagenet, his son?	
ELIZABETH	Where is the gentle Rivers, Vaughan, Grey?	

Richard tries to drown out the women's words with drums and trumpets. His mother catalogues all his faults from birth onwards. She demands a final hearing, and vows never to speak to him afterwards.

剧情简介：理查想以鼓号声压过几个女人的说话声。他的母亲罗列他出生以来所有的过错，要求做最后陈辞，发誓之后再不会同他讲话。

1 A mother's view (in small groups)

In lines 168–73, the Duchess of York's view of her son, Richard, is a chilling one. She lists his characteristics from birth to the present, piling up the adjectives that made 'the earth my hell'. She divides his life into four periods:

1 'infancy' – bad-tempered and disobedient
2 'schooldays' – rebellious
3 'prime of manhood' (青年时期) – always taking risks
4 'age confirmed' (maturity) – cunning and untrustworthy.

On television in the UK there used to be a programme called *This Is Your Life*, where famous people's lives were celebrated by friends, family and other celebrities. Each person recounted an incident from the celebrity's life, or introduced a short piece of film. A studio presenter hosted the show.

- In your groups, put together a *Richard III: This Is Your Life* programme, from the perspective of his mother. One person should be the presenter, one Richard's mother and the rest of the group act out four brief scenes from Richard's life. Share your finished programme with the rest of the class.

1	Rail on	批评，责骂
2	Lord's anointed	香脂涂身的君主之君
3	*Flourish*	（喇叭）奏花腔
4	entreat me fair	对我客客气气的
5	report	回响
6	condition	品性
7	brook the accent of reproof	忍受批评
8	stayed	久等
9	the holy rood	神圣的十字架
10	Tetchy and wayward	暴躁而任性
11	age confirmed	成年之后
12	kind in hatred	口蜜腹剑（也可理解为天生狠毒）
13	comfortable	舒心
14	Humphrey Hower	汉弗瑞·豪威尔（当时 dining with Duke Humphrey 表示没饭吃，这里可能是在开玩笑）
15	forth of	远离
16	disgracious	让人厌恶

DUCHESS	Where is kind Hastings?	
RICHARD	A flourish, trumpets! Strike alarum, drums!	
	Let not the heavens hear these telltale women	150
	Rail on¹ the Lord's anointed². Strike, I say!	
	Flourish³. Alarums	
	Either be patient and entreat me fair⁴,	
	Or with the clamorous report⁵ of war	
	Thus will I drown your exclamations.	
DUCHESS	Art thou my son?	155
RICHARD	Ay, I thank God, my father, and yourself.	
DUCHESS	Then patiently hear my impatience.	
RICHARD	Madam, I have a touch of your condition⁶,	
	That cannot brook the accent of reproof⁷.	
DUCHESS	Oh, let me speak.	
RICHARD	Do then, but I'll not hear.	160
DUCHESS	I will be mild and gentle in my words.	
RICHARD	And brief, good mother, for I am in haste.	
DUCHESS	Art thou so hasty? I have stayed⁸ for thee,	
	God knows, in torment and in agony.	
RICHARD	And came I not at last to comfort you?	165
DUCHESS	No, by the holy rood⁹, thou know'st it well,	
	Thou cam'st on earth to make the earth my hell.	
	A grievous burden was thy birth to me.	
	Tetchy and wayward¹⁰ was thy infancy;	
	Thy schooldays frightful, desperate, wild, and furious;	170
	Thy prime of manhood, daring, bold, and venturous;	
	Thy age confirmed¹¹, proud, subtle, sly, and bloody:	
	More mild, but yet more harmful, kind in hatred¹².	
	What comfortable¹³ hour canst thou name	
	That ever graced me with thy company?	175
RICHARD	Faith, none but Humphrey Hower¹⁴, that called your grace	
	To breakfast once, forth of¹⁵ my company.	
	If I be so disgracious¹⁶ in your eye,	
	Let me march on and not offend you, madam.	
	Strike up the drum!	
DUCHESS	I prithee, hear me speak.	180
RICHARD	You speak too bitterly.	
DUCHESS	Hear me a word,	
	For I shall never speak to thee again.	
RICHARD	So.	

The Duchess prophesies she will never see Richard again. She lays a curse to ensure his defeat. Elizabeth echoes the curse. She says she will do anything to save her daughter's life, and blames Richard for her son's death.

剧情简介：公爵夫人预言她与理查永不再见。她诅咒理查必定失败。伊丽莎白附和，说自己会全力保护女儿的生命安全，还将其儿子的死归罪于理查。

1 A mother's last words to her son (in fours)

- The Duchess of York's farewell to her son is in the form of a curse (lines 184–96). Read her speech through at least twice, handing over to the next person at each full stop. Discuss what each section of the curse means, then memorise your lines.

- Explore ways of performing the speech together, using movement, choral speech and gestures. Can you find a piece of music to accompany your performance? What overall tone are you hoping to achieve? Share your performances, and discuss how you think Richard might react to each.

2 Richard versus Elizabeth (in pairs)

To gain a first impression of this long exchange between Richard and Elizabeth, take parts and read it straight through. Then work on one or more of the following activities.

a Talk together about whether you think Elizabeth has any suspicion of Richard's marriage intentions towards her daughter in the script opposite.

b Richard and Elizabeth's verbal battle in lines 212–22 recalls the rapidly alternating lines (known as stichomythia) between Richard and Anne in the 'wooing scene' (Act 1 Scene 2). Speak the lines in turn to bring out their speed and balance.

c Watch two different filmed productions of this scene. Write at least three paragraphs comparing how the directors set the scene and present the character of Elizabeth. Try to include quotations from the original script to illustrate how the director has made changes.

3 Mock innocence? (in pairs)

Elizabeth refers to her sons' death (lines 219–21), to which Richard replies, 'You speak as if that I had slain my cousins' (line 222). How does he say this line? In pairs try it in various ways:

- with mock innocence
- with knowing menace (as if daring Elizabeth to accuse him to his face)
- flatly and inscrutably (难以捉摸)
- casual and uncaring.

Decide which delivery you like best. Discuss what this line says about Richard and the way you would want to present him on stage.

---

1 ordinance 旨意，指示
2 turn 归来
3 perish 死亡
4 tire thee 让你疲惫
5 còmplete 从头到脚
6 adverse party 对手
7 Whisper 对……耳语
8 attend 侍奉
9 For my 至于我的
10 level not 不要算计
11 veil of infamy 恶名做成的面纱
12 So 如果
13 in her birth 当她处在生来的高位上时
14 good stars were opposite 星象不利
15 ill friends 坏朋友
16 unavoided 无法避免
17 avoided grace 不敬上帝

DUCHESS	Either thou wilt die by God's just ordinance[1]	
	Ere from this war thou turn[2] a conqueror,	185
	Or I with grief and extreme age shall perish[3]	
	And nevermore behold thy face again.	
	Therefore take with thee my most grievous curse,	
	Which in the day of battle tire thee[4] more	
	Than all the còmplete[5] armour that thou wear'st.	190
	My prayers on the adverse party[6] fight,	
	And there the little souls of Edward's children	
	Whisper[7] the spirits of thine enemies	
	And promise them success and victory.	
	Bloody thou art, bloody will be thy end;	195
	Shame serves thy life and doth thy death attend[8]. *Exit*	
ELIZABETH	Though far more cause, yet much less spirit to curse	
	Abides in me. I say amen to her.	
RICHARD	Stay, madam. I must talk a word with you.	
ELIZABETH	I have no more sons of the royal blood	200
	For thee to slaughter. For my[9] daughters, Richard,	
	They shall be praying nuns, not weeping queens,	
	And therefore level not[10] to hit their lives.	
RICHARD	You have a daughter called Elizabeth,	
	Virtuous and fair, royal and gracious.	205
ELIZABETH	And must she die for this? Oh, let her live,	
	And I'll corrupt her manners, stain her beauty,	
	Slander myself as false to Edward's bed,	
	Throw over her the veil of infamy[11].	
	So[12] she may live unscarred of bleeding slaughter,	210
	I will confess she was not Edward's daughter.	
RICHARD	Wrong not her birth; she is a royal princess.	
ELIZABETH	To save her life, I'll say she is not so.	
RICHARD	Her life is safest only in her birth[13].	
ELIZABETH	And only in that safety died her brothers.	215
RICHARD	Lo, at their birth good stars were opposite[14].	
ELIZABETH	No, to their lives ill friends[15] were contrary.	
RICHARD	All unavoided[16] is the doom of destiny.	
ELIZABETH	True, when avoided grace[17] makes destiny.	
	My babes were destined to a fairer death,	220
	If grace had blest thee with a fairer life.	
RICHARD	You speak as if that I had slain my cousins.	

Elizabeth continues to accuse Richard of the murder of the princes and wishes she could die assaulting him. Richard declares that he will banish her grief by giving all honour and dignity to her daughter, Elizabeth.

剧情简介： 伊丽莎白继续指控理查谋杀两位王子，情愿与他同归于尽。理查说他要把所有的荣耀和尊严都给她女儿伊丽莎白，以此来消解她的悲伤。

Characters 人物分析

Interpreting Elizabeth (in pairs)

a Read through the script opposite and discuss what impressions you gain of Elizabeth at this point in the play. Do you see her as:

- a strong, principled woman, not afraid to stand up to Richard
- nervous and fearful, pleading with Richard at times to spare her daughter
- scheming just as much as Richard, thinking that she might win some advantage by marrying her daughter to him
- behaving in another way?

b Find examples from the text to support your interpretation and note them down. Prepare a short presentation to deliver to the class. When everyone has given their presentations, discuss any differences in interpretation. Why is it possible to read the script in a number of different ways?

1. cozened 被骗去
2. kindred 家人
3. Whose hand soever 无论是谁的手
4. lanch'd 刺穿
5. direction 命令
6. whetted 磨利
7. But that 不过是因为
8. still use of grief 一波接一波的悲痛
9. in such a desperate bay 身陷绝境
10. bark 小船
11. tackling reft 绳索被拆除
12. so thrive I in my 让我在……获得成功
13. As 因为（或 "仅就……而言"）
14. discovered 揭露
15. high imperial type 那种高高在上的王家的……
16. demise 许给
17. So 条件是
18. Lethe 丽息河（又译作 "遗忘河"，希腊神话中冥界的五条河之一，死者到达冥界时会被要求喝这条河的水，以忘却尘世之事）
19. thy kindness' date 你善意的期限
20. from = apart from

Richard argues that he should marry Elizabeth's daughter to consolidate (巩固) his position as King. Choose a line to make an effective caption for the picture.

King Richard III Act 4 Scene 4
理查三世

ELIZABETH	Cousins indeed, and by their uncle cozened[1]
	Of comfort, kingdom, kindred[2], freedom, life.
	Whose hand soever[3] lanch'd[4] their tender hearts, 225
	Thy head all indirectly gave direction[5].
	No doubt the murderous knife was dull and blunt
	Till it was whetted[6] on thy stone-hard heart
	To revel in the entrails of my lambs.
	But that[7] still use of grief[8] makes wild grief tame, 230
	My tongue should to thy ears not name my boys
	Till that my nails were anchored in thine eyes,
	And I in such a desperate bay[9] of death,
	Like a poor bark[10] of sails and tackling reft[11],
	Rush all to pieces on thy rocky bosom. 235
RICHARD	Madam, so thrive I in my[12] enterprise
	And dangerous success of bloody wars
	As[13] I intend more good to you and yours
	Than ever you and yours by me were harmed.
ELIZABETH	What good is covered with the face of heaven 240
	To be discovered[14], that can do me good?
RICHARD	Th'advancement of your children, gentle lady.
ELIZABETH	Up to some scaffold, there to lose their heads.
RICHARD	Unto the dignity and height of fortune,
	The high imperial type[15] of this earth's glory. 245
ELIZABETH	Flatter my sorrow with report of it.
	Tell me what state, what dignity, what honour,
	Canst thou demise[16] to any child of mine?
RICHARD	Even all I have, ay, and myself and all,
	Will I withal endow a child of thine, 250
	So[17] in the Lethe[18] of thy angry soul
	Thou drown the sad remembrance of those wrongs
	Which thou supposest I have done to thee.
ELIZABETH	Be brief, lest that the process of thy kindness
	Last longer telling than thy kindness' date[19]. 255
RICHARD	Then know that from[20] my soul I love thy daughter.
ELIZABETH	My daughter's mother thinks it with her soul.
RICHARD	What do you think?
ELIZABETH	That thou dost love my daughter from thy soul.
	So from thy soul's love didst thou love her brothers, 260
	And from my heart's love I do thank thee for it.

Richard states his intention to marry Elizabeth's daughter and make her Queen. Elizabeth mockingly suggests ways in which he should woo her daughter. Richard promises to make amends through the marriage.

剧情简介：理查宣布他准备娶伊丽莎白的女儿并封她为王后。伊丽莎白语带嘲讽地教他怎样讨好她女儿。理查承诺通过这次婚姻弥补过错。

Write about it 写作练习

A grisly love letter

Richard now reveals that he wants to marry Elizabeth's daughter and make her Queen of England. On the grounds that a mother best knows how to win her daughter's heart, Richard asks for help in proposing marriage. Elizabeth's reply is probably not quite what he had in mind …

- Sketch and label Elizabeth's suggested gifts as outlined in lines 274–86 Then write the accompanying letter from Richard to the young Elizabeth.

1 Play it for laughs? (in pairs)

Faced with Elizabeth's elaborate challenge to his proposals, Richard's response in lines 287–8 could be delivered in a 'deadpan' (不动声色) tone to cause amusement. In the following lines, Richard goes on to defend himself. Such bloody acts have been committed because of his love for Elizabeth's daughter (line 292). When Elizabeth rejects this excuse, he suggests that sometimes men can act thoughtlessly ('Men shall deal unadvisedly sometimes'). This line usually gains a laugh in the theatre because 'deal unadvisedly' is totally out of proportion to the enormity of his crimes.

a Take parts and play around with this section of script (lines 270–99), trying to emphasise the preposterous nature of Richard's proposal and the possible humour in this part of the scene.

b Talk together about the advantages and disadvantages of highlighting the humour here.

Stagecraft 导演技巧

Direct the army

Richard entered at line 135 with his followers ('*train*'), which presumably included armed soldiers and military drummers, but there has been no stage direction to indicate what the army is doing all this time.

- Step into role as director and decide on some possible solutions. Make notes in your Director's Journal.

1 confound 误会
2 humour 性情
3 by 以……的名义
4 purple sap 紫色血液（指血液；当时人们相信贵族的血液是紫色的）
5 sweet brother (指爱德华王子)
6 mad'st away 让……消失
7 Mad'st quick conveyance with 急急忙忙废黜了
8 spoil 毁灭
9 Look what 无论（做了）什么
10 deal unadvisedly 草率行事

178

RICHARD	Be not so hasty to confound[1] my meaning.	
	I mean that with my soul I love thy daughter	
	And do intend to make her Queen of England.	
ELIZABETH	Well then, who dost thou mean shall be her king?	265
RICHARD	Even he that makes her queen. Who else should be?	
ELIZABETH	What, thou?	
RICHARD	Even so. How think you of it?	
ELIZABETH	How canst thou woo her?	
RICHARD	That I would learn of you,	270
	As one being best acquainted with her humour[2].	
ELIZABETH	And wilt thou learn of me?	
RICHARD	Madam, with all my heart.	
ELIZABETH	Send to her by[3] the man that slew her brothers	
	A pair of bleeding hearts; thereon engrave	275
	Edward and York; then haply will she weep.	
	Therefore present to her, as sometime Margaret	
	Did to thy father, steeped in Rutland's blood,	
	A handkerchief, which, say to her, did drain	
	The purple sap[4] from her sweet brother's[5] body,	280
	And bid her wipe her weeping eyes withal.	
	If this inducement move her not to love,	
	Send her a letter of thy noble deeds.	
	Tell her thou mad'st away[6] her uncle Clarence,	
	Her uncle Rivers, ay, and for her sake	285
	Mad'st quick conveyance with[7] her good aunt Anne.	
RICHARD	You mock me, madam, this is not the way	
	To win your daughter.	
ELIZABETH	There is no other way,	
	Unless thou couldst put on some other shape	290
	And not be Richard that hath done all this.	
RICHARD	Say that I did all this for love of her.	
ELIZABETH	Nay, then indeed she cannot choose but hate thee,	
	Having bought love with such a bloody spoil[8].	
RICHARD	Look what[9] is done, cannot be now amended.	295
	Men shall deal unadvisedly[10] sometimes,	
	Which after-hours gives leisure to repent.	
	If I did take the kingdom from your sons,	
	To make amends I'll give it to your daughter.	

Richard lists all the gains Queen Elizabeth will enjoy if her daughter becomes his wife. Her son, Dorset, will also benefit. He asks her to prepare Elizabeth for his wooing while he defeats Buckingham.

剧情简介：理查列出伊丽莎白王后能得到的所有好处，前提是她女儿成为他妻子。她儿子多塞也将受益。他要求她在其与白金汉作战期间做好女儿的思想工作。

1 Intercut Richard's argument (in pairs)

Read lines 300–40, in which Richard lays out his argument as to why Elizabeth should accept his offer. He speaks without interruption, but what might Elizabeth be thinking all this time?

a Divide Richard's speech into sections and work out what Elizabeth's unspoken response might be. Use the following summary to help you understand Richard's lines:

- **Lines 298–9** If I took the kingdom from your sons, I'll make your daughter Queen.
- **Lines 300–2** If I killed your children, I will now give life to heirs through your daughter.
- **Lines 303–8** A grandmother is loved only a little less than a child's mother, but the grandmother does not have to suffer the pain of labour to produce a grandchild.
- **Lines 309–10** Your children were an annoyance when you were young. Grandchildren will comfort you in age.
- **Lines 311–12** Your loss is not having a son as King, but that has resulted in your daughter becoming Queen.
- **Lines 313–14** I can't offer you what I'd really like, but please accept what I'm able to offer.
- **Lines 315–20** Your son, Dorset, can return home to a position of power, as brother-in-law to the King.
- **Lines 321–3** You will be the mother-in-law to the King and the troubles of the past will be resolved.
- **Lines 324–8** The future will be far, far better and happier than the past.
- **Lines 329–34** Go to your daughter and use your maturity to prepare her to be wooed. Make her ambitious to be Queen and tell her of the joys of marriage.
- **Lines 335–40** When I've defeated Buckingham, I'll marry your daughter and she will be my commander.

Look back at Elizabeth's responses to Richard so far in this scene. How has she addressed Richard up to now? What is her manner and what kind of language does she use? Perform Richard's speech, pausing at the end of each section to allow Elizabeth to voice her innermost thoughts.

b Turn the page to find out how Elizabeth actually responds. As a class, discuss any major differences between the script and your prediction.

1 **quicken your increase** 让您加快繁衍生息
2 **doting title** 让人溺爱的名号
3 **They** （即孙子孙女）
4 **metal** 品格
5 **Of all one pain** 会同样让人心痛
6 **bid like sorrow** 忍受相似的痛苦
7 **discontented steps** 心怀不满的追随者
8 **Familiarly** 以家人的方式
9 **orient** 亮晶晶
10 **Advantaging** 涨价
11 **my mother** 我的岳母
12 **aspiring flame** 野心的火苗
13 **triumphant garlands** 得胜的花环
14 **retail** 复述

If I have killed the issue of your womb, 300
To quicken your increase[1] I will beget
Mine issue of your blood upon your daughter.
A grandam's name is little less in love
Than is the doting title[2] of a mother;
They[3] are as children but one step below, 305
Even of your metal[4], of your very blood,
Of all one pain[5], save for a night of groans
Endured of her for whom you bid like sorrow[6].
Your children were vexation to your youth,
But mine shall be a comfort to your age. 310
The loss you have is but a son being king,
And by that loss your daughter is made queen.
I cannot make you what amends I would;
Therefore accept such kindness as I can.
Dorset, your son, that with a fearful soul 315
Leads discontented steps[7] in foreign soil,
This fair alliance quickly shall call home
To high promotions and great dignity.
The king that calls your beauteous daughter wife
Familiarly[8] shall call thy Dorset brother. 320
Again shall you be mother to a king,
And all the ruins of distressful times
Repaired with double riches of content.
What? We have many goodly days to see.
The liquid drops of tears that you have shed 325
Shall come again, transformed to orient[9] pearl,
Advantaging[10] their love with interest
Of ten times double gain of happiness.
Go then, my mother[11], to thy daughter go.
Make bold her bashful years with your experience; 330
Prepare her ears to hear a wooer's tale;
Put in her tender heart th'aspiring flame[12]
Of golden sovereignty; acquaint the princess
With the sweet silent hours of marriage joys.
And when this arm of mine hath chastisèd 335
The petty rebel, dull-brained Buckingham,
Bound with triumphant garlands[13] will I come
And lead thy daughter to a conqueror's bed;
To whom I will retail[14] my conquest won,
And she shall be sole victoress, Caesar's Caesar. 340

Elizabeth again mocks Richard's proposal to woo Princess Elizabeth. She challenges every one of his arguments and statements, and dismisses his attempt to swear on the symbols of kingship.

剧情简介：伊丽莎白再一次嘲笑理查追求伊丽莎白公主的打算。她质疑他给出的所有的理由和承诺，不理会他以王权的种种象征发的誓。

Language in the play 剧中语言

Claims and counter-claims (whole class, then in pairs)

Elizabeth's list of questions (lines 341–6) is a response to Richard's long speech ending in the proposal that he should marry young Elizabeth. What follows returns to the quick-fire exchanges, often using balanced, antithetical (对偶的) pairing of sentences. This rapid exchange ends on a set of split lines (378–81).

a Divide the class into two and stand on different sides of the classroom in two long opposing lines:

- One line reads Richard's words, the other line reads Elizabeth's (lines 347–71). Start off quite slowly to get used to the words, but as you become more confident, start to experiment with pace, volume and tone, and how each side answers the other.
- Can you add gestures to the words? Remember, everyone on your side of the room needs to do the same. Make sure there is no gap between one side speaking and the other taking over. Aim for a slight overlap so that the rapid exchange is maintained.

b Divide into pairs and look again at each two-line claim and counter-claim separately.

- Talk together about the way one line leads to the next (that is, how one character picks up a word or phrase spoken by the other and returns it in a different form).
- Dramatically, what is the effect of this style of writing? What does it convey to an audience about Elizabeth and Richard? Make notes in your Director's Journal.

1 Infer   暗示
2 still-lasting   经久不衰
3 the king's King   万王之王（指上帝）
4 vail   失去
5 speeds best   最能成功
6 quick   仓促
7 Harp not on that string   别总是老调重弹
8 George   圣乔治（英格兰的主保圣人）
9 Garter   嘉德勋章（骑士的最高荣誉）
10 Profaned   被亵渎
11 his = its

ELIZABETH	What were I best to say? Her father's brother	
	Would be her lord? Or shall I say her uncle?	
	Or he that slew her brothers and her uncles?	
	Under what title shall I woo for thee	
	That God, the law, my honour, and her love	345
	Can make seem pleasing to her tender years?	
RICHARD	Infer¹ fair England's peace by this alliance.	
ELIZABETH	Which she shall purchase with still-lasting² war.	
RICHARD	Tell her the king, that may command, entreats.	
ELIZABETH	That at her hands which the king's King³ forbids.	350
RICHARD	Say she shall be a high and mighty queen.	
ELIZABETH	To vail⁴ the title, as her mother doth.	
RICHARD	Say I will love her everlastingly.	
ELIZABETH	But how long shall that title ever last?	
RICHARD	Sweetly in force unto her fair life's end.	355
ELIZABETH	But how long fairly shall her sweet life last?	
RICHARD	As long as heaven and nature lengthens it.	
ELIZABETH	As long as hell and Richard likes of it.	
RICHARD	Say I, her sovereign, am her subject low.	
ELIZABETH	But she, your subject, loathes such sovereignty,	360
RICHARD	Be eloquent in my behalf to her.	
ELIZABETH	An honest tale speeds best⁵ being plainly told.	
RICHARD	Then plainly to her tell my loving tale.	
ELIZABETH	Plain and not honest is too harsh a style.	
RICHARD	Your reasons are too shallow and too quick⁶.	365
ELIZABETH	Oh, no, my reasons are too deep and dead,	
	Too deep and dead, poor infants, in their graves.	
RICHARD	Harp not on that string⁷, madam. That is past.	
ELIZABETH	Harp on it still shall I till heartstrings break.	
RICHARD	Now, by my George⁸, my Garter⁹, and my crown –	370
ELIZABETH	Profaned¹⁰, dishonoured, and the third usurped.	
RICHARD	I swear –	
ELIZABETH	By nothing, for this is no oath.	
	Thy George, profaned, hath lost his lordly honour;	
	Thy Garter, blemished, pawned his knightly virtue;	
	Thy crown, usurped, disgraced his¹¹ kingly glory:	375
	If something thou wouldst swear to be believed,	
	Swear then by something that thou hast not wronged.	

Elizabeth will not accept any oath sworn by Richard based on himself, the world, his father's death, on God or the future. Richard claims that he intends to reform if he is successful in battle.

 剧情简介：理查用他自己、世界、父亲的死、上帝和未来发誓，但伊丽莎白均不接受。理查声称自己如果凯旋就会力图改革。

1 God, honour and the state

In line 345, Elizabeth accused Richard of disregarding three basic principles that govern a stable society ('God', 'law', 'honour'). Later, in line 370, Richard swears by Saint George (Church), his Garter (honour) and his crown (law and kingship). By swearing on these symbols of his kingship, Richard is not only invoking the Church, chivalry and honour, but also the divinity connected with kingship.

a Carry out an Internet search to find out more about St George and what he stands for as the patron saint of England. Do the same for the Order of the Garter.

b Identify the three reasons Elizabeth gives in lines 373–5 that show Richard's oath is worthless.

c Using the symbolism of St George, the Garter and the crown, design a graphic representation (a drawing or a collage) of Richard's crown, religion and knightly honour all profaned and tarnished.

2 Richard's oath (in pairs)

Richard continues to search for an oath that is acceptable to Elizabeth. Today an oath is mainly sworn in a formal situation, such as when swearing in a jury or making marriage vows. The swearers pledge their word by using something they venerate (崇敬) as a symbol, perhaps a holy book or the safety of those they love.

Elizabeth says that Richard cannot swear an oath, as through his actions he has devalued all he might swear by. He has destroyed the value of himself, his kingdom and the honour of his dead father (lines 378–80). Richard does not answer Elizabeth's charges, but tries another oath based on the future. She dismisses this with contempt, because the future will be filled with the children and parents grieving for their loved ones whom Richard has killed.

- Take parts as Richard and Elizabeth, and speak the whole 'oath' episode (lines 370–401). Emphasise Richard's increasing desperation and Elizabeth's determined rejection of each attempt.
- As you rehearse this episode, experiment with positioning – for example, with the two characters standing very close to each other, then gradually further apart. Also, try making them move onto different levels. Who might gain the highest position by the end of this exchange?

1 Thyself is self-misused 你把自己用错了地方
2 Him (指上帝)
3 Th'imperial metal 王冠
4 bedfellows for dust 结伴长眠于尘土之中
5 time o'erpast 过去
6 Hereafter time 以后的日子
7 Ungoverned 没人管教
8 by times ill-used repassed 过去错误花费的时间
9 bar me 挡住我
10 opposite (与我)作对
11 proceeding 成功
12 Immaculate devotion 虔诚的祷告
13 tender not 痛失

RICHARD	Then by myself.	
ELIZABETH	Thyself is self-misused[1].	
RICHARD	Now, by the world –	
ELIZABETH	'Tis full of thy foul wrongs.	
RICHARD	My father's death.	
ELIZABETH	Thy life hath it dishonoured.	380
RICHARD	Why then, by heaven.	
ELIZABETH	Heaven's wrong is most of all.	
	If thou didst fear to break an oath with Him[2],	
	The unity the king my husband made	
	Thou hadst not broken, nor my brothers died.	
	If thou hadst feared to break an oath by Him,	385
	Th'imperial metal[3] circling now thy head	
	Had graced the tender temples of my child,	
	And both the princes had been breathing here,	
	Which now, two tender bedfellows for dust[4],	
	Thy broken faith hath made the prey for worms.	390
	What canst thou swear by now?	
RICHARD	The time to come.	
ELIZABETH	That thou hast wrongèd in the time o'erpast[5],	
	For I myself have many tears to wash	
	Hereafter time[6], for time past wronged by thee.	395
	The children live whose fathers thou hast slaughtered,	
	Ungoverned[7] youth, to wail it with their age;	
	The parents live whose children thou hast butchered,	
	Old barren plants, to wail it with their age.	
	Swear not by time to come, for that thou hast	400
	Misused ere used, by times ill-used repassed[8].	
RICHARD	As I intend to prosper and repent,	
	So thrive I in my dangerous affairs	
	Of hostile arms. Myself myself confound!	
	Heaven and fortune bar me[9] happy hours!	405
	Day, yield me not thy light, nor night, thy rest!	
	Be opposite[10], all planets of good luck	
	To my proceeding[11] if, with dear heart's love,	
	Immaculate devotion[12], holy thoughts,	
	I tender not[13] thy beauteous, princely daughter!	410
	In her consists my happiness and thine.	

Richard says that total destruction will result if he does not marry young Elizabeth. Her mother says she will let Richard know later. Ratcliffe brings news of a threatened invasion and unreliable allies.

 剧情简介：理查说如果她娶不到少女伊丽莎白，就会导致世界的毁灭。伊丽莎白说会晚些时候告诉理查结果。拉克利夫禀告叛军入侵、盟军散伙的消息。

Stagecraft 导演技巧
Is Elizabeth persuaded? (in pairs)

For the Plantagenets, marriages of political expediency (权宜) were commonplace and morally acceptable. Therefore, Richard's final argument to Elizabeth is the strongest – without this alliance the state will collapse. Richard paints a picture of the country ruined if Princess Elizabeth will not marry him.

In the end, does Richard feel he has been successful? His comment about Elizabeth at line 436 ('Relenting fool and shallow, changing woman') suggests that he thinks he has won her over.

- With a partner, take parts and read through the script from line 423 to Elizabeth's exit. Rehearse a version that suggests Elizabeth has been persuaded by Richard and will allow him to marry her daughter.
- Then rehearse a second version, in which it is clear that Elizabeth has rejected the idea. Think carefully about how Elizabeth speaks her lines and about the way she exits in each version.

1 mother　岳母
2 attorney　代理人；媒人
3 necessity and state of times　当前的危机
4 be … designs　大事当前不可意气用事
5 in … breed　在那凤凰的巢中他们将得以重生
6 recomforture　新的福祉
7 Relenting　心软
8 puissant　强大
9 shores　海滩
10 hollow-hearted　内心空虚
11 admiral　舰队司令
12 hull　在锚点漂泊
13 expecting but　就等着
14 light-foot　快步如飞

Characters 人物分析
'Rounding out' Elizabeth

Many commentators claim that until Act 4 Scene 4, the female roles are rather 'flat' and formulaic (公式化), fulfilling a specific thematic function. Here, however, the actor playing Elizabeth is given space to develop the character dramatically.

Write approximately four paragraphs outlining how you think the role of Elizabeth should be played. Focus your attention on Act 4 and provide evidence from the script to support your view of her. You might find it helpful to look at the following episodes:

- **Act 4 Scene 1** The three women meet outside the Tower, where Elizabeth's sons are imprisoned.
- **Act 4 Scene 4** Elizabeth and the Duchess meet Margaret. Note particularly the points where Elizabeth mourns her sons; where she takes cursing lessons, and how she immediately responds to Richard's entrance; and where she sustains a verbal fencing match with Richard.

King Richard III Act 4 Scene 4
理查三世

	Without her follows to myself and thee,	
	Herself, the land, and many a Christian soul,	
	Death, desolation, ruin, and decay.	
	It cannot be avoided but by this.	415
	It will not be avoided but by this.	
	Therefore, dear mother[1], I must call you so,	
	Be the attorney[2] of my love to her.	
	Plead what I will be, not what I have been,	
	Not my deserts, but what I will deserve.	420
	Urge the necessity and state of times[3],	
	And be not peevish found in great designs[4].	
ELIZABETH	Shall I be tempted of the devil thus?	
RICHARD	Ay, if the devil tempt you to do good.	
ELIZABETH	Shall I forget myself to be myself?	425
RICHARD	Ay, if your self's remembrance wrong yourself.	
ELIZABETH	Yet thou didst kill my children.	
RICHARD	But in your daughter's womb I bury them,	
	Where in that nest of spicery they will breed[5]	
	Selves of themselves, to your recomforture[6].	430
ELIZABETH	Shall I go win my daughter to thy will?	
RICHARD	And be a happy mother by the deed.	
ELIZABETH	I go. Write to me very shortly,	
	And you shall understand from me her mind.	
RICHARD	Bear her my true love's kiss, and so farewell.	435

Exit Q[ueen Elizabeth]

Relenting[7] fool and shallow, changing woman.
How now, what news?

Enter RATCLIFFE [*and* CATESBY]

RATCLIFFE	Most mighty sovereign, on the western coast	
	Rideth a puissant[8] navy. To our shores[9]	
	Throng many doubtful, hollow-hearted[10] friends,	440
	Unarmed and unresolved to beat them back.	
	'Tis thought that Richmond is their admiral[11];	
	And there they hull[12], expecting but[13] the aid	
	Of Buckingham to welcome them ashore.	
RICHARD	Some light-foot[14] friend post to the Duke of Norfolk:	445
	Ratcliffe, thyself, or Catesby; where is he?	
CATESBY	Here, my good lord.	

Richard's orders to Catesby and Ratcliffe cause them some puzzlement. Stanley confirms that Richmond is leading a force by sea to seize the crown. Richard suspects Stanley's loyalty.

剧情简介：理查向凯茨贝和拉克利夫下达的命令让他们不知所措。斯坦雷证实瑞奇蒙正率领一支部队从海路而来，要争夺王位。理查怀疑斯坦雷的忠诚。

Characters 人物分析
Is Richard an effective general? (in threes)

a Catesby and Ratcliffe have problems with Richard's orders. Take parts and read lines 437–62 aloud. Think about:
- the clarity of Richard's commands
- possible reasons for Richard's forgetfulness
- how Catesby and Ratcliffe react to each other and to Richard
- how effective you think Richard is as a military commander.

b Write two paragraphs about the way Richard appears to be developing at this point in the play. Try to include quotations to support your comments.

1 Is Stanley loyal? (in fours)

In Act 3, Stanley urged Hastings to flee to the north to escape Richard's vindictiveness (怀恨在心) (Act 3 Scene 2, lines 17–18), yet here he appears to still be working for Richard and passing on valuable information.

a Two group members take on the roles of Richard and Stanley. Read the script through, pausing at the end of each character's lines. In the pause, the other two group members voice the inner thoughts of the character. How far does what they say match what they really mean? How does this contribute to the theme of appearance and reality as the play moves towards its conclusion?

b Do you think Stanley is loyal to Richard? How much does Richard suspect him?

Stagecraft 导演技巧
'Is the chair empty?'

Line 476 can be a great moment on stage, and every actor playing Richard tries to create a striking dramatic effect with the words 'Is the chair empty?'.

- What would you do to make this a thrilling dramatic moment? What stage sets or delivery might give meaning to Richard's line? Write some notes in your Director's Journal.

1 liege 陛下
2 deliver 传达
3 levy straight 立即征召
4 make 召集
5 Hoyday 哎哟（表示不耐烦）
6 nearest 最简单直接
7 White-livered runagate 吓破了胆的逃兵
8 makes for 前往
9 chair 王位
10 unswayed 没有挥舞
11 The empire unpossessed? 江山无主了？
12 York 约克家族
13 makes he = is he doing
14 Welshman 威尔士人（指瑞奇蒙，欧文·都铎的孙子）

King Richard III Act 4 Scene 4
理查三世

RICHARD	Catesby, fly to the duke.	
CATESBY	I will, my lord, with all convenient haste.	
RICHARD	Ratcliffe, come hither. Post to Salisbury.	450
	When thou com'st thither – Dull, unmindful villain,	
	Why stay'st thou here, and go'st not to the duke?	
CATESBY	First, mighty liege[1], tell me your highness' pleasure,	
	What from your grace I shall deliver[2] to him.	
RICHARD	Oh, true, good Catesby. Bid him levy straight[3]	455
	The greatest strength and power that he can make[4]	
	And meet me suddenly at Salisbury.	
CATESBY	I go. *Exit*	
RATCLIFFE	What, may it please you, shall I do at Salisbury?	
RICHARD	Why, what wouldst thou do there before I go?	460
RATCLIFFE	Your highness told me I should post before.	
RICHARD	My mind is changed.	

Enter LORD STANLEY [EARL OF DERBY]

	Stanley, what news with you?	
STANLEY	None good, my liege, to please you with the hearing,	
	Nor none so bad but well may be reported.	465
RICHARD	Hoyday[5], a riddle! Neither good nor bad.	
	What need'st thou run so many miles about,	
	When thou mayst tell thy tale the nearest[6] way?	
	Once more, what news?	
STANLEY	Richmond is on the seas.	
RICHARD	There let him sink, and be the seas on him!	470
	White-livered runagate[7], what doth he there?	
STANLEY	I know not, mighty sovereign, but by guess.	
RICHARD	Well, as you guess.	
STANLEY	Stirred up by Dorset, Buckingham, and Morton,	
	He makes for[8] England, here to claim the crown.	475
RICHARD	Is the chair[9] empty? Is the sword unswayed[10]?	
	Is the king dead? The empire unpossessed?[11]	
	What heir of York[12] is there alive but we?	
	And who is England's king but great York's heir?	
	Then tell me, what makes he[13] upon the seas?	480
STANLEY	Unless for that, my liege, I cannot guess.	
RICHARD	Unless for that he comes to be your liege,	
	You cannot guess wherefore the Welshman[14] comes.	
	Thou wilt revolt and fly to him, I fear.	

Richard continues to criticise Stanley, accusing him of using his troops to support Richmond. He takes Stanley's son as a hostage. Messengers bring news of more support for Richmond throughout the country.

 剧情简介：理查继续批评斯坦雷，指责他调动部队支持瑞奇蒙。他把斯坦雷的儿子当作人质。信使又带来些全国各地内支持瑞奇蒙的消息。

Stagecraft 导演技巧

Growing distrust? (in pairs)

Richard accuses Stanley of sending his army to help Richmond's troops disembark (登陆) safely in Wales. Stanley claims to be loyal and says he will raise an army to fight against Richmond. Still distrusting Stanley, Richard insists that his son, George, be left as a hostage to be killed if Stanley is disloyal.

- Take parts as Stanley and Richard and speak lines 463–505, emphasising Richard's distrust and Stanley's evasive (避而不谈) replies. What stage business could you include to show that Richard means his threat? How might Stanley react?

1. power　军力
2. tenants　佃户
3. Safe-cònducting　为……安全带路
4. Cold　不友好
5. Pleaseth = If it pleases
6. muster up　召集
7. false　不忠
8. assurance　安全
9. advertisèd　消息灵通
10. haughty prelate　骄傲的主教
11. confederates, are in arms　伙同党羽起兵作乱
12. competitors　响应者，同伙
13. ye = you　(你们)
14. owls　猫头鹰（其叫声被认为是死亡的预言）

1 Mapping the action (in pairs)

- Create a large-scale map based on the one on pages 2–3. Locate all the places mentioned in the script and where the separate forces ranged against Richard are active. (Richard is in London.)
- Use the Internet to find production photographs of different characters from the play. Print them out and attach them to the map in such a way that they can be moved around. Consider ways of colour-coding those loyal to Richard and those fighting with Richmond.
- Put the clearest versions up on the wall and add/move/remove characters as the next act unfolds.

2 Don't shoot the messenger (in sixes)

Two messengers tell of increasing support for Richmond 'in Devonshire' and 'In Kent'. The Third Messenger brings news of Buckingham, but Richard strikes him, fearing more bad news.

- Freeze the moment when Richard strikes the Third Messenger. Work out who else is on stage at this moment. How exactly does Richard strike him and does the messenger stay on his feet or fall over? Show the expressions of those nearby as they see Richard strike the messenger.
- Bring some characters in the tableau to life and explain what they are thinking at this moment.
- What does this action contribute to an audience's impression of Richard?

KING RICHARD III ACT 4 SCENE 4
理查三世

STANLEY	No, my good lord; therefore mistrust me not.	485
RICHARD	Where is thy power¹ then, to beat him back?	
	Where be thy tenants² and thy followers?	
	Are they not now upon the western shore,	
	Safe-cònducting³ the rebels from their ships?	
STANLEY	No, my good lord, my friends are in the north.	490
RICHARD	Cold⁴ friends to me. What do they in the north	
	When they should serve their sovereign in the west?	
STANLEY	They have not been commanded, mighty king.	
	Pleaseth⁵ your majesty to give me leave,	
	I'll muster up⁶ my friends and meet your grace	495
	Where and what time your majesty shall please.	
RICHARD	Ay, thou wouldst be gone, to join with Richmond.	
	But I'll not trust thee.	
STANLEY	Most mighty sovereign,	
	You have no cause to hold my friendship doubtful.	500
	I never was nor never will be false⁷.	
RICHARD	Go then and muster men, but leave behind	
	Your son George Stanley. Look your heart be firm,	
	Or else his head's assurance⁸ is but frail.	
STANLEY	So deal with him as I prove true to you. *Exit Stanley*	505

Enter a MESSENGER

MESSENGER	My gracious sovereign, now in Devonshire,	
	As I by friends am well advertisèd⁹,	
	Sir Edward Courtney and the haughty prelate¹⁰,	
	Bishop of Exeter, his elder brother,	
	With many more confederates, are in arms¹¹.	510

Enter another MESSENGER

SECOND MESSENGER	In Kent, my liege, the Guilfords are in arms,	
	And every hour more competitors¹²	
	Flock to the rebels, and their power grows strong.	

Enter another MESSENGER

THIRD MESSENGER	My lord, the army of great Buckingham –	
RICHARD	Out on ye¹³, owls¹⁴, nothing but songs of death!	515
	He striketh him	
	There, take thou that, till thou bring better news.	

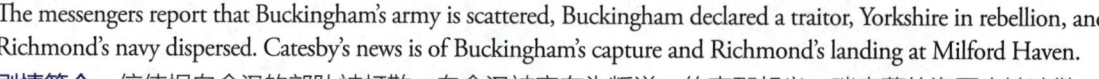

The messengers report that Buckingham's army is scattered, Buckingham declared a traitor, Yorkshire in rebellion, and Richmond's navy dispersed. Catesby's news is of Buckingham's capture and Richmond's landing at Milford Haven.

 剧情简介：信使报白金汉的部队被打散，白金汉被宣布为叛逆，约克郡起义，瑞奇蒙的海军也被冲散了。凯茨贝的消息称白金汉被俘，瑞奇蒙在米尔福德港登陆。

Stagecraft 导演技巧

Unwelcome news (in small groups)

In lines 506–43, four messengers and Catesby report growing unrest and tell of Richmond's invasion. Richard's reactions to the unwelcome news show that he feels under increasing pressure. He gives confused orders and changes his mind. He strikes a messenger. He makes hasty decisions without seeking counsel.

- Take parts as Richard, Catesby and the messengers, then speak lines 506–47. Work out how to stage the sequence to bring out the increasing pace of events, their effect on Richard, and whether he retains any of his grotesque sense of humour.

1 fall of waters 天降大雨
2 dispersed 打散
3 well-advisèd 考虑周全
4 Breton navy 布列塔尼来的舰队
5 assistants 援军
6 Upon his party 增援他
7 Hoised 升起
9 Bretagne 布列塔尼
9 reason 争辩
10 royal battle 争夺王位的战斗

Write about it 写作练习

Wanted!

Richard proclaims that Buckingham is a traitor with a price on his head (lines 523–5).

a Write the proclamation (a brief statement that was 'proclaimed' or shouted out publicly).

b Design a 'Wanted' poster for Buckingham. Include: a picture; a list of his alleged crimes; the price on his head; and where to bring him if caught.

Characters 人物分析

Richard in Scene 4: a reminder

Scene 4 is a very long scene in which a great deal happens. Richard's fortunes change dramatically. Glance back over the whole scene to remind yourself of its major episodes:

- **Lines 1–135** Margaret, Elizabeth and the Duchess's grieving (and cursing of Richard).
- **Lines 136–96** Richard's relationship with his mother.
- **Lines 197–436** Richard's proposal of marriage
- **Lines 437–547** Richard dealing with military matters.

Write four paragraphs, briefly describing each sequence and explaining what each reveals about Richard. Include evidence from the script to support your ideas.

THIRD MESSENGER   The news I have to tell your majesty
                  Is that by sudden floods and fall of waters[1]
                  Buckingham's army is dispersed[2] and scattered,
                  And he himself wandered away alone,   520
                  No man knows whither.
RICHARD   I cry thee mercy.
                  There is my purse to cure that blow of thine.
                  Hath any well-advisèd[3] friend proclaimed
                  Reward to him that brings the traitor in?   525
THIRD MESSENGER   Such proclamation hath been made, my lord.

Enter another MESSENGER

FOURTH MESSENGER   Sir Thomas Lovell and Lord Marquess Dorset,
                   'Tis said, my liege, in Yorkshire are in arms.
                   But this good comfort bring I to your highness:
                   The Breton navy[4] is dispersed by tempest.   530
                   Richmond, in Dorsetshire, sent out a boat
                   Unto the shore, to ask those on the banks
                   If they were his assistants[5], yea or no,
                   Who answered him they came from Buckingham
                   Upon his party[6]. He, mistrusting them,   535
                   Hoised[7] sail and made his course again for Bretagne[8].
RICHARD   March on, march on, since we are up in arms,
                   If not to fight with foreign enemies,
                   Yet to beat down these rebels here at home.

Enter CATESBY

CATESBY   My liege, the Duke of Buckingham is taken.   540
                  That is the best news. That the Earl of Richmond
                  Is with a mighty power landed at Milford
                  Is colder news, but yet they must be told.
RICHARD   Away towards Salisbury! While we reason[9] here
                  A royal battle[10] might be won and lost.   545
                  Someone take order Buckingham be brought
                  To Salisbury. The rest march on with me.

                                                    Flourish. Exeunt

Stanley discloses that his son is Richard's hostage, so he cannot openly support Richmond, and that Queen Elizabeth has agreed to Richmond marrying her daughter. Urswick reports that Richmond's army is marching to London.

 剧情简介：斯坦雷透露他儿子被理查扣作人质，所以他不能公开支持瑞奇蒙。伊丽莎白王后同意把女儿嫁给瑞奇蒙。额斯维报瑞奇蒙的军队在向伦敦进发。

Stagecraft 导演技巧
Scene change

A very swift change of scene is suggested here, where Stanley feels safe enough to confess his disloyalty to Richard. This change of location is easy to effect in a film, but how might a director manage it on stage without holding up the action? Consider some of the following suggestions and make some notes in your Director's Journal:

- Use a change of lighting (for example, dim the lights to suggest an indoor scene).
- Bring on two or three pieces of furniture to suggest a domestic interior.
- Simply have Stanley return once Richard and his followers have left.

Write about it 写作练习
Stanley's letter

In the previous scene, Stanley declared his loyalty to Richard. Now he shows that he is really loyal to Richmond, but cannot openly support his stepson because Richard has taken his son, George, hostage and threatens to execute him if Stanley is disloyal.

- Imagine that Stanley sends a letter to Richmond to explain his predicament. Write the letter. Refer to the growing number of nobles who are turning against Richard in order to bolster Richmond's confidence in attacking Richard's army. What frame of mind do you believe Richard to be in? Why do you think this?

1 Growing opposition

Sir Christopher Urswick reports that more noblemen are joining Richmond. (Urswick is the Stanley family priest, used as a messenger.)

- Create a chart (or add to the map you began on p. 190), in which you collect the growing list of Richard's enemies. Use the list of characters on pages 4–5 to help you identify who's who.

1 franked up in hold 关在监狱
2 present aid 立即驰援
3 espouse 迎娶
4 Pembroke 彭布罗克（威尔士一镇）
5 Ha'rfordwest = Haverfordwest 哈弗福韦斯特（西威尔士的一个海边城镇）
6 men of name 名声显赫的人
7 redoubted 勇敢
8 ap （威尔士语，相当于英语的 of，常用在姓氏前）
9 bend their power 行军
10 by the way 沿途
11 hie thee to thy lord = go to Richmond

Act 4 Scene 5
The house of Stanley, Earl of Derby

Enter STANLEY EARL OF DERBY, *and* SIR CHRISTOPHER URSWICK, *a priest*

STANLEY Sir Christopher, tell Richmond this from me,
That in the sty of the most deadly boar
My son George Stanley is franked up in hold[1].
If I revolt, off goes young George's head;
The fear of that holds off my present aid[2]. 5
So get thee gone; commend me to thy lord.
Withal say that the queen hath heartily consented
He should espouse[3] Elizabeth her daughter.
But tell me, where is princely Richmond now?

CHRISTOPHER At Pembroke[4], or at Ha'rfordwest[5], in Wales. 10

STANLEY What men of name[6] resort to him?

CHRISTOPHER Sir Walter Herbert, a renownèd soldier,
Sir Gilbert Talbot, Sir William Stanley,
Oxford, redoubted[7] Pembroke, Sir James Blunt,
And Rice ap[8] Thomas, with a valiant crew, 15
And many other of great name and worth;
And towards London do they bend their power[9],
If by the way[10] they be not fought withal.

STANLEY Well, hie thee to thy lord[11]; I kiss his hand.
My letter will resolve him of my mind. 20
Farewell.

Exeunt

King Richard III
理查三世

Looking back at Act 4 第4幕回顾
Activities for groups or individuals

1 Grieving women

Anne, the Duchess of York, Elizabeth and Margaret do not appear again after this act (although Anne returns as a ghost in Act 5). This activity is designed to help you consider the four women characters and what dramatic tension they add to the play in Act 4.

a Make a list or draw a diagram for each of the women to illustrate what each says she has suffered or is about to suffer. The following table may help you locate relevant information in the script.

	Scene 1	Scene 4
Anne	Lines 66–87	
Elizabeth	Lines 98–104	Lines 9–14; 206–11
Duchess		Lines 43–4; lines 166–75
Margaret		see her asides on page 165; lines 35–70

b In groups of four, select a key line or phrase for each woman that you agree best sums up the nature of her grief. Create a tableau entitled 'Grief', making sure all four group members are included. Once you are happy with the look of the tableau (think about shapes, posture, facial expressions), you can add the words you selected from the script and begin to move and speak. Compare your performance with other groups'. Which one seems to convey most effectively the overwhelming emotion of the four female characters?

2 Richard as King

Imagine you are a spy in Richard's camp, secretly working for Richmond. You see everything, from Richard's entrance in Scene 3 to the end of the act. Write a report explaining Richard's military and political situation and describing his mental state. You might like to include:

- how Richard greets the news of the princes' deaths
- the various pieces of bad news Richard receives and how he reacts to them.
- Richard's public encounter with his mother
- any other gossip you have picked up (e.g. about Lord Stanley)
- what conclusions you come to: should Richmond feel confident about victory?

3 Richard as lover

In Act 1, Richard's brazen (厚颜无耻) wooing results in Anne succumbing to (屈服于) his menacing charm and agreeing to marry him. In Act 4 Scene 3, he is confidently making plans to go wooing again. But in Scene 4, he appears to be less successful in his manoeuvres (策略) when he attempts to court the young Elizabeth through her mother. Has he lost his touch or do you think that Elizabeth is, in the end, persuaded of the benefits of allowing Richard to marry her daughter?

Imagine you are directing the play. You are considering three possible interpretations of the scene between Richard and Elizabeth:

- Elizabeth pretends to agree to Richard's proposal in order to stall for time, knowing that Richmond's army is on its way.
- Elizabeth eventually gives in and genuinely agrees to the marriage.
- Richard's power and confidence are visibly weaker in this 'wooing scene', and Elizabeth senses this.

In groups of three, one person takes the role of director, while the other two take the parts of Richard and Elizabeth. Read through lines 197–435 in Scene 4, then choose one of the interpretations listed above. Work out a way of enacting the script so that this interpretation is clearly conveyed to an audience. Get together with another group that has chosen a different interpretation and compare a short section of your performances. In what ways do they differ?

Buckingham, escorted to execution, begs all Richard's dead victims to mock him. He remembers he wished God to punish him when he was proved a traitor, and recalls Margaret's prophecy that Richard would betray him.

剧情简介：白金汉被押赴刑场，他乞求所有被理查杀害的死者一齐嘲笑他。他想起自己曾希望一旦自己被证明是叛徒，就受到上帝的惩罚，还记起玛格蕊曾预言理查会背叛他。

Stagecraft 导演技巧

Set the scene (in pairs)

The setting for Act 5 Scene 1 in this edition of the play is 'Salisbury: a place of execution', and from Buckingham's words we know he is about to be beheaded ('the block of shame', line 28). In a film version of the play, it would be easy to show this change of scene from Stanley's house in Act 4 Scene 5, but on stage this is more complicated.

- Take on the roles of director and set designer. Talk about your ideas for this scene change on stage, bearing in mind that it needs to be swift. How might you use lighting, sound, props and/or set change in a way that effectively, but efficiently, conveys meaning?

1 How does Buckingham leave?

The tone of this short scene is important. It helps to establish whether or not the director wants the audience to sympathise with the figure of Buckingham.

- Talk about how you could portray Buckingham (for example, how the guards deal with him, how he moves and speaks, what lighting and sounds could highlight the desperateness of his situation). In Buckingham's final line, does he say that he gets what he deserves? How would you stage his departure for execution?

2 All Souls' Day (in pairs)

Buckingham reveals that he is about to be executed on the Christian festival of All Souls' Day (line 12).

- Use the Internet to conduct some research into All Souls' Day. Suggest why this might be an appropriate day for Buckingham's death.

Themes 主题分析

Curses

Buckingham remembers Margaret's earlier curse as he walks to his execution (line 25).

- Turn back to Act 1 Scene 3, lines 299–301 to check how accurately he remembers her words. As you read on through Act 5, keep a record of all the curses that come true.

1 thy = King Henry's
2 miscarrièd 被杀害
3 moody = angry
4 All Souls' day 万灵节（11月2日）
5 doomsday 末日
6 fall on me 判我死刑
7 determined respite of my wrongs 我受处罚缓刑的结束之日
8 All-Seer 无所不见之主（指上帝）
9 dallied 戏耍
10 in earnest 真的
11 block of shame 断头台

Act 5 Scene 1
Salisbury: a place of execution

Enter SHERIFF *and officers lead* BUCKINGHAM *to execution*

BUCKINGHAM Will not King Richard let me speak with him?
SHERIFF No, my good lord. Therefore be patient.
BUCKINGHAM Hastings and Edward's children, Grey and Rivers,
Holy King Henry, and thy[1] fair son Edward,
Vaughan, and all that have miscarrièd[2] 5
By underhand corrupted foul injustice,
If that your moody[3], discontented souls
Do through the clouds behold this present hour,
Even for revenge mock my destruction.
This is All Souls' Day[4], fellow, is it not? 10
SHERIFF It is.
BUCKINGHAM Why, then, All Souls' Day is my body's doomsday[5].
This is the day which, in King Edward's time,
I wished might fall on me[6] when I was found
False to his children and his wife's allies. 15
This is the day wherein I wished to fall
By the false faith of him whom most I trusted.
This, this All Souls' Day to my fearful soul
Is the determined respite of my wrongs[7].
That high All-Seer[8] which I dallied[9] with 20
Hath turned my feignèd prayer on my head
And given in earnest[10] what I begged in jest.
Thus doth he force the swords of wicked men
To turn their own points in their masters' bosoms.
Thus Margaret's curse falls heavy on my neck: 25
'When he', quoth she, 'shall split thy heart with sorrow,
Remember Margaret was a prophetess.'
Come, lead me, officers, to the block of shame[11];
Wrong hath but wrong, and blames the due of blame.

Exeunt Buckingham with officers

Richmond has received a letter of support from Stanley. He vows to defeat Richard's troops and bring peace. Doubts are voiced about the loyalty of Richard's followers.

 剧情简介： 瑞奇蒙收到斯坦雷的拥戴信。他发誓要打败理查的军队，让国家太平。理查追随者对主子的忠诚受到质疑。

Characters 人物分析
Richmond rallies his troops (in groups of four or five)

a Read through Richmond's speech in lines 1–16. Identify each of the following features of his speech:
- the way he refers to Richard
- how he talks about peace
- what he says about trust and hope
- how he mentions God and faith.

b Read the speech aloud in your group, with one person in role as Richmond. The rest of the group (as soldiers) should cheer at any references to God, peace, trust, faith/hope and Richard.

c At the end of the speech, the person reading Richmond should add the final three lines on the page (lines 22–4). How does his 'soldier audience' react? Discuss Richmond's choice of words – how good is he at motivating his men?

1	bowels	腹地
2	Lines of fair comfort	声援信
3	spoiled	毁掉
4	Swills	贪婪地吞食
5	wash	泔水
6	embowelled bosoms	被掏空的身体
7	cheerly	抖擞精神
8	homicide	凶手
9	dearest	紧要关头
10	meaner	更卑下的

Language in the play 剧中语言
Richard as rampaging boar (in threes)

Richmond employs a particularly vivid extended metaphor to describe Richard's rule over England (lines 7–12).

a Use pictures from magazines or the Internet to create a large collage that captures all the different aspects of the metaphor. Underneath your collage, add a few lines of writing explaining the effect your group was hoping to achieve with your collage.

b Consider how effective Richmond's words are in creating a particular view of Richard. Write a paragraph either for display or as notes in your Director's Journal.

Stagecraft 导演技巧
Richmond's 'colours'

The stage direction in this edition directs Richmond and his followers to enter with drums and banners.

- Suggest an appropriate colour for Richmond (different from Richard's white rose) and an appropriate image. What qualities do you want to suggest?

Act 5 Scene 2
Tamworth: the camp of Richmond

Enter RICHMOND, OXFORD, BLUNT, HERBERT, *and others,*
with drum and colours

RICHMOND	Fellows in arms, and my most loving friends,	
	Bruised underneath the yoke of tyranny,	
	Thus far into the bowels[1] of the land	
	Have we marched on without impediment;	
	And here receive we from our father Stanley	5
	Lines of fair comfort[2] and encouragement.	
	The wretched, bloody, and usurping boar,	
	That spoiled[3] your summer fields and fruitful vines,	
	Swills[4] your warm blood like wash[5], and makes his trough	
	In your embowelled bosoms[6], this foul swine	10
	Is now even in the centre of this isle,	
	Near to the town of Leicester, as we learn.	
	From Tamworth thither is but one day's march.	
	In God's name, cheerly[7] on, courageous friends,	
	To reap the harvest of perpetual peace	15
	By this one bloody trial of sharp war.	
OXFORD	Every man's conscience is a thousand men	
	To fight against this guilty homicide[8].	
HERBERT	I doubt not but his friends will turn to us.	
BLUNT	He hath no friends but what are friends for fear,	20
	Which in his dearest[9] need will fly from him.	
RICHMOND	All for our vantage. Then in God's name march!	
	True hope is swift and flies with swallow's wings;	
	Kings it makes gods, and meaner[10] creatures kings.	
	Exeunt	

Richard orders his tent to be pitched and declares his army to be three times larger than Richmond's. He begins his battle plans. Richmond also begins to prepare for the coming battle.

剧情简介：理查下令安营，称自己的兵力是瑞奇蒙的三倍。他开始制定作战计划。瑞奇蒙也准备迎战。

1 Rival camps, sunset to sunrise

Scene 3 portrays events from sunset to early morning. The action alternates between the rival camps of Richard and Richmond, as the two leaders reflect upon their personal situations and prepare for the coming battle.

a Time passing As you read the whole scene, look out for ways in which Shakespeare's language indicates the passage of time (sunset, 9 o'clock at night, midnight, 4 o'clock in the morning, dawn). Make a note of how this is indicated in the words and stage directions.

b Staging Many modern productions have two tents erected on either side of the stage. Whether inside or outside their tents, Richard and Richmond are in full view of the audience, but do not acknowledge each other's presence. Design the insignia (徽章，标记) on the two tents to denote Richard and Richmond. Think about appropriate symbols, colours, coats of arms and mottos.

2 Similarities and differences

The alternating episodes in the scene, between Richard and Richmond and their troops, enable the audience to make direct comparisons and contrasts between the rival camps.

- Copy the table below and make notes on the differences and similarities between the two leaders and their followers as you read through the scene. Begin with Richard and Richmond's initial comments in the script opposite.

Richmond as leader	Richard as leader
	Dismisses number of traitors as unimportant; boasts that his status as King more than makes up for it (11–13).
Discusses battle strategy with trusted nobles (22–34).	Talks battle tactics with trusted nobles (14–18).
Regards the beautiful sunset as a good omen (19–21).	

1 have knocks 受到打击
2 all's one for that 随它去吧
3 descried 发现
4 battalia 大军
5 account 数目
6 vantage 有利位置；优势
7 men of sound direction 有完美方向感的人（也可引申为"善于指挥的人"）
8 tract 轨迹
9 car 战车
10 standard 军旗
11 form and model 形式和模式
12 Limit 分配
13 several charge 各自职责
14 part … power 把有限的兵力合理分配

Act 5 Scene 3
Bosworth Field

Enter RICHARD *in arms, with* NORFOLK, RATCLIFFE, *the* EARL OF SURREY *and others*

RICHARD Here pitch our tent, even here in Bosworth field.
My lord of Surrey, why look you so sad?
SURREY My heart is ten times lighter than my looks.
RICHARD My lord of Norfolk.
NORFOLK Here, most gracious liege.
RICHARD Norfolk, we must have knocks[1], ha, must we not? 5
NORFOLK We must both give and take, my loving lord.
RICHARD Up with my tent. Here will I lie tonight,
But where tomorrow? Well, all's one for that[2].
Who hath descried[3] the number of the traitors?
NORFOLK Six or seven thousand is their utmost power. 10
RICHARD Why, our battalia[4] trebles that account[5].
Besides, the king's name is a tower of strength,
Which they upon the adverse faction want.
Up with the tent. Come, noble gentlemen,
Let us survey the vantage[6] of the ground. 15
Call for some men of sound direction[7].
Let's lack no discipline, make no delay,
For lords, tomorrow is a busy day.

Exeunt

Enter RICHMOND, SIR WILLIAM BRANDON, OXFORD, *and* DORSET, [HERBERT, BLUNT, *and others*]

RICHMOND The weary sun hath made a golden set,
And by the bright tract[8] of his fiery car[9], 20
Gives token of a goodly day tomorrow.
Sir William Brandon, you shall bear my standard[10].
Give me some ink and paper in my tent.
I'll draw the form and model[11] of our battle,
Limit[12] each leader to his several charge[13], 25
And part in just proportion our small power[14].
My lord of Oxford, you, Sir William Brandon,
And you, Sir Walter Herbert, stay with me.

Richmond asks Blunt to attempt to take an important message to Stanley. He proposes a battle-plan meeting. Richard checks his armour is ready and orders trustworthy guards to be placed on watch.

剧情简介：瑞奇蒙让布琅设法给斯坦雷传递重要情报。他提议开会商讨作战计划。理查检查盔甲并命亲信夜间守卫。

1 **keeps his regiment** 留在他的军团中
2 **quartered** 驻扎，扎营（斯坦雷还不能公开支持瑞奇蒙，因为他儿子仍被理查扣为人质）
3 **colours** 旗帜
4 **make some good means** 尽你最大努力
5 **needful** 重要
6 **beaver** 面甲
7 **easier** 更好用
8 **hie thee to thy charge** 快去执行你的任务
9 **sentinels** 警卫
10 **warrant** 保证

▲ Richard (top left) and Richmond (top right) encourage their supporters to fight. How would you design the set for this scene to show the difference between rival camps?

1 Meanwhile, back at Richard's camp … (in pairs)

In sharp contrast to Richmond, all is not well with Richard.

a Many productions show Richard's camp with a boar symbol. Discuss why this is appropriate for Richard. In particular, consider the animal imagery that has been used earlier in the play.

b Suggest what Richard's manner of speaking and general behaviour should be like at this point in the play. Make some notes in your Director's Journal, using what you have learned about Richard as the play has progressed.

KING RICHARD III ACT 5 SCENE 3
理查三世

	The Earl of Pembroke keeps his regiment[1].	
	Good Captain Blunt, bear my goodnight to him	30
	And by the second hour in the morning	
	Desire the earl to see me in my tent.	
	Yet one thing more, good captain, do for me:	
	Where is Lord Stanley quartered[2], do you know?	
BLUNT	Unless I have mista'en his colours[3] much,	35
	Which well I am assured I have not done,	
	His regiment lies half a mile at least	
	South from the mighty power of the king.	
RICHMOND	If without peril it be possible,	
	Sweet Blunt, make some good means[4] to speak with him	40
	And give him from me this most needful[5] note.	
BLUNT	Upon my life, my lord, I'll undertake it.	
	And so, God give you quiet rest tonight.	
RICHMOND	Good night, good Captain Blunt.	
	Come, gentlemen,	45
	Let us consult upon tomorrow's business.	
	Into my tent; the dew is raw and cold.	

They withdraw into the tent

Enter RICHARD, RATCLIFFE, NORFOLK, *and* CATESBY

RICHARD	What is't o'clock?	
CATESBY	It's supper time, my lord; it's nine o'clock.	
RICHARD	I will not sup tonight.	50
	Give me some ink and paper.	
	What, is my beaver[6] easier[7] than it was,	
	And all my armour laid into my tent?	
CATESBY	It is, my liege, and all things are in readiness.	
RICHARD	Good Norfolk, hie thee to thy charge[8].	55
	Use careful watch; choose trusty sentinels[9].	
NORFOLK	I go, my lord.	
RICHARD	Stir with the lark tomorrow, gentle Norfolk.	
NORFOLK	I warrant[10] you, my lord.	

Exit

RICHARD	Ratcliffe.	60
RATCLIFFE	My lord.	

Richard sends a message that Stanley's son will be killed if Stanley does not bring troops to him. He reflects on the loss of his previously high spirits. Stanley pledges, if possible, to aid Richmond in the battle.

 剧情简介：理查传信给斯坦雷称如果他拒不出兵相助就杀掉他儿子。他反思着自己不似往日兴致高昂。斯坦雷承诺如果可能的话会在战场上助瑞奇蒙一臂之力。

Characters 人物分析

Richard: a changed man? (in pairs)

Richard observes that he has lost his normal cheerfulness of mind ('alacrity of spirit').

a Take parts and read aloud lines 62–81. Make a list of key words or phrases from the script that convey Richard's mood at this point in the play.

b What advice would you give to the actor playing Richard here? How should he act and speak during this scene? Write notes for the actor, emphasising the importance of certain lines, words or phrases.

1 Stanley: the balance of power? (in threes)

Stanley acts as a catalyst (促使变化的人) to reveal the differences between Richard and Richmond. Both commanders need his support, but they try to win this support in very different ways. Stanley's relationship with Richmond (lines 82–105) provides a sharp contrast to the way he relates to Richard.

a Each person takes the role of Richmond, Richard or Stanley. Create two tableaux: one of Stanley and Richard together, the other depicting an 'eve-of-war' photograph showing Stanley with Richmond. Think about the way they stand (or perhaps one is seated?), the distance between the two men, their facial expressions and the direction of their gaze. When you present your tableaux, it should be obvious to other groups who each character is. If you have a camera, take a photograph of each pairing.

b Produce a slow-motion transition sequence between the first tableau (Stanley and Richard) and the second (Stanley with Richmond). As Stanley moves, what might Richard and Richmond do?

c Talk together about the relationship between the three men at this point in the play. How does it contribute to the dramatic tension?

d Continue adding to your notes on the similarities and differences between Richard and Richmond (see p. 202).

1 **pursuivant at arms** 武装扈从（低于最高军官武装之王 [king of arms] 和中级军官武装使节 [herald of arms] 的下级军官）
2 **watch** 蜡烛钟（在蜡烛上标记小段来计算时间）
3 **white Surrey** 白萨里马（一种特殊的马）
4 **staves** 长矛
5 **Saw'st** = Have you seen
6 **cockshut** 黄昏
7 **alacrity** 轻松，快乐
8 **Fortune … helm** 愿幸运与胜利降临于你
9 **by attorney** 通过代理
10 **flaky darkness** 黑暗的碎片
11 **Prepare thy battle** 拉开阵势
12 **arbitrement** 裁决
13 **mortal-staring** 要命地盯着看
14 **With best advantage** 趁最佳机会

King Richard III Act 5 Scene 3
理查三世

RICHARD	Send out a pursuivant at arms[1]
	To Stanley's regiment. Bid him bring his power
	Before sunrising, lest his son George fall
	Into the blind cave of eternal night. 65
	Fill me a bowl of wine. Give me a watch[2].
	Saddle white Surrey[3] for the field tomorrow.
	Look that my staves[4] be sound and not too heavy. Ratcliffe!
RATCLIFFE	My lord.
RICHARD	Saw'st[5] the melancholy Lord Northumberland? 70
RATCLIFFE	Thomas the Earl of Surrey and himself,
	Much about cockshut[6] time, from troop to troop
	Went through the army, cheering up the soldiers.
RICHARD	So, I am satisfied. Give me a bowl of wine.
	I have not that alacrity[7] of spirit 75
	Nor cheer of mind that I was wont to have.
	Set it down. Is ink and paper ready?
RATCLIFFE	It is, my lord.
RICHARD	Bid my guard watch. Leave me.
	Ratcliffe, about the mid of night come to my tent 80
	And help to arm me. Leave me, I say.

Exeunt Ratcliffe [and Catesby]

Enter [STANLEY EARL OF] DERBY to RICHMOND in his tent

STANLEY	Fortune and victory sit on thy helm[8].
RICHMOND	All comfort that the dark night can afford
	Be to thy person, noble father-in-law.
	Tell me, how fares our noble mother? 85
STANLEY	I by attorney[9] bless thee from thy mother,
	Who prays continually for Richmond's good.
	So much for that. The silent hours steal on,
	And flaky darkness[10] breaks within the east.
	In brief, for so the season bids us be, 90
	Prepare thy battle[11] early in the morning,
	And put thy fortune to th'arbitrement[12]
	Of bloody strokes and mortal-staring[13] war.
	I, as I may (that which I would I cannot),
	With best advantage[14] will deceive the time 95
	And aid thee in this doubtful shock of arms.

Stanley says the threat to his son prevents him openly supporting Richmond. He hopes for long friendship. Richmond prays for success in battle. The ghost of Prince Edward visits Richard and Richmond.

 剧情简介： 斯坦雷说儿子受到威胁，自己无法公开支持瑞奇蒙。他希望保持长久的友谊。瑞奇蒙祈祷战斗胜利。爱德华王子的鬼魂向理查和瑞奇蒙显灵。

Themes 主题分析

Sin and salvation: Richmond's prayer (in pairs)

In lines 111–20, Richmond prays to God, asking him to bless his army ('Look on my forces with a gracious eye') and support them as they fight against Richard. The army will then be agents of God ('ministers of chastisement') and it will be God's victory that is celebrated.

- Discuss possible reasons why Shakespeare gave Richmond a prayer here, but not Richard.

1 Ghostly visitors (in large groups)

In lines 121–79, the action continues to alternate between the rival camps as no fewer than eleven ghosts of Richard's victims visit the two sleeping leaders, condemning Richard and supporting Richmond.

- Divide the parts up between your group members and read lines 121–79.
- Split into pairs. Share out the different ghosts between you and, for each one, pick out a key phrase or line that he or she says to the sleeping Richard or Richmond.
- Each pair then presents to the larger group a brief scene in which the ghosts chant their phrase repeatedly. Compare each pair's chosen words and decide which you think is truly key to that particular ghost.
- Draw a table similar to the one below on a large sheet of paper. The whole group should now contribute to completing it.

Lines	Ghost	What does s/he say to Richard?	What does s/he say to Richmond?
121–6	Prince Edward	'thou stab'st me in my prime of youth … Despair … and die'	'King Henry's issue … comforts thee'
127–33	Henry VI		
	Clarence		

1 forward 明目张胆
2 brother （乔治·斯坦雷，瑞奇蒙同母异父的兄弟）
3 tender 年幼
4 leisure 空闲
5 ample interchange of sweet discourse 长期离别的朋友应有诉不尽的衷肠
6 sundered 别离
7 speed 胜利
8 strive 做斗争
9 peise 压垮
10 thou （指上帝）
11 captain 先锋官
12 bruising irons 杀伤敌人的武器
13 chastisement 惩罚
14 commend 托付
15 windows 眼睑

KING RICHARD III ACT 5 SCENE 3
理查三世

But on thy side I may not be too forward[1],
Lest being seen, thy brother[2], tender[3] George,
Be executed in his father's sight.
Farewell. The leisure[4] and the fearful time   100
Cuts off the ceremonious vows of love
And ample interchange of sweet discourse[5]
Which so long sundered[6] friends should dwell upon.
God give us leisure for these rites of love.
Once more adieu. Be valiant, and speed[7] well.   105

RICHMOND   Good lords, conduct him to his regiment.
I'll strive[8] with troubled noise to take a nap,
Lest leaden slumber peise[9] me down tomorrow,
When I should mount with wings of victory.
Once more, good night, kind lords and gentlemen.   110
                                    Exeunt [all but Richmond]
O thou[10] whose captain[11] I account myself,
Look on my forces with a gracious eye.
Put in their hands thy bruising irons[12] of wrath,
That they may crush down with a heavy fall
Th'usurping helmets of our adversaries.   115
Make us thy ministers of chastisement[13],
That we may praise thee in thy victory.
To thee I do commend[14] my watchful soul
Ere I let fall the windows[15] of mine eyes.
Sleeping, and waking, oh, defend me still. *Sleeps*   120

Enter the GHOST OF PRINCE EDWARD, *son to Henry the Sixth*

GHOST [OF PRINCE EDWARD] (*To Richard*) Let me sit heavy on thy
          soul tomorrow.
Think how thou stab'st me in my prime of youth
At Tewkesbury. Despair therefore, and die.
(*To Richmond*) Be cheerful, Richmond, for the wrongèd souls
Of butchered princes fight in thy behalf.   125
King Henry's issue, Richmond, comforts thee.

The ghosts of Henry VI, Clarence, Rivers, Grey, Vaughan and Hastings visit Richard and Richmond. All wish for despair and death for Richard and success for Richmond.

剧情简介：亨利六世、克莱润、瑞沃、格雷、沃恩和海斯廷的鬼魂向理查和瑞奇蒙显灵。他们都希望理查陷入困境、战败而亡，而祝愿瑞奇蒙赢取胜利。

Stagecraft 导演技巧
The ghosts (in pairs)

The ghost sequence offers any director an exciting opportunity to think creatively. On stage, the ghosts have been presented in many different ways. In one production, they did not appear to the dreaming commanders in their tents, but took part in the Battle of Bosworth (which happens in Scenes 4 and 5). They wounded Richard in the fighting, emphasising that although Richmond physically killed Richard in a real sword fight, Richard had already been defeated psychologically. How would you present the ghosts?

- What do they look like? Would you use real actors or not? Alternatives might be puppets or film projected onto a large screen.
- How do they dress? Are the ghosts all very similar or different to each other?
- How do they move? What gestures do they use?
- How do they speak? Do they talk individually or in chorus? Do they speak in different tones when wishing good luck to Richmond or repeatedly cursing Richard?
- Do they simply walk on stage and stand near the sleeping Richard or Richmond? Or do they appear on a balcony, or emerge through the audience? Are they all on stage together?

1 mortal 活着
2 punchèd 刺透
3 washed 淹死
4 fulsome 满到嗓子眼儿
5 guile 谎言
6 fall thy edgeless sword 丢掉你那把没刃的剑
7 battle 部队
8 bosom 良心

Enter the GHOST OF HENRY THE SIXTH

GHOST [OF HENRY] [*To Richard*] When I was mortal¹, my anointed body
    By thee was punchèd² full of holes.
    Think on the Tower and me. Despair, and die.
    Harry the Sixth bids thee despair and die.   130
    (*To Richmond*) Virtuous and holy, be thou conqueror.
    Harry, that prophesied thou shouldst be king,
    Doth comfort thee in sleep. Live and flourish.

Enter the GHOST OF CLARENCE

GHOST [OF CLARENCE] [*To Richard*] Let me sit heavy in thy soul tomorrow,
    I, that was washed³ to death with fulsome⁴ wine,   135
    Poor Clarence, by thy guile⁵ betrayed to death.
    Tomorrow in the battle think on me,
    And fall thy edgeless sword⁶, despair, and die.
    (*To Richmond*) Thou offspring of the house of Lancaster,
    The wrongèd heirs of York do pray for thee.   140
    Good angels guard thy battle⁷. Live and flourish.

Enter the GHOSTS OF RIVERS, GREY, *and* VAUGHAN

[GHOST OF] RIV[ERS] [*To Richard*] Let me sit heavy in thy soul tomorrow.
    Rivers that died at Pomfret. Despair, and die.
[GHOST OF] GREY   Think upon Grey, and let thy soul despair.
[GHOST OF] VAUGHAN   Think upon Vaughan, and with guilty fear   145
    Let fall thy lance. Despair, and die.
ALL [THREE GHOSTS] (*To Richmond*) Awake, and think our wrongs in
    Richard's bosom⁸
    Will conquer him. Awake, and win the day.

Enter the GHOST OF LORD HASTINGS

GHOST [OF HASTINGS] [*To Richard*] Bloody and guilty, guiltily awake
    And in a bloody battle end thy days.   150
    Think on Lord Hastings. Despair, and die.
    (*Hast*[*ings*] *to Richmond*) Quiet untroubled soul, awake, awake.
    Arm, fight, and conquer, for fair England's sake.

The ghosts of the princes in the Tower, Anne and Buckingham bring messages of death and despair to Richard and success to Richmond.

 剧情简介： 伦敦塔遇害的两位王子、安娜和白金汉的鬼魂给理查带来了死亡和绝望的讯息，给瑞奇蒙带来了胜利的讯息。

Language in the play 剧中语言
The ghosts' messages

The ghosts' messages to the sleeping commanders are delivered in formal, highly patterned language.

a Re-read the ghosts' speeches and find an example of each of the following linguistic devices:
- repetition
- balance and contrast.

b Write two paragraphs describing the ghosts' language, suggesting why the ghosts speak in this way. Share what you have written with two or three other students.

1. the boar's annoy 野猪（这里指理查）的伤害
2. beget 生下
3. race of kings 王室血脉
4. perturbations 焦虑
5. adversary 敌人
6. Fainting 心虚，胆怯
7. yield 放弃
8. I died ... aid 在能帮助你之前我已死去
9. Richard fall 理查要覆灭

1 More ghosts

The picture below shows a stylised, formal presentation of the ghost scene, where all the ghosts gather on stage together to accuse Richard (seated, wearing crown).

- Compare this picture with the ghosts shown in the image on page xii (left) in the photo gallery and that of the ghost on page 210. How do these images compare with your own ideas for staging and representing the ghosts?

Enter the GHOSTS OF THE TWO YOUNG PRINCES

GHOSTS [OF PRINCES] [*To Richard*] Dream on thy cousins smothered in
    the Tower.
    Let us be laid within thy bosom, Richard,   155
    And weigh thee down to ruin, shame, and death.
    Thy nephews' soul bids thee despair and die.
    (*To Richmond*) Sleep, Richmond, sleep in peace, and wake in joy.
    Good angels guard thee from the boar's annoy[1].
    Live, and beget[2] a happy race of kings[3].   160
    Edward's unhappy sons do bid thee flourish.

Enter the GHOST OF ANNE, *his wife*

GHOST [OF ANNE] (*To Richard*) Richard, thy wife, that wretched Anne, thy wife,
    That never slept a quiet hour with thee,
    Now fills thy sleep with perturbations[4].
    Tomorrow in the battle think on me,   165
    And fall thy edgeless sword. Despair, and die.
    (*To Richmond*) Thou quiet soul, sleep thou a quiet sleep.
    Dream of success and happy victory.
    Thy adversary's[5] wife doth pray for thee.

Enter the GHOST OF BUCKINGHAM

GHOST [OF BUCKINGHAM] (*To Richard*) The first was I that helped thee to
    the crown.   170
    The last was I that felt thy tyranny.
    Oh, in the battle think on Buckingham,
    And die in terror of thy guiltiness.
    Dream on, dream on, of bloody deeds and death.
    Fainting[6], despair; despairing, yield[7] thy breath.   175
    (*To Richmond*) I died for hope ere I could lend thee aid[8].
    But cheer thy heart and be thou not dismayed.
    God and good angels fight on Richmond's side,
    And Richard fall[9] in height of all his pride.

Richard starts from sleep and questions the reasons for his fear. He wrestles with his troubled conscience, which reminds him of the ghosts' accusations of murder and threats of vengeance.

剧情简介：理查从睡梦中惊醒，疑惑自己担心的缘由。他饱受煎熬的良知提醒他，鬼魂控诉他杀人并威胁要复仇。他努力与良知搏斗。

Language in the play 剧中语言

Dramatic punctuation (whole class)

You will need a large space for this activity, such as a hall, drama studio, or cleared classroom. All class members should hold a copy of Richard's soliloquy in lines 180–209.

a Everyone walks around the room while reading the first few lines of the script in unison. At every punctuation mark, change direction (don't change direction at speech marks or apostrophes [撇号]).

b Now, try the whole speech – but this time it's a race to see who can perform the speech fastest, making sure everyone continues to turn at each punctuation mark. As you finish, freeze and wait for everyone else to reach the end.

c Discuss the way this speech is punctuated, including sentence length and structure, use of questions and exclamations. How does the punctuation (and repeated use of first person pronoun) help guide an actor playing the part of Richard?

d On your own, write two paragraphs analysing the way this speech is written and what it suggests about Richard's state of mind at this point in the play.

1 **afflict** 折磨
2 **The lights burn blue** 烛光幽蓝（被认为是鬼魂出现的标志）
3 **not dead midnight** 并非正好子夜
4 **none else by** 身旁并无旁人
5 **several** 各种，不同
6 **all used in each degree** 轻重不一
7 **Throng** 拥向
8 **bar** 审判席
9 **done salutation** 恭迎

Themes 主题分析

'Shadows', dreams and sleep (in pairs)

Earlier in this scene, the ghost of Anne takes delight in disturbing Richard's sleep, while wishing dreams of success for Richmond (lines 162–9). Earlier in the play (Act 1 Scene 4), Clarence wakes from a hellish dream and realises he should repent his sins. Here, Richard also wakes from a terrible dream.

a Read from line 180 to line 220 and consider how Richard reacts to his nightmares, firstly during his soliloquy (up to line 209) and secondly in dialogue with Ratcliffe (210–20).

b Read lines 224–34 and summarise how Richmond reacts to his dreams.

c Devise a short presentation for the rest of the class, in which you talk about Richard's dream and the significance of dreams in the play as a whole. Include two or three short quotations from both Richard's and Richmond's speeches.

Richard starts out of his dream

RICHARD Give me another horse! Bind up my wounds! 180
Have mercy, Jesu! Soft, I did but dream.
O coward conscience, how dost thou afflict[1] me?
The lights burn blue[2]. It is not dead midnight[3].
Cold, fearful drops stand on my trembling flesh.
What? Do I fear myself? There's none else by[4]. 185
Richard loves Richard, that is, I am I.
Is there a murderer here? No. Yes, I am.
Then fly. What, from myself? Great reason why:
Lest I revenge. What, myself upon myself?
Alack, I love myself. Wherefore? For any good 190
That I myself have done unto myself?
Oh, no. Alas, I rather hate myself
For hateful deeds committed by myself.
I am a villain. Yet I lie, I am not.
Fool, of thyself speak well. Fool, do not flatter. 195
My conscience hath a thousand several[5] tongues,
And every tongue brings in a several tale,
And every tale condemns me for a villain.
Perjury in the highest degree,
Murder, stern murder, in the direst degree, 200
All several sins, all used in each degree[6],
Throng[7] all to th'bar[8], crying all 'Guilty, guilty!'
I shall despair. There is no creature loves me,
And if I die no soul shall pity me.
Nay, wherefore should they, since that I myself 205
Find in myself no pity to myself?
Methought the souls of all that I had murdered
Came to my tent, and every one did threat
Tomorrow's vengeance on the head of Richard.

Enter RATCLIFFE

RATCLIFFE My lord. 210
RICHARD Who's there?
RATCLIFFE Ratcliffe, my lord, 'tis I. The early village cock
Hath twice done salutation[9] to the morn.
Your friends are up and buckle on their armour.
RICHARD O Ratcliffe, I fear, I fear. 215

Richard plans to eavesdrop on his troops to discover deserters. Richmond tells of his happiness about his dream and its message of victory. He tells his army that God and right are on their side.

 剧情简介：理查打算偷听士兵的谈话，查处逃兵。瑞奇蒙讲述他做的好梦和梦中胜利的讯息。他告诉自己的部下上帝和正义与他们同在。

1 Motivating the troops (in pairs)

Richmond motivates his soldiers through a formal address ('oration') before the battle (Richard also speaks an oration to his troops later). In pairs, practise reading the speech in lines 238–71 in a manner that will instil confidence in those who hear it. Use the following outline of the speech to help you decide what tone and manner to use for each section:

- **Lines 238–40** He regrets he has little time for his speech.
- **Lines 240–3** He assures the soldiers that God is on their side and that they fight for a just cause.
- **Lines 244–53** He claims that all Richard's followers want Richmond to win because they know Richard is a usurper and not the true King.
- **Lines 254–63** He again reminds his soldiers that God is on their side, and he lists the advantages for the future that will be gained by fighting now.
- **Lines 264–71** If he succeeds, the soldiers will all share his victory; they should go cheerfully into battle for the sake of God, their country, Richmond and victory.

1 shadows 幻影
2 apostle Paul 圣保罗
3 Armèd in proof 身披坚甲
4 shallow 浅薄
5 shrink from 从……退缩
6 ta'en a tardy sluggard 抓住一个睡懒觉的人
7 fairest-boding 最好的征兆
8 cried on 欢呼
9 leisure ... time 时间的闲暇和限制（指时间紧迫）
10 high-reared bulwarks 高耸的城垛（一般用来抵御进攻）
11 except 除外
12 raised in blood 靠屠杀起家
13 made means 使用阴谋

Write about it 写作练习

A soldier's letter home

It is customary for soldiers to write letters to their loved ones on the eve of battle, in case they never return. Imagine you are a soldier in Richmond's army. You have just listened to his speech and now have just enough time to write your letter home. You might like to use the following prompts to help you shape your letter, but feel free to develop ideas of your own:

- What is your impression of Richmond as a leader – do you feel confident with him in charge?
- Were you impressed by his speech to the troops? What kind of things did he say?
- What is the mood of the troops around you?
- Why did you join up to fight against the King? Do you still believe it was the right thing to do?
- End by sending loving messages to your family.

King Richard III Act 5 Scene 3
理查三世

RATCLIFFE Nay, good my lord, be not afraid of shadows¹.
RICHARD By the apostle Paul², shadows tonight
Have struck more terror to the soul of Richard
Than can the substance of ten thousand soldiers
Armèd in proof³ and led by shallow⁴ Richmond. 220
'Tis not yet near day. Come, go with me.
Under our tents I'll play the eavesdropper,
To hear if any mean to shrink from⁵ me.
Exeunt Richard and Ratcliffe

Enter the LORDS *to Richmond sitting in his tent*

LORDS Good morrow, Richmond.
RICHMOND Cry mercy, lords and watchful gentlemen, 225
That you have ta'en a tardy sluggard⁶ here.
LORD How have you slept, my lord?
RICHMOND The sweetest sleep and fairest-boding⁷ dreams
That ever entered in a drowsy head
Have I since your departure had, my lords. 230
Methought their souls whose bodies Richard murdered
Came to my tent and cried on⁸ victory.
I promise you, my heart is very jocund
In the remembrance of so fair a dream.
How far into the morning is it, lords? 235
LORD Upon the stroke of four.
RICHMOND Why, then 'tis time to arm and give direction.
His oration to his soldiers
More than I have said, loving countrymen,
The leisure and enforcement of the time⁹
Forbids to dwell upon. Yet remember this: 240
God and our good cause fight upon our side.
The prayers of holy saints and wrongèd souls,
Like high-reared bulwarks¹⁰, stand before our faces.
Richard except¹¹, those whom we fight against
Had rather have us win than him they follow. 245
For what is he they follow? Truly, gentlemen,
A bloody tyrant, and a homicide;
One raised in blood¹², and one in blood established;
One that made means¹³ to come by what he hath,
And slaughtered those that were the means to help him; 250

Richmond tells his troops that Richard is a usurper and an enemy to God. He lists the advantages they will gain from fighting Richard. Richard sees disaster ahead for somebody.

剧情简介：瑞奇蒙对部下说理查乃篡位之人，是上帝的敌人。他罗列了战胜理查后的好处。理查预见了某人的灾难。

Write about it 写作练习

Motivational speech

Imagine you manage a sports team, or you have organised a big charity event. You need to make a key motivational speech before the event opens or the match begins. You want to make people feel confident, believe that the event is important and that it will be a great success – and to assure them that the hard work will be worthwhile.

- Write the speech (it should last no more than two minutes when read aloud). Make it as inspirational as possible.
- Summarise the speech on cards, and practise performing it so that you are confident enough to make eye contact with your audience as you speak.
- Listen to each other's speeches, then discuss what features help to make a motivational speech really effective. Relate your conclusions to Richmond's speech in the play. What specific persuasive and motivational elements can you find in his speech.

1 **stone** 宝石
2 **foil / Of England's chair** 王位的衬托
3 **ward** 保护
4 **Your country's fat** 您的国家（英格兰）的财富
5 **hire** 补偿
6 **quits** 回报
7 **age** 年老
8 **ransom** 兵败的赎金
9 **Tell the clock** 数一数钟敲了几下
10 **calendar** 历书（当时的历书跟中国的传统皇历一样，含有多种关于天象和凶吉征兆的描述）
11 **by the book** 历书上说
12 **braved** 照亮

▼ Richmond is often portrayed as the bright young hero saving England from Richard's dark oppression. Discuss the way Richmond is presented in this production photograph. How would you describe him in this picture? Could there be another way of presenting Richmond? How do you imagine him? Find the lines in the script that have shaped your views.

King Richard III Act 5 Scene 3
理查三世

A base, foul stone[1] made precious by the foil
Of England's chair[2], where he is falsely set;
One that hath ever been God's enemy.
Then if you fight against God's enemy,
God will in justice ward[3] you as his soldiers; 255
If you do swear to put a tyrant down,
You sleep in peace, the tyrant being slain;
If you do fight against your country's foes,
Your country's fat[4] shall pay your pains the hire[5];
If you do fight in safeguard of your wives, 260
Your wives shall welcome home the conquerors;
If you do free your children from the sword,
Your children's children quits[6] it in your age[7].
Then in the name of God and all these rights,
Advance your standards, draw your willing swords. 265
For me, the ransom[8] of my bold attempt
Shall be this cold corpse on the earth's cold face.
But if I thrive, the gain of my attempt
The least of you shall share his part thereof.
Sound drums and trumpets boldly and cheerfully. 270
God and Saint George, Richmond and victory!

Enter RICHARD, RATCLIFFE, *and* CATESBY

RICHARD	What said Northumberland as touching Richmond?
RATCLIFFE	That he was never trainèd up in arms.
RICHARD	He said the truth. And what said Surrey then?
RATCLIFFE	He smiled and said 'The better for our purpose'. 275
RICHARD	He was in the right, and so indeed it is. Tell the clock[9] there.

Clock strikes

Give me a calendar[10]. Who saw the sun today?

RATCLIFFE	Not I, my lord.
RICHARD	Then he disdains to shine, for by the book[11] 280 He should have braved[12] the east an hour ago. A black day will it be to somebody. Ratcliffe!
RATCLIFFE	My lord.

Richard tries to calm his misgivings about the lack of sun. He sets out his battle plan and dismisses a mocking verse. His address to his troops begins by insulting Richmond's followers.

剧情简介：理查努力打消自己对阴郁天气的不满。他部署自己的作战计划，并对一首讽刺诗不屑一顾。他激励部下，开场便羞辱瑞奇蒙的追随者。

Characters 人物分析
Richard's changing mood (in pairs)

Read the script from line 272 to line 343. This activity will help you analyse Richard's changing mood.

a Find lines in the script that suggest the following:
- Richard is concerned about traitors and deserters.
- Richard takes notice of good or bad omens.
- Richard is an experienced general and is happiest when he is busy issuing commands.
- Richard is a confident tactician (战术家).
- Richard is back to his old swaggering self.
- Richard cynically claims that only cowards have a conscience.
- Richard believes that his troops are better fighters than Richmond's.

b For each statement above, write a sentence explaining whether you think this is a fair comment about Richard. Provide a short quotation from the script as evidence to support each of your points.

c Sum up what you think about Richard's state of mind at this point in the play. Has he completely recovered from his nightmares or not?

Write about it 写作练习
Richard's diary

Write Richard's diary entry for the day of the battle, just before the fighting starts. What are his hopes and fears? You might like to mention:
- his dreams and how he feels about them
- his concern about disloyalty in his ranks
- his superstitious belief in omens (for example, the lack of sun, his consultation of a calendar)
- what he thinks about Richmond as a military man
- what he thinks about Richmond's troops (see Richard's speech in lines 316–39).

1 from 从……消失
2 vaunts 大摇大摆，趾高气扬
3 bustle 赶快
4 Caparison 披挂
5 foreward 先锋
6 drawn 拉开
7 horse and foot 骑兵和步兵
8 main battle 主力部队
9 puissance 人马
10 well-wingèd with 由……在两翼提供良好支援
11 chiefest horse 精锐骑兵
12 This … boot! 这样，再加上圣乔治的护佑！（英格兰以圣乔治作为本国的守护神）
13 direction 作战计划
14 Jockey (John的昵称)
15 Dickon (对理查的蔑称)
16 bought and sold 完蛋
17 Join 参战
18 pell mell 奋力厮杀
19 inferred 说过
20 cope withal 与……作战
21 A sort of 一帮子
22 lackey 狗腿子

220

RICHARD	The sun will not be seen today;	
	The sky doth frown and lour upon our army.	285
	I would these dewy tears were from¹ the ground.	
	Not shine today? Why, what is that to me	
	More than to Richmond? For the self-same heaven	
	That frowns on me looks sadly upon him.	

Enter NORFOLK

NORFOLK	Arm, arm, my lord! The foe vaunts² in the field!	290
RICHARD	Come, bustle³, bustle. Caparison⁴ my horse.	
	Call up Lord Stanley; bid him bring his power.	
	I will lead forth my soldiers to the plain,	
	And thus my battle shall be orderèd:	
	My foreward⁵ shall be drawn⁶ in length,	295
	Consisting equally of horse and foot⁷;	
	Our archers shall be placèd in the midst.	
	John Duke of Norfolk, Thomas Earl of Surrey,	
	Shall have the leading of the foot and horse.	
	They thus directed, we will follow	300
	In the main battle⁸, whose puissance⁹ on either side	
	Shall be well-wingèd with¹⁰ our chiefest horse¹¹.	
	This, and Saint George to boot!¹² What think'st thou, Norfolk?	
NORFOLK	A good direction¹³, warlike sovereign.	
	This found I on my tent this morning:	305
	'Jockey¹⁴ of Norfolk, be not so bold,	
	For Dickon¹⁵ thy master is bought and sold¹⁶.'	
RICHARD	A thing devisèd by the enemy.	
	Go, gentlemen, every man to his charge.	
	Let not our babbling dreams affright our souls,	310
	For conscience is a word that cowards use,	
	Devised at first to keep the strong in awe.	
	Our strong arms be our conscience, swords our law!	
	March on! Join¹⁷ bravely! Let us to't pell mell¹⁸,	
	If not to heaven, then hand in hand to hell.	315

[*His oration to his army*]

What shall I say more than I have inferred¹⁹?
Remember whom you are to cope withal²⁰:
A sort of²¹ vagabonds, rascals, and runaways,
A scum of Bretons and base lackey²² peasants,

Richard calls Richmond's followers beggars and rapists. He mocks Richmond as a spoilt weakling and reminds his soldiers of past victories over the French. Hearing of Stanley's refusal to join him, Richard orders Stanley's son's death.

剧情简介：理查称瑞奇蒙的追随者为乞丐、强奸犯，讥笑瑞奇蒙是一个被宠坏的懦夫，提醒自己的士兵曾经击败过法国。得知斯坦雷不愿入伙后，理查下令杀掉他的儿子。

1 Richard spurs on his troops (in threes)

In a stirring oration (lines 316–43), Richard attempts to galvanise (激励) his troops into action.

a Read Richard's speech, then pick out all the words or phrases he uses to describe Richmond's army. Discuss what he is trying to suggest by these descriptions. You might find it helpful to copy out and complete the table below.

Lines	Richard's description of the enemy	What he means
318	vagabonds, rascals and runaways; famished beggars	They are all beggars and thieves
331		
319	scum (人渣), lackey peasants	The lowest of the low
319	Bretons	They are not even English
	their o'ercloyèd country vomits forth	
	led by a 'milksop'	
	rats	

b Create a tableau that represents Richard's view of Richmond's army. Remember, a tableau does not have to be realistic – it should be suggestive of some of the images Richard uses. Make sure everyone in your group is involved.

c Share your tableau with others in the class and talk about how successful Richard is in making the enemy seem less of a threat.

d Re-read Richmond's oration and compare it with Richard's. Add some more information to your table, charting the differences between the two men (see p. 202).

---

1 o'ercloyèd 撑得要吐
2 restrain 抢夺
3 distain 污辱
4 paltry 一文不值；微不足道
5 our mother's 我们祖国的
6 milksop 窝囊废
7 overweening 不知天高地厚
8 fond exploit 愚蠢的入侵
9 means 吃穿用度
10 bobbed 猛揍
11 on recòrd 正如史籍所录
12 yeomen 自耕农（比绅士低一等级）
13 welkin 天

Whom their o'ercloyèd¹ country vomits forth 320
To desperate adventures and assured destruction.
You sleeping safe, they bring you to unrest;
You having lands, and blest with beauteous wives,
They would restrain² the one, distain³ the other.
And who doth lead them but a paltry⁴ fellow, 325
Long kept in Bretagne at our mother's⁵ cost?
A milksop⁶, one that never in his life
Felt so much cold as over shoes in snow.
Let's whip these stragglers o'er the seas again;
Lash hence these overweening⁷ rags of France, 330
These famished beggars, weary of their lives,
Who, but for dreaming on this fond exploit⁸,
For want of means⁹, poor rats, had hanged themselves.
If we be conquered, let men conquer us,
And not these bastard Bretons, whom our fathers 335
Have in their own land beaten, bobbed¹⁰, and thumped,
And on recòrd¹¹ left them the heirs of shame.
Shall these enjoy our lands, lie with our wives?
Ravish our daughters?

(*Drum afar off*)
            Hark, I hear their drum!
Fight, gentlemen of England! Fight boldly, yeomen¹²! 340
Draw, archers, draw your arrows to the head!
Spur your proud horses hard and ride in blood;
Amaze the welkin¹³ with your broken staves!

Enter a MESSENGER

What says Lord Stanley? Will he bring his power?

MESSENGER My lord, he doth deny to come. 345
RICHARD Off with his son George's head!
NORFOLK My lord, the enemy is past the marsh;
After the battle let George Stanley die.
RICHARD A thousand hearts are great within my bosom.
Advance our standards! Set upon our foes! 350
Our ancient word of courage, fair Saint George,
Inspire us with the spleen of fiery dragons!
Upon them! Victory sits on our helms!

[*Exeunt*]

Richard has fought bravely. His horse has been killed but he searches for Richmond, intending to slay him. Richmond kills Richard. Stanley presents Richmond with the crown, which he has taken from Richard.

剧情简介： 理查作战英勇。他的马死了，可他还是在搜寻瑞奇蒙并要杀死他。瑞奇蒙杀了理查。斯坦雷将王冠从理查头上拿下，献给瑞奇蒙。

1 'my kingdom for a horse!' (in pairs)

The actor Anthony Sher, who played Richard III, once remarked that 'A horse, a horse, my kingdom for a horse!' is one of the most famous of all Shakespeare's lines. How can an actor make it sound fresh and new? Take parts as Richard and Catesby and read Scene 4. Explore ways of speaking Richard's lines to find the most dramatically effective delivery. For example, is Richard:

- bullish, overly confident and deluding (欺骗) himself
- terrified and panicking
- full of despair
- resigned to his fate
- noble, dignified?

1 *Excursions* 战斗
2 Daring an opposite 挑战对手
3 Slave 奴才
4 cast 孤注一掷
5 stand … die 死也在所不惜
6 well hast thou acquit thee 你干得漂亮
7 usurpèd royalties 被篡夺的王冠

Stagecraft 导演技巧

Richard's death (in small groups)

In some stage productions, Richard and Richmond perform a choreographed (精心设计的) fight in heavy medieval armour. In the 1997 film version, Ian McKellen plays Richard in a jeep like a World War II general. Eventually, he greets death with a sardonic (轻蔑) smile. Al Pacino (*Looking for Richard*, 1996) portrays him in medieval costume with arrows in his chest and back, killed by Richmond's longsword.

a The stage direction calls for '*Excursions*', or battles. Would you have some fighting on stage, or simply use sound effects to suggest the battle is happening off stage? Why?

b Work out how you would stage Richard's death. Turn back to the picture on page xii (right) in the photo gallery, showing how one stage production portrayed Richard's death. Then work out your own imaginative staging of that moment.

c Create a series of three tableaux capturing the moment of Richard's death. As a class, select one group's tableau and ask them to extend the final frame. One person in the role of Stanley mimes removing the crown from dead Richard's head and ceremonially presents it to Richmond. Read Stanley's lines 3–7. As a class, discuss the dramatic effect you would want to achieve here.

Act 5 Scene 4
Bosworth: the battlefield

Alarum. Excursions[1]. Enter CATESBY

CATESBY   Rescue, my lord of Norfolk, rescue, rescue!
           The king enacts more wonders than a man,
           Daring an opposite[2] to every danger.
           His horse is slain, and all on foot he fights,
           Seeking for Richmond in the throat of death.   5
           Rescue, fair lord, or else the day is lost.

Alarums. Enter RICHARD

RICHARD   A horse, a horse, my kingdom for a horse!
CATESBY   Withdraw, my lord; I'll help you to a horse.
RICHARD   Slave[3], I have set my life upon a cast[4],
           And I will stand the hazard of the die[5].   10
           I think there be six Richmonds in the field;
           Five have I slain today instead of him.
           A horse, a horse, my kingdom for a horse!

[*Exeunt*]

Act 5 Scene 5
Bosworth: the battlefield

Alarum. Enter RICHARD *and* RICHMOND. *They fight.*
Richard is slain. A trumpet sounds retreat. Enter STANLEY EARL
OF DERBY *bearing the crown, with several other lords*

RICHMOND   God and your arms be praised, victorious friends!
           The day is ours; the bloody dog is dead.
STANLEY   Courageous Richmond, well hast thou acquit thee[6].
           Lo, here these long usurpèd royalties[7]
           From the dead temples of this bloody wretch   5
           Have I plucked off to grace thy brows withal.
           Wear it and make much of it.

Richmond learns that George Stanley is safe but that four noblemen have died. He declares the civil war at an end, and that his marriage to Elizabeth will unite the houses of York and Lancaster.

剧情简介：瑞奇蒙获悉乔治·斯坦雷没有死，但四位贵族已经战死。他宣布内战结束，他与伊丽莎白的婚姻也将团结约克与兰开斯特两大家族。

1 A new beginning

Richmond's crowning is highly significant historically, as it marks the end of the Wars of the Roses and the beginning of Tudor rule. His actions and language are intended to bring peace after bloody civil war.

a By marrying Elizabeth, Richmond will unite the houses of York and Lancaster. Use the family tree on page 266 to discover just how the 'white rose and the red' are now united. Design a new emblem that could be used to mark the unification of the white and red rose.

b One commentator suggests that Richmond's closing speech refers to 'all things an Elizabethan cared about', in that it upholds the 'Tudor myth' (see pp. 236–7). Pick out three aspects of Richmond's speech that you think support this view.

Stagecraft 导演技巧

The final image (in small groups)

The final 'stage picture' can underline the director's overall approach and interpretation of the main themes. For example, a director might want to end the play on an optimistic note, suggesting that England's troubles are now over and a good King is in place. Or a director might want to raise doubts about the ambitious Richmond, emphasising the fact that he, too, has gained the throne by use of bloody force.

a What final image would the audience see at the end of your production of *King Richard III*? Firstly, create a freeze-frame of Richmond's final words, 'God say amen'. Consider who is on stage and where they are standing. Think about body language and facial expressions.

b What do you plan to do with the dead Richard? Is his corpse on stage right to the end? If so, where and why? For example, does he have prominence in the scene or is he already an irrelevance?

c Consider what lighting and sound or music you might use as Richmond finishes his speech. What tone or mood do you want to create – and why? How do characters leave the stage?

d Show your freeze-frames to the rest of the class and explain your ideas, trying to relate them to your overall understanding of the play.

1	men of name	有名望的人物
2	Inter	埋葬
3	in submission	败仗投降
4	ta'en the sacrament	发誓言
5	Smile heaven	愿上天微笑
6	conjunction	结合
7	enmity	仇恨
8	sire	父亲
9	fair ordinance	令人愉快的旨意
10	conjoin	联姻
11	smooth-faced	无忧无虑
12	Abate the edge	毁了刀刃
13	reduce	重回
14	increase	丰收
15	civil wounds	内战的创伤
16	are stopped	已经结痂

RICHMOND	Great God of heaven, say amen to all.	
	But tell me, is young George Stanley living?	
STANLEY	He is, my lord, and safe in Leicester town,	10
	Whither, if you please, we may withdraw us.	
RICHMOND	What men of name[1] are slain on either side?	
STANLEY	John Duke of Norfolk, Walter Lord Ferris,	
	Sir Robert Brakenbury, and Sir William Brandon.	
RICHMOND	Inter[2] their bodies as become their births.	15

Proclaim a pardon to the soldiers fled
That in submission[3] will return to us,
And then, as we have ta'en the sacrament[4],
We will unite the white rose and the red.
Smile heaven[5] upon this fair conjunction[6], 20
That long have frowned upon their enmity[7].
What traitor hears me and says not amen?
England hath long been mad, and scarred herself;
The brother blindly shed the brother's blood;
The father rashly slaughtered his own son; 25
The son, compelled, been butcher to the sire[8];
All this divided York and Lancaster,
Divided in their dire division.
Oh, now let Richmond and Elizabeth,
The true succeeders of each royal house, 30
By God's fair ordinance[9] conjoin[10] together.
And let thy heirs, God, if thy will be so,
Enrich the time to come with smooth-faced[11] peace,
With smiling plenty and fair prosperous days.
Abate the edge[12] of traitors, gracious Lord, 35
That would reduce[13] these bloody days again
And make poor England weep in streams of blood.
Let them not live to taste this land's increase[14]
That would with treason wound this fair land's peace.
Now civil wounds[15] are stopped[16]; peace lives again. 40
That she may long live here, God say amen.

Exeunt

FINIS.

King Richard III
理查三世

Looking back at the play 本剧回顾
Activities for groups or individuals

1 Headlines

Split into five groups. Each group is assigned a different act. Your challenge is to tell the story of each act in four or five headlines that could be used on the main evening television news. For example, the group assigned Act 1 might begin with the following two headlines:

'The Royal Family is in turmoil today as the Duke of Clarence is arrested on the grounds of possible treason.'

'And today's long-term weather forecast is for glorious summer…'

Present your headlines in the style of your favourite newsreader. Share the headlines in the order of the five acts. After each presentation, other groups could suggest a 'missing' headline – what they would have included if they had been working on your act.

2 The case against Hastings and Buckingham

Imagine that Hastings and Buckingham are brought to public trial, accused of treason against Richard. The King would not appear in court in person to give evidence, but he might submit a written statement in which he gives details of the men's crimes. Write Richard's two statements. Consider how he might describe certain events in such a way as to hide his own complicity in some of their crimes.

3 Changing fortunes

a Characters' fortunes (status, happiness and so on) rise and fall frequently in the play. Chart the fluctuating fortunes of Hastings, Buckingham and Anne in graph form, accompanied by quotations to illustrate their changing circumstances.

b Do you see Richard as a tragic hero figure (as suggested by the picture opposite, for example)? Or more as a comic rogue (as suggested in the picture on p. 197)?

4 Tragedy, history or comedy?

The title of the play is sometimes printed as *The Tragedy of Richard III*. Some critics view this play as a tragedy, others as a history play – some even see it as a comedy.

a Use the Internet to find out what the literary definition is of 'tragedy', 'comedy' and 'history play'.

b Suggest three or four reasons that could support each view of the play and use the table below to record your ideas. Look at various photographs in this edition to help you form ideas about what kind of play this is.

	Reason 1	Reason 2	Reason 3
Tragedy	Richard, the main character, dies at the end		
Comedy			
History			

c Give your own view about the genre of the play and suggest what aspects (for example, what episodes or what feature of Richard's character) you would need to emphasise in order to support that interpretation of the play in performance. Share these ideas with others in your class.

King Richard III 理查三世

Perspectives and themes 视角与主题

What is the play about?

The obvious answer to this question might seem to be that this is a play about the rise and fall of a man who will stop at nothing to gain power. However, since the play was first performed, a number of different interpretations have been proposed – and there is no 'correct' way of thinking about any work of literature. How you personally read or interpret *King Richard III* may depend upon your own values and beliefs, the society in which you live, or even the way you have been taught to think about Shakespeare at school. For example, references to sin and redemption abound in the play, but how you understand and respond to these ideas will be shaped by your own religious faith (or lack of it). It is unlikely that many people watching a modern performance of this play believe in the divine right of kings (that a monarch is God's representative on Earth), but in Shakespeare's day, almost everyone held that belief.

This section investigates some of the different ways of thinking about *King Richard III*.

Themes

Themes are important ideas or concepts that recur throughout the play and help link all the different elements into a coherent whole. Themes may be developed both verbally and/or visually. For example, the boar image repeatedly linked to Richard contributes to our understanding of the savage nature of his power. This image recurs in the language and is often visually represented on stage. Themes can emerge through imagery, characters and events, adding texture and complexity to the play, with the result that *King Richard III* becomes much more than 'just' a story about a man who murders his way to the throne.

Main themes of *King Richard III* include:
- the pursuit of power
- appearance and reality
- attitudes to women
- sin and salvation
- Church versus state
- nemesis (报应), fate and free will
- dreams and the supernatural
- words as weapons.

◆ In small groups, choose one of the themes listed above. Look through the play and locate an example of the following that illustrates your chosen theme and its importance to the play:
- an event
- a character and a character's action
- an image or other quotation from the script.

Record your ideas on large sheets of paper, add visual images (for example, search the Internet for production photographs) and then share your presentation with other groups. Display the sheets on your classroom wall.

The pursuit of power

The play could be seen as a study in the harsh realities of power politics: what life is like under a brutal King ruling a deeply corrupt state. Richard exploits the historical divisions caused by feuding political factions, manipulates individuals and the system, seizing the opportunity to make himself King. He is a Machiavellian (马基雅弗利主义的；不择手段) figure – a cynical politician who uses any method to gain and maintain power, even to the point of eliminating friends and allies. Richard's antithesis is Richmond (Henry VII), a monarch apparently divinely appointed by God whose reign promises lasting peace and stability. Because Henry VII's reign marked the beginning of the Tudor dynasty, Shakespeare is likely to have been flattering Queen Elizabeth I, Henry's granddaughter.

Some commentators see in Richard parallels with political figures in more recent times, whose huge ambition has led them to use ruthless means to achieve their goal. From this viewpoint, Richmond could be seen, for all his talk of peace and unity, as yet another politically ambitious figure, staging a coup to gain control of a profoundly unjust state.

In small groups, compose a series of three or four tableaux to illustrate your understanding of the contrasting types of power held by:

- Richard
- Richmond
- Queen Elizabeth.

Think about the nature (physical or not), the extent (individual or collective, personal or political) and the effect (harmful or protective) of the power held by each character.

◆ Discuss key differences between your tableaux, making direct reference to specific characters and events in the play to support your ideas. Find a key quotation from the script to use as an appropriate caption for each tableau.

apparent intention in saying or doing these things, and the effects of their deception. Consider the following lines as a starting point:

- Elizabeth: Act 4 Scene 4, lines 197–436
- Stanley: Act 3 Scene 2, lines 17–18; Act 4 Scene 4, lines 463–505; Act 4 Scene 5
- Bishop of Ely (Morton): Act 3 Scene 4, lines 1–78; Act 4 Scene 3, lines 45–57.

◆ Write at least three paragraphs outlining the ways in which these three characters contribute to the theme of appearance and reality in the play. Include embedded quotations in your writing.

Appearance and reality

Richard is an arch-deceiver. His skills as actor and manipulator enable him to use false words and appearances to fool other characters. His enthusiasm for sharing these skills with an audience – while other characters are on stage and unaware of what is happening – provides much of the play's entertainment. However, Richard is not the only character who hides true feelings beneath an outward show. Other figures, including Stanley, Queen Elizabeth and the Bishop of Ely, all successfully hide their true motives from Richard. Acting is a recurring motif in the play, creating a double layer of deceit, as real actors portray characters who are dishonestly performing a role.

◆ Compile notes on the way in which Elizabeth, Stanley and the Bishop of Ely (a female character, a member of the nobility close to Richard, and a representative of the Church) all consciously set out to deceive others. Note down in three columns their deceptive words or actions, their

King Richard III
理查三世

Attitudes to women

Richard introduces this theme in Act 1 Scene 1, by referring to women as a source of trouble for men, as if possessing a malevolent power: 'Why, this it is when men are ruled by women' (line 62). The position of women in the play has been vigorously debated by critics over the past fifty years. Are women merely powerless victims (for example, grieving mothers and widows) or do they provide emotional strength in the play, in direct contrast to Richard and his male followers?

The diagram opposite suggests a number of roles that women fulfil in the play. Below it and on the page opposite are a number of quotations from the play that refer to, or are spoken by, women. Look at the diagram and the quotations and then carry out the activities below.

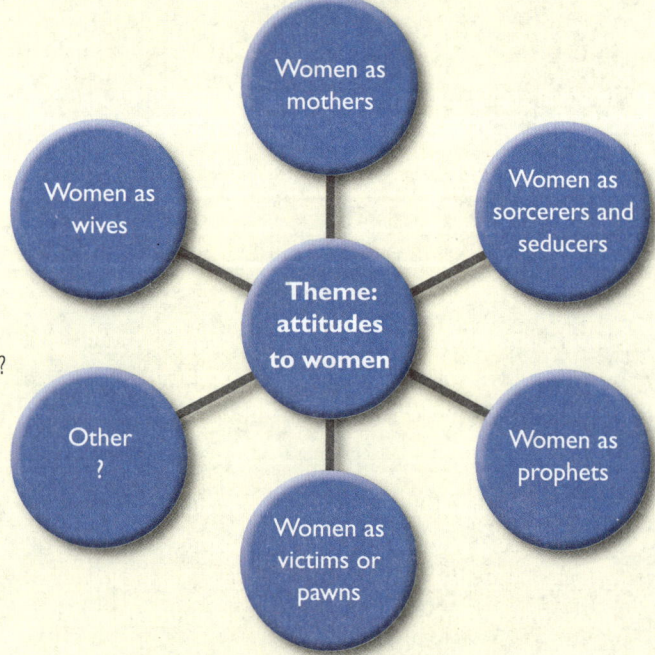

- Identify who says each quotation and when. Find some other quotations to add to this list.

- Match the quotations to the different female roles. Some might fit in more than one category. One circle has been left blank in case you feel that another role needs to be included.

- Take each category one by one, and discuss what aspects of that specific role or 'type' seem to be proposed in the play. For example, motherhood is not presented as a straightforward concept: mothers love and grieve for their children; equally, a mother may wish a child dead. Investigate each category, locate conflicting views and suggest where one category overlaps with another.

- In groups, select one category of womanhood and create a movement piece that encapsulates (概括) the various aspects you have discussed. The only words you speak must be the relevant quotations. Make sure all group members are involved, both in speaking and moving.

Why, this it is when men are ruled by women.
'Tis not the king that sends you to the Tower.
My lady Grey, his wife ... 'tis she
That tempts him to this harsh extremity.

Then be your eyes the witness of their evil.
Look how I am bewitched. Behold, mine arm
Is like a blasted sapling, withered up.
And this is Edward's wife, that monstrous witch,
Consorted with that harlot, strumpet Shore

... Oh, let her live,
And I'll corrupt her manners, stain her beauty,
Slander myself as false to Edward's bed

The jealous, o'er-worn widow

Naught to do with Mistress Shore?

ANNE   Oh, wonderful, when devils tell the truth!
RICHARD   More wonderful, when angels are so angry.

O my accursèd womb, the bed of death.
A cockatrice hast thou hatched to the world

Perspectives and themes

Ah, my poor princes! Ah, my tender babes!
My unblown flowers, new-appearing sweets!
… hear your mother's lamentation.

Oh, would to God that the inclusive verge
Of golden metal that must round my brow
Were red-hot steel, to sear me to the brains.
Anointed let me be with deadly venom
And die ere men can say 'God save the queen.'

Thou protector of this damnèd strumpet,
… Thou art a traitor.

Relenting fool and shallow, changing woman.

RICHARD   Who intercepts me in my expedition?
DUCHESS   Oh, she that might have intercepted thee,
                 By strangling thee in her accursèd womb

For then I'll marry Warwick's youngest daughter.
What though I killed her husband and her father?

To hear the lamentations of poor Anne,
Wife to thy Edward, to thy slaughtered son,
Stabbed by the selfsame hand that made these wounds.
Lo, in these windows that led forth thy life,
I pour the helpless balm of my poor eyes.

Play the maid's part: still answer nay and take it.

A care-crazed mother to a many sons,
A beauty-waning and distressèd widow,
Even in the afternoon of her best days,
Made prize and purchase of his wanton eye,
Seduced the pitch and height of his degree
To base declension and loathed bigamy.

Bear with me, I am hungry for revenge

From forth the kennel of thy womb hath crept
A hell-hound that doth hunt us all to death

Oh, now let Richmond and Elizabeth,
The true succeeders of each royal house,
By God's fair ordinance conjoin together.

If ancient sorrow be most reverend,
Give mine the benefit of seniory,
And let my griefs frown on the upper hand

Earth gapes, hell burns, fiends roar, saints pray,
To have him suddenly conveyed from hence.
Cancel his bond of life, dear God, I pray,
That I may live and say the dog is dead.

      … the queen hath heartily consented
He should espouse Elizabeth her daughter.

King Richard III
理查三世

Sin and salvation

Elizabethans believed that the soul lives on after death and may be rewarded or punished by God. All hope of salvation depended on the individual's spiritual state at the moment of death. If sins were confessed and then forgiven by a priest (shriven), or the sacrament of bread and wine celebrated, then the person died in a state of grace and the soul enjoyed an eternity of peace in heaven. Dying with sins unconfessed and unforgiven damned the soul to everlasting suffering in hell. Those who had not fully confessed before dying went to Purgatory (炼狱), where they suffered until the unconfessed minor sins were burnt away (purged) by remorse.

Characters in the play are constantly reminded of their past sins. Richard recalls Margaret's cruel acts against his family (Act 1 Scene 3). Margaret's curses and prophecies remind the feuding nobles of their past crimes (Act 1 Scene 3). United in suffering, Queen Elizabeth, the Duchess of York and Queen Margaret lament wrongs committed against them (Act 4 Scene 4). Reminded of past sins and fearing everlasting damnation, characters attempt last-minute salvation for their terrible deeds. Clarence, Grey and Rivers, Hastings and Buckingham all refer to the importance of prayer, confession of sins and divine forgiveness before they die.

◆ Look back at the last (or almost last) words of Clarence (Act 1 Scene 4, lines 170–257), Buckingham (Act 5 Scene 1) and Richard (Act 5 Scene 3, lines 180–209). In pairs, discuss which lines or phrases offer the most striking glimpse of that character's vision of what awaits him. Select four or five of these lines and create a dramatic presentation in which you are only able to use those words (although some can be repeated).

◆ Consider how these final words work in the context of the play's themes and characters. For example, does the acknowledgement of sin help us (as readers or viewers) to sympathise with certain characters? Does it give the play a moral centre (reassuring the audience that sinful people will ultimately be punished)? In your opinion, which characters are most likely to gain salvation? Compile some notes based on your ideas, quoting some of the words or phrases used in the drama activity as evidence.

◆ Draw up an essay plan in response to the following essay question: How important is the theme of sin and salvation in *King Richard III*? If you are studying the play for an examination or other form of formal assessment, remind yourself of the assessment criteria before you start. Share your essay plans with other students in your class and discuss key differences.

Church versus state

The play exposes the tension between Church and state. The belief in the 'divine right of kings' held that the monarch was God's representative on Earth. As such, a crime against the King was a crime against God. The crown, orb (王权宝球) and sceptre and anointing with holy oil at the monarch's coronation symbolised the bond between the secular and the spiritual.

The play constantly reminds the audience of the power and powerlessness of Church against state when the King is evil. Richard's hellish origins ('cacodemon', 'hellhound') contrast with references to heaven, angels and saints that resonate throughout the play. In addition to the named archbishops, bishops and priests who are present in crucial scenes, a director has many opportunities to include churchmen in the several processions, executions and crowd scenes.

Priests have to please both God and man. Witnessing a succession of churchmen lending their holy office for Richard's advancement creates episodes rich in irony. The Bishop of Ely, anxious to gather strawberries for his monarch (Act 3 Scene 4), and two churchmen supporting a 'pious' Richard (Act 3 Scene 7) reveal a Church impotent against Richard's power, as well as how Richard manipulates the Church for his own purposes.

Perspectives and themes

The powerlessness of the Church is forcefully realised on stage in Act 3 Scene 1, which examines the right to sanctuary. A person accused of crimes could be protected from civil justice by sheltering in a church. Queen Elizabeth and the young Duke of York seek this sanctuary, but Richard and Buckingham successfully persuade the Church to yield up 'sanctuary children'.

- ◆ Improvise a conversation between the Bishop of Ely and the two bishops who appear on either side of Richard when he is pretending to be reluctant to take the throne (Act 3 Scene 7, lines 94–220). The conversation takes place after Richard has been defeated at the Battle of Bosworth. What do the clerics have to say about their roles in Richard's rise and fall. Could they have behaved differently? How do they defend their various actions?

Nemesis, fate and free will

The play examines political and religious issues, but nemesis and the working of fate are also major themes. Nemesis is retribution (the punishment for wrongdoing), and fate is the power that makes such punishment inevitable. This was the defining pattern of Greek drama, in which the inevitable workings of fate brought suffering and death.

In *King Richard III*, lamentation, cursing, dreams, prophecies and omens – often written in stylised and ritualistic form – express the hatred and desire for retribution that dominates many events in the play. The 'prophetess' Queen Margaret is the 'voice' of nemesis as she remembers past bloody deeds that call out for revenge. She prophesies that vengeance shall fall on the house of York for the wrongs done to the house of Lancaster (Act 1 Scene 3), and each victim remembers Margaret's prophecy at their moment of death.

But if Margaret is the voice or 'chorus', Richard is the agent of nemesis. He has the political power to destroy his enemies. Richard is at the centre of the action as death follows death, but he fails to see that he, too, is part of the pattern and it is inevitable that he too must die.

- ◆ In Richard's opening soliloquy, he says that he is 'determinèd' to be a villain (line 31). This can either mean that Richard is predestined to be a villain, or that he has made up his mind to be one. Prepare a class debate. Is Richard merely behaving according to fate and predestination, or is he a Machiavellian character enacting his free will? Find evidence that supports both readings, then decide which side of the argument you are going to support.

- ◆ Once you have discussed this as a class, consider how a director could suggest either reading on stage. If you wanted to emphasise the role of fate, are there any episodes or characters you would choose to cut? Similarly, if you wanted to present Richard as a man exercising his own free will, are there any episodes or characters you would cut? Write at least five paragraphs outlining your editorial/directorial decisions and explaining the reasons for them.

King Richard III
理查三世

The contexts of *King Richard III*
《理查三世》的创作背景

Shakespeare's sources

One way of thinking about *King Richard III* is to set it in the context of its time. This involves looking at the world that Shakespeare knew and the way history was interpreted to make sense of this world.

Historical accounts of English history were vital sources for Shakespeare as he wrote *King Richard III*. Raphael Holinshed's *The Third Volume of Chronicles* (1587) and Edward Hall's *The Union of the Two Noble and Illustrate Famelies of Lancastre and Yorke* (1548) were particularly important. Shakespeare took these narrative accounts of English history and turned them into compelling drama. *King Richard III* is just one of the many history plays he wrote, and it shows the free use of historical sources that characterises them all. Shakespeare followed in Holinshed's footsteps when he represented Richard III as an evil King, but he goes further in his dramatic portrayal of him as a murderous usurper and tyrannical ruler.

The Tudor myth

Under Henry VII (Richmond – the man who killed Richard and established the Tudor dynasty) and his son Henry VIII, successive historians and writers established the now-traditional view of Richard as an evil, unpopular King. Such writers described him as a usurper (a person who wrongfully seizes power) who murdered Henry VI, the princes in the Tower and his wife Anne. Sir Thomas More's *History of Richard III* (written 1513–18) describes Richard as 'deformed' and evil from birth. Another 'history' claimed that Richard was born with teeth and with hair down to his shoulders. Other histories written during the reign of Henry VIII were responsible for the popular image of Richard as a hunchback.

The Tudor point of view also emphasised their right to rule. It focused on the horrors of civil war and praised the Tudors as the bringers of peace and prosperity to England. Polydore Vergil's *Historia Anglia* (1534) claims that Henry IV's illegal seizure of the crown from Richard II broke the God-given order of the universe. This supposedly resulted in all the disasters that followed: the early death of Henry V, the bloody civil war known as the Wars of the Roses and Richard III's murderous, despotic (暴虐) reign. According to Vergil, England was rescued by Henry Tudor, who was God's instrument on Earth and who brought peace and plenty by uniting the houses of York and Lancaster.

The claims of the new King Henry VII to the throne were insecure and it was essential for Henry to destroy Richard's reputation. Under Elizabeth I, the historians Edward Hall and Raphael Holinshed incorporated the interpretations of More and Vergil so completely into their history books that by the end of the sixteenth century, this negative portrayal of Richard's appearance and actions was almost universally accepted. This version of history was Shakespeare's major resource as he wrote his play.

▼ Portraits of Richard III are believed to have been altered in Tudor times to make him look more sinister and evil.

The contexts of King Richard III

Whatever his own views about Richard, Shakespeare was more interested in creating drama that would grip and thrill his audience. To achieve that dramatic intensity, and to give Richard his magnetic stage personality, he compressed historical events and made many alterations to produce fast-paced action. He invented Richard's wooing of Anne, the imprisonment of Hastings, Clarence's dream and murder. He also included Queen Margaret in the events of the play (even though she died in 1482) and compressed Richmond's invasion (November 1483), Buckingham's execution (August 1485) and the Battle of Bosworth (22 August 1485) into five scenes.

◆ What evidence do we have today that might help us to rewrite history and see Richard III from a different perspective? Research the recent discovery of Richard III's skeleton beneath a car park in Leicester to see what evidence that presents for a different understanding of the last Plantagenet King of England. Below are some points to start with:

- The skeleton was found with significant battle wounds – eight in the head.
- The skeleton had a contorted spine (suggesting a disease called scoliosis [脊柱側彎]).
- The frame of the skeleton indicated a slender build.
- The arms of the skeleton were crossed, which could indicate the wrists were still tied at burial.
- The teeth of the skeleton were ground down (possibly from anxiety or stress) and showed extensive tooth decay.

Shakespeare's inspiration

Layers of interpretive possibilities within the script are also built on past dramatic performances as well as on contemporary accounts of the Wars of the Roses. Shakespeare was influenced by classical dramatists such as Seneca, a first-century Roman much loved by Elizabethan audiences for his use of violence, bloodshed and physical horrors in his plays. Ghosts and the supernatural, omens, prophecies and vivid descriptions of the underworld often appear in Seneca's plays, together with descriptions of bloody deeds committed offstage or in the past.

English dramatic traditions also influenced Shakespeare as he wrote *King Richard III*. The medieval mystery plays were religious dramas that told the story of the Bible from creation to the end of the world. One character from these plays that was imprinted in the popular imagination was Herod – the tyrant king who was brutally violent and responsible for the massacre of innocent children. This character, shouting and stamping across the stage, spoke directly to the audience, telling them what he was going to do and revelling in his own wickedness.

Shakespeare was also influenced by medieval morality plays, which personified a range of vices (including the seven deadly sins) and virtues in stories of temptation and ongoing conflict between good and evil.

By the mid-sixteenth century, the character Vice had become the star turn of morality plays, and audiences relished his theatrical delight in his own malice and trickery. Vice (sometimes called Iniquity) was a representative of the devil, whose function was to entrap people into sin through charm, wit and double-dealing. When he says 'Thus, like the formal Vice, Iniquity / I moralise two meanings in one word', Richard invites the audience to see him in the same way they see this character from the morality plays.

King Richard III
理查三世

In one of Richard III's soliloquies in *Henry VI, Part 3*, Shakespeare elaborates on this aspect of his character. Richard shows his craftiness and his ability to deceive and betray when he says:

> I can add colours to the chameleon,
> Change shapes with Proteus for advantages,
> And set the murderous Machiavel to school.
> Can I do this and cannot get a crown?
> Tut! Were it farther off, I'll pluck it down.
>
> Act 3 Scene 2, lines 191–5

Richard refers to Proteus (a Greek god who was said to constantly change his shape) as he revels in his ability to hide his intensions and to deceive others for his own advantage. He also refers to Machiavelli (whose name is synonymous with deception and manipulation) as he boasts that he will surpass him in his murderous schemes. Like the character Vice, Richard also revels in his own machinations and reveals his intentions to the audience in soliloquies and asides.

It is evidence of Shakespeare's dramatic genius that he was able to create such a magnetic and compelling stage personality out of historical accounts of the last of the Plantagenet kings and out of past performances of charismatic evil on the English stage.

Characters 人物分析

Character study as an approach

One traditional way of interpreting Shakespeare's plays has been by closely examining the main characters: what they say and do, how they behave and how they relate to one another.

This approach to literary criticism was developed over one hundred years ago by A. C. Bradley (*Shakespearean Tragedy*, 1904), but has remained a popular way of thinking about the plays, particularly in school. It tends to treat dramatic roles as if they are real people who have lives beyond the world of the play. One advantage of focusing on characters is that it helps readers to make connections with the world of the plays, sympathising with human problems and emotions.

However, in recent years, approaches to 'character study' have undergone significant revision. Some critics have argued that character-based approaches focus attention too much on emotions rather than ideas, and may give the impression that Shakespeare's dramatic scope is rather domestic and narrow. Furthermore, it has been argued by theatre historians that Elizabethan and Jacobean playwrights were not concerned with constructing psychologically consistent characters. Instead, certain character traits would be conveyed to audiences on Shakespeare's stage through 'stock' gestures and signalled by types of costume. Therefore, achieving realistic characterisation (as we might get in a modern novel or a television drama) was unlikely to have been Shakespeare's aim.

It may be that the fascination with tragic heroes emerged some time during the nineteenth century – the time of the great Victorian actor-managers, famed for their starring roles – and was further influenced by the kind of characterisation developed in the novels of the time. Some critics and historians have suggested that Victorian moralists were interested in using Shakespeare's characters as examples for moral guidance.

This section offers a number of activities that will help you explore different views of 'character', combining more traditional ideas about characterisation with broader considerations of the thematic, dramatic and political functions of the various roles in *King Richard III*.

Richard – a man of many parts

Although there is a huge cast of characters in this play, Richard dominates. Unusually for a Shakespeare play, there are no sub-plots, and this enables Richard to appear in fifteen of the twenty-five scenes overall (and, arguably, to be essential to the remaining ten). In his soliloquies, Richard frequently refers to plays and acting ('part', 'tragedy', 'pageant'), as if drawing attention to the fact that he is play-acting in order to deceive those around him. Consider some of the various parts or roles Richard adopts in the course of the drama:

Richard the actor Part of Richard's enduring fascination lies in his great acting skills. He pretends to be the caring brother, devoted lover, the innocent who is unjustly accused, a pious man of God, and the simple man who is too modest to become King.

Richard the charmer Richard's delight in his own abilities is infectious and gives him great audience appeal. He can, for example, charm the audience as he shares his plots with them in language that is often mocking, sardonic and full of wit.

Richard the lover Anne regrets succumbing to Richard's 'honey-words'. We observe Richard making two boldly persuasive marriage propositions in the course of the play.

Richard the brave warrior Richard's intellectual energy is matched by his physical vitality. He is constantly planning and always busy, restless in mind and body, fearless on the battlefield.

King Richard III
理查三世

Richard the physically disabled man
Despite his proven prowess on the battlefield, at times Richard goes out of his way to draw attention to his disabilities, downplaying the extent of his power in order to manipulate people's reactions to him.

Richard the solitary man In *Henry IV, Part 3* (Act 5 Scene 6, line 83), immediately after he has murdered King Henry, Richard declares 'I am myself alone'. *King Richard III* starkly portrays how he puts that self-centred philosophy into action.

Richard the machiavellian politician
Niccolo Machiavelli (1469–1527), in *The Prince*, stated that politics must be separated from ethics, that the end justifies the means, and decisions based on the needs of the state come above conscience. This idea of a cunning, manipulative ruler was taken up by Elizabethan dramatists, who created self-centred, immoral villains like Richard.

◆ As a class, divide into seven groups. Look at the photographs in this edition and select at least one image that your group believes illustrates an aspect of Richard that is described above. Each group takes one of the listed roles to focus on. Create a presentation for the rest of the class that explores the way in which Richard plays this particular role. Your presentation should last three to four minutes. Use the following points to help you shape your presentation:

- Find a key episode or scene in which Richard plays this role. Summarise Richard's actions in words, mime, or a series of tableaux.
- Pick out key quotations – things Richard says that emphasise the characteristic you are exploring.
- Choose relevant photographs and other images from this edition and/or from the Internet.
- evaluate how successful Richard is at playing that particular part – what does he achieve by acting in this way?

On the psychiatrist's (精神科医生) couch
◆ One branch of literary criticism that developed in the late twentieth century is concerned with using psychology as a tool to help us understand particular characters, their motivation and the way they act. Put Richard on the psychiatrist's couch. One person takes the role of Richard before the Battle of Bosworth, the other becomes the psychiatrist, asking questions about his relationships, desires and fears. Use the bullet points below to help you prepare, then role-play the encounter and show it to others in your class.

- How does Richard feel about what his mother says about him? Does this make him feel resentful about his favoured brothers? Is he jealous? (Look at Act 2 Scene 2, lines 49–56; Act 4 Scene 1, lines 54–6; Act 4 Scene 4, lines 136–96.)
- Richard gives the impression that he is very self-conscious about his physical appearance. Was his childhood difficult? What are the most hurtful things people have said about him? Has he ever felt pressure to prove himself capable of doing things that other people take for granted? (Look at Act 1 Scene 1, lines 14–31; Act 1 Scene 3, lines 47–53; Act 1 Scene 2, lines 34–67 and 105.)
- How would Richard describe his love life? What kind of relationships does he enjoy with women? Does he have women friends or does he just see women as sex objects? (Look at Act 1 Scene 1, lines 62–100 and 154–61; Act 1 Scene 2; Act 4 Scene 2, lines 52–64.)
- What are his greatest fears? What do Richard's dreams say about his subconscious fears? (Look at Act 5 Scene 3, lines 121–223 and 284–9; Act 1 Scene 3, lines 202–39).

Characters

Richard's social media profile

◆ Imagine Richard lived in the digital age. Create his profile and home page as it might appear on a social media website. Your mocked-up page(s) will probably contain some of the following:

- friends
- likes (for example, music, TV programmes, films, hobbies, favourite historical figures, political affiliations, religious beliefs)
- pictures from key moments in Richard's life
- comments
- notifications (who might have liked Richard's comments or replied to them)
- messages from others to Richard
- friend requests from people who want to be Richard's friends.

◆ As an extension, create a similar profile for Richard's brother Clarence, and include messages he might have sent to Richard following his imprisonment.

Richard's relationship with Buckingham

Although Buckingham appears to adopt a politically neutral position at the beginning of the play, he goes on to sustain a relationship with Richard longer than any other character. In the end, however, Buckingham becomes a victim of Richard's merciless plotting, just as Clarence and Hastings did before him.

◆ With a partner, trace the relationship between Buckingham and Richard. Look at the way Buckingham responds to Margaret's warnings early on in the play (Act 1 Scene 3, lines 280–304). At what point do we begin to see Buckingham and Richard forming an alliance?

◆ Pick a memorable episode or scene that shows Buckingham and Richard working closely together. What role does Buckingham adopt in his relationship with Richard? What qualities of Buckingham effectively complement those of Richard? In what ways is he different? Where does it all start to go wrong?

◆ Study the photographs of Richard and Buckingham in this edition. Make some suggestions about how you would present Buckingham on stage and give reasons for your choices.

King Richard III
理查三世

- Using the notes and ideas generated by your discussions, write an essay with at least five paragraphs outlining the way Buckingham's relationship with Richard develops. Make sure you include quotations from the play to support your points in each paragraph. You might find it helpful to use the scaffold below:
    - **Paragraph 1:** introduce the important role that Buckingham plays and how he relates to Richard.
    - **Paragraph 2:** what kind of man does Buckingham appear to be at the beginning of the play. How is he drawn to Richard?
    - **Paragraph 3:** give an example of the way Richard and Buckingham operate as a team; how do they complement each other? How do their antics contribute to the dramatic qualities of the play?
    - **Paragraph 4:** describe what goes wrong. Does Buckingham change (or is it Richard)? Who is to blame for Buckingham's downfall? Does Buckingham repent at the end? Is Richard a changed man without Buckingham?
    - **Paragraph 5:** sum up what Buckingham's relationship with Richard contributes to the play (such as dramatic tension, humour, tragedy, themes, development of Richard's character).

The women in the play

Feminist approaches to literary criticism attempt to focus on the contribution female characters make to a text, to consider the role of women as portrayed in a piece of work and to expose the way traditional readings of plays (often from a male perspective) represent women. In the early twentieth century, the female characters in *King Richard III* tended to be regarded as powerless victims. This view has been challenged by many critics in the past fifty years.

Queen Margaret

Margaret is the French wife of the murdered Henry VI, who is bitterly opposed to the house of York. In *Henry VI, Part 3*, Margaret led armies and had great power. Here she has lost all, and is reduced to using only the power of words to curse and prophesy the doom of others. She is chorus, prophetess and nemesis, cursing all whom she believes have plotted against her. She fiercely and passionately denounces and curses Richard, who has killed her husband and son. Like the other women in the play, Margaret is a victim of misogyny in a state where men have all the power. But it seems that Margaret influences the women so that they finally support each other, and it is Margaret who inspires Elizabeth to stand up to Richard in Act 4.

In many productions of *King Richard III*, Margaret's part is heavily cut. In the 1995 film version, Margaret is omitted completely. However, some recent directors have argued strongly that Margaret's role in the play is crucial, both dramatically and thematically. For example, like Richard, at times Margaret is a character who is given the privilege of speaking directly to the audience.

- Imagine you are about to direct a new film version of *King Richard III*. The script editor and the producer both think that Margaret's part should be omitted. You disagree. Prepare an argument for preserving the part of Margaret and then suggest a shortlist of actors who you think would be good for the role.

- To help you consider Margaret's importance, draw a table like the one opposite and collect evidence for each of the roles Margaret fulfils.

CHARACTERS

Role	Explanation of role	Evidence from the play
'Chorus' (a figure from classical drama)	Comments on events; provides historical background…	Her asides Act 1 Scene 3…
Prophet		
'Nemesis' (a figure from classical drama)	Figure of divine retribution, demanding justice	
Motivator to the other women		
Dramatic counter-balance to Richard	Strong female figure; represents house of Lancaster…	
Other…		

- Using your notes from the table, write a letter to the script editor explaining why you believe the character or role of Margaret to be essential to an understanding of the play overall.

- Look through the various photographs in this edition showing Margaret in different productions. What aspects of her role does each emphasise? Propose the names of two or three well-known actors who you might want to cast in the part. Explain what appropriate qualities they have.

Queen Elizabeth

Elizabeth Woodville married Edward IV and used her power to ensure that her family achieved high-ranking positions. The promotion of her relatives caused resentment among the traditional nobility. The only occasion on which Richard and Margaret agree is when they mock the *parvenu* (people who rise above their original status through sudden wealth or position) Woodvilles (Act 1 Scene 3, lines 255–65). Richard uses the unpopularity of the Woodvilles to gain the support of Hastings and Buckingham, and he orders the executions of Elizabeth's son (Grey), brother (Rivers) and supporter (Vaughan), but he does not harm Elizabeth.

When husbands lose power, so do their wives. After King Edward's death, Queen Elizabeth is forced to face the consequences of the loss of her personal and political power. She foresaw her future powerlessness as King Edward lay dying: 'I fear our happiness is at the height' (Act 1 Scene 3, line 41).

Grieving the death of her two young sons (Act 4 Scene 4), she joins Margaret and the Duchess of York in a highly patterned lamentation as the three women remember their dead. Elizabeth bravely stands up to Richard ('Tell me, thou villain slave, where are my children?'), outwits him as he woos her for her daughter, and is rewarded when her daughter marries Richmond, the new King Henry VII.

The Duchess of York

The Duchess is the widowed mother of Richard, King Edward and Clarence. Her husband had been humiliated and killed by Margaret (in *Henry VI, Part 3*). In *King Richard III*, she suffers the deaths of Clarence and her two male grandchildren on the orders of Richard, and has to endure Richard spreading rumours that she was unfaithful and her eldest son is illegitimate. The Duchess joins the grieving of Margaret and Elizabeth, but she is vilified by Margaret for giving birth to Richard. Her final words to Richard are a curse and her desire for his death and defeat in battle: 'Bloody thou art, bloody will be thy end'.

King Richard III
理查三世

Lady Anne Neville

Anne was betrothed to Prince Edward, the son of Henry VI. Both Edward and Henry were killed by Richard. In Act 1 Scene 2, she mourns over the corpse of Henry. Richard engages her in a war of words, resolved only when she agrees to become his wife. Later in the play, Anne shows courage and determination when she visits the princes in the Tower (Act 4 Scene 1), challenging Brakenbury to allow her to enter. About to be crowned Queen, she reveals that the curse she placed on Richard's future wife is ironically upon herself, seduced by his 'honey words'. Richard's 'timorous dreams' deny her sleep and, in almost her last utterance, she fears he will 'shortly be rid of me'. She is all too right. He arranges her death so that he can marry the young Elizabeth.

◆ In small groups, consider the following statements about the female characters in the play (Anne, Elizabeth, the Duchess of York and Margaret). Discuss the statements in turn and select those with which you most strongly agree and disagree:

- Men hold all the power in the play.
- Anne's role is the only important one; the rest of the women's parts could all usefully be cut in a production.
- The women are bound by a sense of feminine solidarity.
- The women provide a dramatic contrast to Richard and his male followers.
- The women all hate one another as much as they hate Richard.
- By the end of Act 4, the women gain strength by supporting each other, acting collectively.
- Women help change the course of the play.
- Men and women are portrayed as socially equal in the play.
- Although we never actually see Jane Shore, she is an important female character.
- The audience gets to hear Richard's innermost thoughts at different points of the play, but all the women remain as one-dimensional, 'flat' characters.

◆ Prepare to explain your choices to the rest of the class, making reference to events in the play. What are the sharpest points of disagreement?

The men in the play

Clarence, Hastings and Buckingham in turn become victims of Richard's merciless plotting. Shakespeare exposes the ironies implicit in appearance and reality, as each is fooled and blinded by Richard's false friendship. Finally, just before execution, each man is forced by his conscience to examine his own moral nature.

Clarence

Clarence's first appearance emphasises his trusting faith in a scheming brother who is about to have him executed. His gullibility generates situations where irony is at once funny and macabre. He tells the two Murderers whom Richard has sent to kill him that Richard is loving and kindly and 'would labour my delivery', not realising that Richard's 'delivery' means death. Shakespeare's transforming imagination underplays Clarence's involvement in past events (perjury and murder in *Henry VI, Part 3*), focusing instead on his dream; in an episode rich in imagery (Act 1 Scene 4, lines 9–74), Clarence finds belief in Christianity and understands the power of conscience, repenting his past crimes.

Hastings

Imprisoned through the intrigues of the Woodvilles ('By the suggestion of the Queen's allies'), Hastings is a faithful supporter of the house of York. His overconfidence and blindness to the real motives of others, allied to his bitter opposition to the Woodvilles, make him an easy victim of Richard's plans. He rejoices at the executions of Rivers, Grey and Vaughan, and is convinced of his own invulnerability. But Hastings's misinterpretations of every warning sustain the humour and grim irony that characterise the play. He fails to take the advice of Stanley to flee north, and he refuses Catesby's appeal to support Richard's bid for the crown (Act 3 Scene 2). In a deeply ironic episode at the council, he believes that Richard is incapable of hiding his true feelings, and intends harm to no one present (Act 3 Scene 4). Realising his mistakes too late, he recalls Margaret's curse as he prophesies 'the fearful'st time' for England under Richard.

CHARACTERS

Buckingham

Buckingham's ability to dissemble almost rivals Richard's own. He possesses great political awareness and diplomatic skill, and appears first as peacemaker (Act 1 Scene 3), bringing messages from Edward IV to appease the various rivalries. He stands aloof from the bitter family arguments. Buckingham is the only important person not cursed by Margaret, but his neutrality evaporates (Act 2 Scene 2) when he seizes the opportunity to join with Richard in isolating Edward, Prince of Wales, from his family. He becomes Richard's right-hand man, and much of the humour and irony of Acts 2 and 3 derive from the energy and verve Buckingham and Richard generate as they embark on a spree (一通，一阵) of outrageous play-acting and stage-management that has lethal outcomes. They order the imprisonment and execution of Rivers, Grey and Vaughan (Act 2 Scene 4). They send the princes to the Tower (Act 3 Scene 1) and contrive Hastings's execution (Act 3 Scene 4). Persuading the citizens of London there is a plot against them (Act 3 Scene 5), they fool the Lord Mayor and aldermen into making Richard King (Act 3 Scene 7).

When Richard refuses to grant him the promised earldom of Hereford, Buckingham does not hesitate. He raises an army against Richard, but a storm disperses his troops. Before his execution, he recognises the justice of his punishment and reflects that 'Margaret's curse falls heavy on my neck'. Margaret's curse is a persistent reminder throughout the play of the power of nemesis and fate (see p. 235) as characters face the inevitable consequences of their actions. Buckingham's fall marks the beginning of Richard's own decline in fortune. The 'deep-revolving witty Buckingham' is replaced by the sinister figure of Ratcliffe. Richard will rely increasingly on several unprincipled men to carry out his brutal plans.

King Richard III
理查三世

Lord Stanley, Earl of Derby

The husband of Margaret Beaufort and stepfather to Richmond, Stanley is the only character to play Richard at his own game – his words hiding his true intentions. Stanley's loyalty is first challenged by Queen Elizabeth (Act 1 Scene 3), who knows Stanley's wife hates all the Woodvilles. His reply is both tactful and politic, an approach he uses successfully throughout the play to avoid suspicion. His plea to Edward IV to save the life of his servant establishes Stanley as a caring master who is respected by the King. He gradually emerges as an important focus for opposition to Richard, aware almost from the beginning of Richard's true nature.

Stanley shows some of his true feelings when he warns Hastings to be suspicious of Richard (Act 3 Scene 2) and when he encourages Dorset to join Richmond (Act 4 Scene 1). Powerless to stop Richard from becoming King, Stanley waits for the opportune moment. When Richard holds his son hostage and threatens him with execution, Stanley promises the tyrant military support, but he secretly intends to support Richmond. Using Richard's own weapons of double-dealing and hypocrisy, Stanley joins Richmond to defeat Richard, and by good luck his son's life is spared.

Richmond

Richmond – the future Henry VII – appears very late in the play, addressing his troops in Act 5 Scene 2. He seems the all-conquering hero, a *deus ex machina* (天命使者) (god who intervenes in the nick of time) who ends Richard's evil reign. He appears to have all the right credentials: he is highly principled, honourable, moral and righteous, a fighter who wants only his country's good. Believing God will support his just cause, he puts his fate in divine hands. He is not part of the bloody legacy of the Wars of the Roses, and his innocence is acknowledged by the ghosts. An astute tactician who realises the importance of Stanley's forces, he shows genuine affection for his stepfather and is magnanimous in victory.

While some commentators argue that Richmond is the hero saving England from Richard's oppression, others disagree. They claim that the play has been starved of moral language for so long while Richard has delighted audiences with his Machiavellian cunning, that the contest is not a fair one. Such transparent moral righteousness as Richmond possesses seems naive and dramatically unconvincing compared to the much more interesting Richard. What is your view of Richmond?

◆ Imagine Lord Stanley has arranged Richmond's first press conference following the victory at Bosworth. This is a chance for the press to get to know the new King and to glimpse the way Stanley is managing the regime. In groups, two people take roles as Stanley and Richmond; the rest become journalists. Separately, journalists prepare questions while Stanley and Richmond prepare statements for the press (explaining, for example, how the battle was won, what England can look forward to, and so on).

◆ As a whole class, select one Stanley/Richmond pair and improvise the press conference, with the rest of the class in role as journalists. The challenge is for Stanley and Richmond to answer questions in a way that is consistent with the play, and to incorporate some of their original language in the responses.

Exploring themes through character

References to appearance abound in the play, particularly concerning Richard's physical looks and disability. A traditional trick of story-telling in a number of cultures is to portray villains as ugly or disfigured, and this seems to be one way Shakespeare is inviting us to regard Richard: his interior sinfulness is exhibited in his outward features. The discovery of Richard's buried remains in 2013 settled the long-running debate as to whether the real historical figure was disabled or not, but attitudes to disability and disfigurement have changed considerably since Shakespeare's day.

CHARACTERS

How to present Richard to a modern audience, and how to deal with offensive disability-related language ('bunch-backed', 'elvish-marked', 'hedgehog') presents a challenge to directors and actors. Below are some views on Richard from actors and directors.

> *I became very interested in the fact that Richard is a severely disabled man. Some actors underplay this – but if you read Richard's opening speech about himself, he is clearly disabled, and has experienced a lot of prejudice, a lot of hatred. This, in turn, has filled him with self-hatred. It's this that enables him to do such evil to other people. He was used to hatred as a disabled man in an un-PC (un-politically correct) society. There were no Paralympics then.*
>
> Actor Antony Sher

> *I've always been struck by his anger as a character, and in the play he explains that this is because he was born so physically disadvantaged. That wasn't something Shakespeare invented – and so perhaps the play isn't the Tudor propaganda hatchet job that people often assume ... When you play Richard on stage, you have to decide how you want him to look. I had a withered left arm, my left leg was in callipers (金属支架), and I had a huge birthmark across my face, because there's a lot of talk in the play about the circumstances of his birth. The idea was that from one side he'd look almost completely normal, and then he'd spin around and everything would be twisted.*
>
> Actor Jonathan Slinger

> *In Richard, Shakespeare created a monster – but he is a monster in a world that is equally monstrous. Medieval politics can't have been fun: it's a vision of a world of violence and lack of moral scruple ... I wanted him to have the shape of a retired American footballer: very big and heavy, with a huge upper body compared to his legs, and a tiny bald head. People said I looked like Shakespeare's 'bunch-backed toad', as his mother calls him. His disability is incredibly important to the play – it's a motor for his fury.*
>
> Actor Simon Russell Beale

> *Richard III is a supercharged panto/tragedy ... Although Richard III is frequently attacked as a melodramatic and simple-minded play, it is psychologically very acute – ... in the way that it shows how a sociopath can move through normal society with terrifying ease.*
>
> Director Dominic Dromgoole

> *We don't see Richard as a 'wink-wink, I'm a villain' character ... Richard is just a normal guy who has had enough ... like any disabled member of our society even today.*
>
> Director Stephanie Barton-Farcas

- ◆ What similarities and differences are there between the various viewpoints expressed in the statements? Which do you most – or least – agree with?

- ◆ In four out of the five productions referred to above, able-bodied actors were cast as Richard. Discuss whether it would make a difference if Richard was played instead by a disabled actor – or if other cast members were disabled. You might find it useful to look back at some of the production photographs of Richard in this edition.

King Richard III
理查三世

The language of *King Richard III*
《理查三世》的语言

The first thing that might strike you about the language of *King Richard III* is that it is highly patterned and often formal. Its style reflects many of the techniques Shakespeare had learned at his school in Stratford-upon-Avon, where Renaissance rhetoric (the art of using language persuasively) was at the centre of the curriculum. As a schoolboy, he imitated classical models, practising many different ways of using language that he later employed in his plays. Richard's curses, lamentations, entreaties and warnings use language in many ways.

Repetition

Shakespeare's use of **repetition** gives his language great dramatic force. Repeated words, phrases, rhythms and sounds add to the emotional intensity of a moment or scene, heightening theatrical effect. The play is full of examples of highly patterned repetition, and many episodes have a ritualistic quality because of the symmetrical repetition of particular phrases and rhythms. This can be seen most in the following language devices.

Anaphora is the repetition of the same word at the beginning of successive sentences:

> *Was ever woman in this humour wooed?*
> *Was ever woman in this humour won?*
> Act 1 Scene 2, lines 231–2

Epistrophe is the repetition of a word or phrase at the end of a series of sentences or clauses:

> CHILDREN *Ah, for our father, for our dear lord Clarence.*
> DUCHESS *Alas for both, both mine Edward and Clarence.*
> ELIZABETH *What stay had I but Edward? And he's gone.*
> CHILDREN *What stay had we but Clarence? And he's gone.*
> DUCHESS *What stays had I but they? And they are gone.*
> ELIZABETH *Was never widow had so dear a loss.*
> CHILDREN *Were never orphans had so dear a loss.*
> Act 2 Scene 2, lines 72–8

Polyptoton (一词数用) is repetition of words derived from the same root word, but with different endings or forms. In Act 4 Scene 4, the women lament, expressing their sorrow in stylised formal language. In lines 39–46, there are seven uses of 'killed' or 'kill':

> *I had an Edward, till a Richard killed him;*
> *I had a husband, till a Richard killed him*
> *…*
> *Thou hadst a Clarence, too,*
> *And Richard killed him.*

Other examples of repetition are **alliteration** (the repetition of consonants at the beginning of words) and **assonance** (半谐音，半韵) (repeated vowel sounds). Both are evident in the single line:

> *And with a virtuous visor hide deep vice.*
> Act 2 Scene 2, line 28

◆ Turn to a scene you particularly enjoy. How many examples of repetition can you find in it?

Other language devices

Antithesis (对偶)

King Richard III is full of conflicts, and Shakespeare's language powerfully expresses conflict through its use of **antithesis**: the opposition of words or phrases. Every page of the play contains antitheses. For example, 'Your grace attended to their sugared words / But looked not on the poison of their hearts' (Act 3 Scene 1, lines 13–14) sets 'attended to' against 'looked not on', 'sugared' against 'poison', and 'words' against 'hearts'. Richard's first soliloquy, which opens the play, contains many antitheses – for example, from the first sixteen lines:

> *winter/summer*
> *smoothed/wrinkled*
> *bruisèd arms/monuments*
> *stern alarums/merry meetings*

The language of King Richard III

dreadful marches/delightful measures
mounting/capers
rudely stamped/love's majesty

At the end of Act 2 Scene 4 (lines 60–2), the Duchess of York laments her sufferings in tightly packed dramatic antitheses:

My husband lost his life to get the crown,
And often up and down my sons were tossed
For me to joy and weep their gain and loss.

Before the final battle, Richard urges on his troops 'If not to heaven, then hand in hand to hell.' His final words are an ironic antithesis, expressing what his ambition has dwindled to: 'my kingdom for a horse!'

◆ **Choose a particular scene and work through it, identifying how each antithesis adds to the dramatic tension in that part of the play.**

Stichomythia

Another source of conflict and dramatic tension is Shakespeare's use of rapidly alternating single lines spoken by two characters to increase pace and tension in a scene. This is known as **stichomythia** and can be seen in Richard's 'wooings' of Anne and Elizabeth in Act 1 Scene 2, lines 197–205, and Act 4 Scene 4, lines 347–71.

Lists

One of Shakespeare's favourite devices was to accumulate words or phrases rather like a list. He knew that 'piling up' item on item, incident on incident, can intensify description, atmosphere, character and dramatic effect. Shakespeare would probably have known this language device as 'copiousness'. Act 3 Scene 5, lines 1–9 list at least a dozen things that a deceitful actor can do. There are many other kinds of list in the play, often in a single line containing four items ('Deep, hollow, treacherous, and full of guile' Act 2 Scene 1, line 38), and sometimes as a much longer catalogue – for example at Act 4 Scene 4, lines 168–73, when the Duchess of York describes Richard's life:

A grievous burden was thy birth to me.
Tetchy and wayward was thy infancy;
Thy schooldays frightful, desperate, wild, and furious;
Thy prime of manhood, daring, bold, and venturous;
Thy age confirmed, proud, subtle, sly, and bloody

◆ **Read through any act, collecting as many lists as you can. Then work with others to act out a few of the lists.**

Blank verse (无韵诗; 素体诗)

With the exception of the episode with the Murderers in Act 1 Scene 4, the play is written entirely in **blank verse**. Each ten-syllable line has five alternating unstressed (x) and stressed (/) syllables (**iambic pentameter**), as in:

x / x / x / x / x /
A horse, a horse, my kingdom for a horse!

◆ **To experience the rhythm of iambic pentameter, speak a few lines from any verse speech. As you speak, beat out the five-beat rhythm (clap your hands or tap your desk). When you have a feel for the rhythm, invent a few blank-verse lines describing your response to the play.**

◆ *King Richard III* **is an 'early' play, and as in other works written by Shakespeare at the start of his career, many of the lines are 'end-stopped' (尾断行) – that is, they make sense as a line: the meaning does not 'run-on' over into the next line (enjambement*). All actors face the problem of whether they should pause, however briefly, at the end of each line. What do you think? Select a long speech and speak it with a pause at the end of each line, then say whether you think actors should always 'signal' the end of the line in some way.**

* enjambement：跨行，指一行诗在印刷排版中因过长而无法排成一整行而不得不将长出来的部分排到下一行的情况。

King Richard III
理查三世

Imagery

Imagery is the use of emotionally charged words and phrases to conjure up vivid mental pictures and associations. Such images intensify the dramatic and emotional impact of the play. They give insight into characters' feelings and thoughts, and help to create the play's distinctive atmosphere and themes. *King Richard III* is rich in imagery and certain images recur through the play, helping to create its distinctive atmosphere.

Animal imagery

Richard is described in metaphors using animal imagery throughout the play. He is called a 'dog', 'hedgehog', 'hell-hound', 'bunch-backed toad', 'cur', 'rooting hog', 'cockatrice', 'bottled spider'. But the imagery is extended to the many characters who are imprisoned – for example, Clarence and Hastings are 'mewed up' (confined) like captive birds of prey, while those who are free and in power are 'kites and buzzards' or 'eagles'.

Theatrical imagery

Shakespeare's fascination with his own profession provided him with a recurring theme: the world as a stage. On this stage, humans make brief appearances to play their parts and take on different roles in different contexts. Richard is the epitome (典型) of the consummate actor who delights in trickery and duplicity – and invites the audience to delight in it, too.

Similes and metaphors

Shakespeare's imagery uses **metaphor** or **simile**. A simile compares one thing to another using 'like' or 'as': Richard claims he is 'like the formal Vice, Iniquity', and declares he will be led by Buckingham 'as a child'. A metaphor is also a comparison, but suggests that two dissimilar things are actually the same or have much in common. For example, the first two lines of the play compare the 'winter' of past battles with the 'summer' of the present time of peace. Richard uses a metaphor when he speaks of the dead King Edward and his sons: 'The royal tree hath left us royal fruit'.

The house of York's family tree is full of fruit (sons who will become King and continue the royal line) when the play opens. But this powerful visual image shows the tree is bare when Richard enters for his final confrontation with Richmond. Here, the verbal imagery of the play is reinforced by the visual imagery of the stage set.

Personification

Personification is a particular type of imagery. It turns things or ideas into humans, giving them human feelings or body parts. The two Murderers call conscience 'blushing, shamefaced'; Richard speaks of 'dull delay' and 'snail-paced beggary'. The Duchess of York tells of England's earth being 'made drunk'.

◆ Turn to two or three pages at random. Identify the images on each page and suggest how they add to the dramatic appeal of the scene.

Playing with language

Puns

A **pun** is a clever or humorous play on the meaning of words that sound or look similar. Richard is a master of the pun as he turns meaning on its head to ridicule, embarrass, sneer at or attack his opponents. Richard reveals his hatred for the Woodvilles by punning on 'noble' (Act 1 Scene 3, line 81), meaning 'one of the nobility' but also 'a coin of little worth'. He puns on 'son' / 'sun' in the second line of the play. The 'son of York' is King Edward, but the 'sun' was also the Yorkist emblem that would bring light and warmth to Richard's family. Throughout the play, 'blood' can refer to family, gore, rage or the Yorkists in general and Richard in particular. Look out for the many other puns as you read through the play.

Keywords

Certain words echo through the play, often repeated: 'blood', 'grace', 'God', 'hate', 'hell', 'Lord', 'murder'. Richard frequently turns an oath (a formal promise made in the name of a god or holy person) into an irreverent and blasphemous (褻瀆神明) expression.

THE LANGUAGE OF KING RICHARD III

- Look back through the play and make a note of the oaths used by Richard and others, and the dramatic contexts in which they are used. A few examples to get you started are:
  - The old Queen Margaret's curses in Act 1 Scene 3, include the an invocation of God's power
  - In Act 3 Scene 1, Richard says to the young princes: 'God keep you from them and from such false friends'.
  - In Act 4 Scene 4, Richard searches for an oath strong enough to convince Queen Elizabeth to allow him to marry her daughter. He finally says 'Why then, by God', but her answer exposes his hypocrisy and blasphemy.

Dramatic language

Soliloquies and asides

A **soliloquy** is a monologue, a kind of internal debate spoken by a character who is alone (or assumes they are alone) on stage. It gives the audience direct access to the character's mind, revealing their inner thoughts and motives. An **aside** is a brief comment or address to the audience that shows the character's unspoken thoughts, unheard by other characters on stage. The audience is taken into this character's confidence or can see deeper into their motivations and experiences. Asides can also be used for characters to comment on the action as it unfolds. You can see how Richard uses both soliloquies and asides throughout the play.

Irony

King Richard III is a play much concerned with false appearance. Shakespeare fills it with two types of irony: verbal and dramatic. In both, the audience knows something that a character on stage does not. Richard is a master of **verbal irony**, saying one thing and meaning another. Everything he says to Clarence and Hastings in the first scene is charged with double meaning. When he tells Clarence 'I will deliver you or else lie for you', Clarence thinks his brother is promising to free him from prison or take his place there. But Richard has murder ('deliver' from life) and telling lies in mind.

Dramatic irony occurs when what is said contrasts with what happens elsewhere in the play. The young York calls Richard 'gentle uncle' and 'kind uncle', unaware that his uncle wishes him dead. There is huge dramatic irony in the appearance of the wicked Richard between two churchmen: the contrast of all he has said and done with his pretended saintliness.

- Choose two examples of dramatic irony in the play and write notes in your Director's Journal about how you would want the set design, lighting, sound effects and actors to highlight the contrast between what is being said and what is actually happening or intended.

- Use an online version of the play to copy and paste all Richard's soliloquies and asides. Read through them to identify what Richard confides in the audience and how he creates a confidential relationship with them.

King Richard III
理查三世

King Richard III in performance
《理查三世》的演出

King Richard III was probably written and first performed around 1592 or 1593. It is almost certain that the play was performed at the Globe Theatre while Shakespeare was alive. According to contemporary reports and anecdotes, it was a great success for both Shakespeare's playing company and for Richard Burbage – the first actor to play the part of Richard III.

Performance on Shakespeare's stage

During Shakespeare's lifetime, plays in outdoor amphitheatres like the Globe were performed in broad daylight during the summer months. So, at 2 p.m. people would assemble with food and drink to watch a play with no lighting and no rule of silence for the audience. There were high levels of background noise and interaction during performances, and audience members were free to walk in and out of the theatre.

In the Globe, the audience was positioned on three sides of the stage: the 'groundlings' (站票观众) stood in the pit (圆形剧场中的无座观众池) around the stage while those who paid more were seated in three levels around the pit. Actors would see around three thousand faces staring up or down at them. The positioning of the audience made it difficult for everyone to hear all that was going on. Inevitably, the actors would have their backs to sections of the audience at times. The best place for actors to stand, especially for a soliloquy or an aside, was at the front of the stage so that they could directly address almost all of the audience. However, it would be tedious if all the action occurred here!

Shakespeare's use of repetition helped to overcome this problem. There are times when the same idea is stated or developed in three ways in order to allow an actor to address each section of the audience. These repetitions were never simply word for word, but were used to create rhythm, accumulate details and build on an idea through different metaphors and imagery. If you spot significant repetition, it may be a clue that Shakespeare intended the character to move around the stage and engage different parts of the audience.

This illustration from 1647 shows the Globe Theatre, built for the second time in 1614 after the first one burnt down.

King Richard III in performance

'Blocking'* is a term used to describe actors' positions on the stage, and on Shakespeare's stage a character's position gave the audience clues about their role or authority in the play. Upstage is furthest away from the audience and downstage is closer to the audience. Characters absorbed in their own lives, or characters who played out literary or conventional stereotypes, were often placed centre-stage or upstage – furthest away from the audience. Characters who had a comic role, who performed many roles or commented on the action on stage were often played closer to the audience or at the edge of the stage. In this way, they existed on the intersection between stage and audience.

◆ Actors at Shakespeare's Globe often comment on how effectively its stage layout can be made to work dramatically, and especially on the way it encourages a close rapport with the audience. What parts of *King Richard III* do you think would work well on this stage, with the audience so close to the actors, and why? Which parts do you think it would be difficult to stage convincingly, and why?

The popularity of Shakespeare's play is evident in the anecdotes about Richard Burbage in the role of Richard. Burbage was well known for his charismatic and powerful acting, and his portrayal of Richard III was very popular with audiences at the Globe Theatre.

The popularity of the play is also evident in its printed history. It was so popular that six Quarto editions of the play were published before it appeared in the Folio edition of Shakespeare's plays in 1623. 'Quarto' and 'Folio' refer to the paper size: Quarto editions were smaller as well as cheaper and quicker to publish than Folio editions. Often, the Quarto version was written from an actor's memory of the performance or by piecing together a few of the actor's lines with the prompt book. As a result of all these editions, there are different versions of the script in existence today. For example, there are thirty-two lines in the First Quarto that are not in the Folio, and the Folio has about 200 lines that do not appear in the First Quarto.

* **blocking**：戏台调度，指导演对演员在戏台上的动作进行的设计和安排，包括演员与演员、演员与戏台景物之间的相对位置及其变化。

King Richard III
理查三世

King Richard III in the eighteenth century

From 1700 until 1877, all performances of *King Richard III* were based on an adaptation of Shakespeare's play written by Colley Cibber. Cibber was Poet Laureate, as well as a playwright and actor, and his version of the play placed the focus firmly on the character of Richard. It was a star vehicle for him as an actor, and this was the version that many other actors chose to display their virtuosic acting abilities for more than a century and a half.

In Cibber's version, Richard has more than forty per cent of the play's lines – two hundred lines from Shakespeare's other history plays were inserted and Cibber put in over a thousand lines of his own. He cut the parts of Queen Margaret, Edward IV, Clarence, Hastings and the Woodvilles. His Richard was a melodramatic villain to the end, and Cibber captured this with the now-famous line he inserted into the play: 'Off with his head. So much for Buckingham!' Cibber gave his villainous hero another famous line on the eve of the Battle of Bosworth: 'Conscience avant; Richard's himself again'. There is no room for ambiguity or remorse: this Richard shakes his sword at fear and sallies forth to battle.

David Garrick was another star actor who played Richard in Cibber's version of the play. He first performed the role in 1741, using a more naturalistic acting style than was favoured at the time. He brought a new expressiveness to the role, using naturalistic voice, gestures and facial expressions to portray Richard as a human being rather than a stage monster. William Hogarth captured the horror and vulnerability of Garrick's portrayal of Richard just before the Battle of Bosworth in a theatrical portrait in 1745. Garrick's approach was both shocking and inspiring for his audiences, and his performances as Richard were a great success. During his time as actor and stage manager at the Theatre Royal, Drury Lane (between 1747 and 1776), the play was performed 213 times in twenty-nine years!

Hogarth's painting of David Garrick in the title role of *King Richard III*.

King Richard III in the twentieth century

Since 1700, nearly all productions of *King Richard III* have cut characters, scenes and lines in order to focus attention on Richard. However, most productions in the twentieth century have returned to the early Quarto and Folio versions, and perform the play with few cuts. Richard III remains a star role that attracts star actors, all of whom want to give a definitive performance of the character. However, the individualistic melodrama of Cibber's script is now replaced by considerations of the more psychological interpretations of Richard and the political potential of the play in performance.

In 1984, Antony Sher played Richard III in a production with the Royal Shakespeare Company (RSC). His portrayal involved an exploration of the character's motivations and past experiences, and his performances are remembered for his striking mannerisms and costume choice. He used two crutches and the dangling cloth of his costume to create the image of Richard as a 'bottled spider' and 'bunch-backed toad' scuttling around the stage like an insect. The mobility and speed of this obviously handicapped character was shocking and unsettling for the audience. Sher's performance provided a glimpse into Richard's manic and evil nature while also attempting to explore some of the reasons why he was like this.

▲ Aidan McArdle's 2001 portrayal relied less on physical disability and more on purity and saintliness to fool his victims.

In 1996, David Troughton played Richard as Mr Punch, a grotesque clown figure who used disguise and false identities to hide the hollowness within.

◆ Carry out some research into the character of Mr Punch and use your findings to analyse how playing Richard in this way adds to the dramatic effect.

King Richard III
理查三世

In 2002, Kenneth Branagh emphasised Richard's physical limitations; the actor wore an ungainly and confining leg-brace strapped to his torso (躯干).

Henry Holden is a disabled actor who needs crutches to walk in his own life. His 2007 production presented Richard's story as similar to that of any disabled person's story in society today – a struggle to get the things that rightfully belong to them.

◆ The pages in this section all portray very different interpretations of Richard. Which comes closest to your own view of Richard? Discuss the reasons for your choice/s with a partner.

◆ Write notes in your Director's Journal to describe how you would want to see Richard portrayed on stage. Compare these past performances with your own ideas.

The reconstruction of Shakespeare's Globe Theatre, on London's Bankside, allows many of the productions there to show the style and costumes that would have been familiar to Shakespeare's audiences. In Shakespeare's time, boy actors played the women's parts, and modern performances at Shakespeare's Globe have experimented with having an all-male cast for this play.

In 2003, the Globe also made a daring experiment in its production of *King Richard III* when all the parts were played by women. In the photograph top right, Kathryn Hunter portrays a crafty and devious Richard who attempts to persuade a reluctant Queen Elizabeth that her daughter should be his next wife. A similar moment is captured in the photograph on the right from a Shakespeare's Globe production with an all-male cast, with Mark Rylance as Richard III and Samuel Barnett as Queen Elizabeth.

◆ Look at the images on the right from performances with an all-male and an all-female cast at Shakespeare's Globe. What – in your opinion – are the gains or losses when the play is performed by actors all of the same gender?

King Richard III in performance

A production of *King Richard III* in Arabic (with English subtitles) was commissioned by the Royal Shakespeare Company as part of its Complete Works Festival in 2007. This adaptation was called *The Baghdad Richard* and it set the play in the modern world of the Arabian Gulf. According to a synopsis of this performance:

> The play unfolds within the hothouse, feudal atmosphere of desert places in an oil-rich kingdom. In this world of tribal allegiances, family in-fighting and absolute power, the questions of leadership, religion and foreign intervention that are at the heart of Shakespeare's play, take on powerful new meanings in a modern context.

A more recent performance at Shakespeare's Globe was given by the National Theatre of China as part of the World Shakespeare Festival in 2012. In this production, Richard was portrayed without the physical disabilities or bodily impairments that audiences have come to expect. Instead, the actor playing Richard was tall and athletic with an imposing physical presence on stage. And yet there were elements of mental impairment in this portrayal, especially in the mental anguish and psychological turmoil of Richard on the eve of the Battle of Bosworth. The director, Wang Xiaoying (王晓鹰), said in an interview:

> The real Richard in history was not handicapped at all. We don't want to make his disability a reason behind his desire for power. In other words, we don't want to make him starkly (明显) different from ordinary people.

◆ What inspiration do you get from reading about these two recent productions of *King Richard III*? Imagine you have been invited to the next 'World Shakespeare Festival' – which country would you like to represent and how would you like to perform Richard? Think about the language and cultural context as you do so. For example, you might like to think about specific points of history and/or tyrannical regimes that might offer interesting interpretive contexts for a new production of the play.

▼ This is a performance of *King Richard III* at a festival in Portugal.

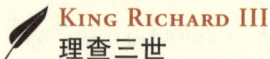

King Richard III
理查三世

King Richard III on film

A silent, black and white film from America in 1911 shows an actor adopting the characteristic appearance for Richard that had developed over the years: Elizabethan doublet and hose, a fur-lined coat and a black wig with shoulder-length hair.

In his 1955 film, Laurence Olivier had the same look, but he added a large and unmistakable nose. The cinematic techniques available to Olivier enabled him to create a character who was at once fascinating and repellent. He took viewers into his confidence through the use of extreme close-ups (特写), yet created a sinister atmosphere as the camera lingered over Richard's misshapen (扭曲，变形) shadow moving through the scenes. Olivier's direct speeches to the camera left no doubt about Richard's evil intentions and power to dissemble, but he was still charismatic and mesmerising.

The film emphasised the importance of the crown as a symbol and Richard's lack of right to rule. It began with an added scene of pomp – the coronation of Edward IV, in which Richard's own coronet falls to the floor. Richard's coronation later was a much less grand affair, and Queen Anne fainted as Richard ascended the throne. At Bosworth, the crown is trampled in the mud before Richard is killed and his body flung over a horse.

Olivier added lines from *Henry VI, Part 3* to the opening soliloquy, to express Richard's duplicity and devious ploys (手段):

> Why, I can smile, and murder whiles I smile,
> And cry, 'Content!' to that which grieves my heart,
> And wet my cheeks with artificial tears,
> And frame my face to all occasions.
>
> Act 3 Scene 2, lines 182–5

He also added lines from Cibber's version to emphasise Richard's deformity, and included a silent yet influential part for Jane Shore, who appears in dramatic and amorous scenes with both King Edward and Hastings.

◆ **Watch Olivier's film of *Richard III*. Give your response to each of Olivier's inventions and additions, saying how helpful you find them.**

King Richard III in performance

Ian McKellen's filmed version of *Richard III* (1995) was an adaptation of Shakespeare's play set in 1930s England. The directors used the cinematic techniques and realistic settings of a contemporary action movie, with fast-paced scenes of violence and war. This, together with Shakespeare's language modernised for contemporary audiences, made the film a box-office success. McKellen hoped that by putting Richard's story in a modern setting, it would help the audience see it as more than just 'old-fashioned Shakespeare'.

McKellen's Richard is a slightly handicapped and stiff-backed officer, who rises to power to become a fascist dictator. The film opens with flashbacks of the recent war in which Richard has cold-bloodedly and violently killed Henry VI and his son Prince Edward. It uses the full opening soliloquy from Act 1 Scene 1 (with additional lines from *Henry VI, Part 3*), spoken first as a public speech and finished as private thoughts spoken aloud in the lavatory. McKellen uses the same technique as Olivier, directly addressing the film audience.

The film ends with an ambiguous and unsettling confrontation between Richmond and Richard. As they face each other towards the end of the Battle of Bosworth, Richard refuses to surrender. Richmond raises his pistol to shoot him, but Richard jumps from the roof of a bombed-out building into the flames below. His final line (taken from the scene that precedes the battle in Shakespeare's play) – 'Let us to't pell mell / If not to heaven, then hand in hand to hell' – is set to jaunty music as he holds out his hand to Richmond. Richmond's smile as he watches Richard fall to his death is hard to decipher. The audience is left with an unsettled feeling: it is unclear what the future holds for England.

▶ Ian McKellen has played Richard on stage and on film.

King Richard III
理查三世

In the docudrama (纪实电影) *Looking for Richard* (1997), Al Pacino played Richard, as well as providing a commentary on his experience of playing the role.

The film merged scenes from Shakespeare's play (in medieval costumes) with episodes in which the actors talked about their characters. Academics were also interviewed about the play. Pacino brought Shakespeare to a modern American audience and raised questions about who has the authority to make interpretive statements on Shakespeare – American actors or British academics.

Pacino's use of the docudrama form allowed him to switch roles from Richard to director, reflecting on his performance (and on the performances of other actors, as well as different interpretations of the play). In his commentary, he talked to viewers and explained his motives and actions in much the same way Richard does in his use of soliloquies and asides in Shakespeare's play.

Throughout history, performances of *King Richard III* have shown a wide range of interpretations and possibilities for dramatic portrayals on stage and on film. In part, this is because the role itself is extremely theatrical. Richard is not only a tyrant king or heroic villain. He is also a consummate actor who plays many parts and revels in each role that allows him to hoodwink his enemies and get rid of those who stand in his way to the throne.

◆ In groups, think about how you would want to stage *King Richard III* for a new production in a city of your choice and with an unlimited budget.

- Describe the setting and time (i.e. the present, the past or the future) and think about how lighting, costume and music could contribute to the overall effect.
- Cast your production with known actors, or other celebrities, and explain your choices. Then identify several speeches you think are particularly important and write instructions on how they should be delivered.
- Draw some costume designs, or use pictures taken from magazines or the Internet.
- Programme notes that are sold at performances of the play might include information on how the stage set links to the director's interpretation and characterisation. Write your own programme notes, in role as a director, using your ideas for a set design above and your knowledge of the play, along with its language, events and characters.

King Richard III in performance

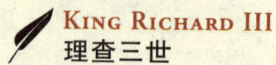

King Richard III
理查三世

Writing about Shakespeare 笔论莎士比亚

The play as text

Shakespeare's plays have always been studied as literary works – as words on a page that need clarification, appreciation and discussion. When you write about the plays, you will be asked to compose short pieces and also longer, more reflective pieces like controlled assessments, examination scripts and coursework – often in the form of essays on themes and/or imagery, character studies, analyses of the structure of the play and on stagecraft. Imagery, stagecraft and character are dealt with elsewhere in this edition. Here, we concentrate on themes and structure. You might find it helpful to look at the 'Write about it' boxes on the left-hand pages throughout the play.

Themes

It is often tempting to say that the theme of a play is a single idea, like 'death' in *Hamlet*, or 'the supernatural' in *Macbeth*, or 'love' in *Romeo and Juliet*. The problem with such a simple approach is that you will miss the complexity of the plays. In *Romeo and Juliet*, for example, the play is about the relationship between love, family loyalty and constraint; it is also about the relationship of youth to age and experience; and the relationship between Romeo and Juliet is also played out against a background of enmity between two families. Between each of these ideas or concepts there are tensions. The tensions are the main focus of attention for Shakespeare and the audience; this is also how the best drama operates – by the presentation of and resolution of tension.

Look back at the 'Themes' boxes throughout the play to see if any of the activities there have given rise to information that you could use as a starting point for further writing about the themes of the specific play you are studying.

Structure

Most Shakespeare plays are in five acts, divided into scenes. These acts were not in the original scripts, but have been included in later editions to make the action more manageable, clearer and more like 'classical' structures. One way to get a sense of the structure of the whole play is to take a printed version (not this one!) and cut it up into scenes and acts, then display each scene and act, in sequence, on a wall, like this:

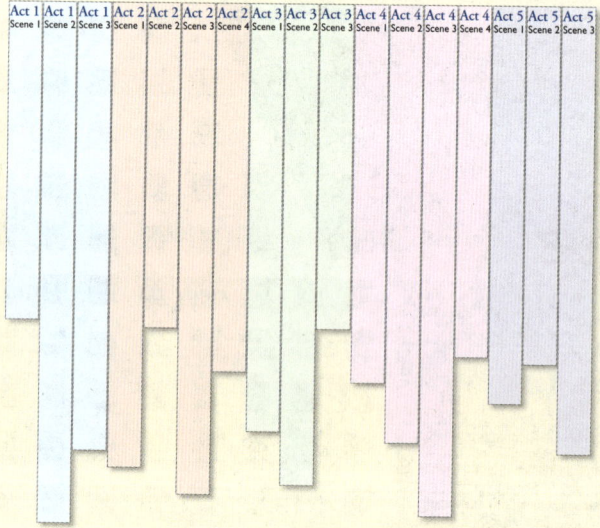

As you set out the whole play, you will be able to see the 'shape' of each act, the relative length of the scenes, and how the acts relate to each other (such as whether one act is shorter, and why that might be). You can annotate the text with comments, observations and questions. You can use a highlighter pen to mark the recurrence of certain words, images or metaphors to see at a glance where and how frequently they appear. You can also follow a particular character's progress through the play.

Such an overview of the play gives you critical perspective: you will be able to see how the parts fit together, to stand back from the play and assess its shape, and to focus on particular parts within the context of the whole. Your writing will reflect a greater awareness of the overall context as a result.

The play as script

There are different, but related, categories when we think of the play as a script for performance. These include *stagecraft* (discussed elsewhere in this edition and throughout the left-hand pages), *lighting*, *focus* (who are we looking at? Where is the attention of the audience?), *music and sound*, *props and costumes*, *casting*, *make-up*, *pace and rhythm*, and other *spatial relationships* (e.g. how actors move around the stage in relation to each other). If you are writing about stagecraft or performance, use the notes you have made as a result of the 'Stagecraft' activities throughout this edition of the play, as well as any information you can find about the plays in performance.

What are the key points of dispute?

Shakespeare is brilliant at capturing a number of key points of dispute in each of his plays. These are the dramatic moments where he concentrates the focus of the audience on difficult (sometimes universal) problems that the characters are facing or embodying.

First, identify these key points in the play you are studying. You can do this as a class by discussing what you consider to be the key points in small groups, then debating the long-list as a whole class, and then coming up with a short-list of what the class thinks are the most significant. (This is a good opportunity for speaking and listening work.) They are likely to be places in the play where the action or reflection is at its most intense, and which capture the complexity of themes, character, structure and performance.

Second, drill down at one of the points of contention and tension. In other words, investigate the complexity of the problem that Shakespeare has presented. What is at stake? Why is it important? Is it a problem that can be resolved, or is it an insoluble one?

Key skills in writing about Shakespeare

Here are some suggestions to help you organise your notes and develop advanced writing skills when working on Shakespeare:

- Compose the title of your writing carefully to maximise your opportunities to be creative and critical about the play. Explore the key words in your title carefully. Decide which aspect of the play – or which combination of aspects – you are focusing on.
- Create a mind map of your ideas, making connections between them.
- If appropriate, arrange your ideas into a hierarchy that shows how some themes or features of the play are 'higher' than others and can incorporate other ideas.
- Sequence your ideas so that you have a plan for writing an essay, review, story – whichever genre you are using. You might like to think about whether to put your strongest points first, in the middle, or later.
- Collect key quotations (it might help to compile this list with a partner), which you can use as evidence to support your argument.
- Compose your first draft, embedding quotations in your text as you go along.
- Revise your draft in the light of your own critical reflections and/or those of others.

The following pages focus on writing about *King Richard III* in particular.

KING RICHARD III
理查三世

Writing about *King Richard III* 笔论《理查三世》

Any kind of writing about *King Richard III* will be informed by your responses to the play. Your understanding of how characters, plot, themes, language and stagecraft are all interrelated will contribute to your unique perspective. This section will help you locate key points of entry into the play so that your writing will be engaging and original.

How do you find your unique perspective? You may want to start by considering this play in the context of Shakespeare's other history plays. *King Richard III* dramatises the final events of the Wars of the Roses, and ends with the marriage of Henry VII (Richmond) and Elizabeth, marking the start of the new Tudor dynasty. The play is coloured by perspectives on Richard that are informed by a Tudor viewpoint: he is represented as a malignant and violent tyrant king who murders eleven people (including his own family members and innocent children) in order to seize the throne.

The real Richard III was not as evil or sinister as Shakespeare has imagined him to be, and his reputation has changed much throughout the centuries since he died. Shakespeare and other sixteenth-century writers embellished this historical figure with dramatic and sensational characteristics, many of which are pure fiction. Shakespeare's Richard III is not only a representation of Tudor perspectives; he is also an inherently theatrical character who delights in his own machinations and in his many performances on stage. He acts out several parts and plays to the audience, seeking its approval and complicity. His many soliloquies and asides that comment on what is happening around him and on his own plans — especially in the first half of the play — are typical of his invitations to the audience to join him in delighting in his own mischief.

In this, Richard is like the Vice character in medieval morality plays and, indeed, Richard makes this comparison himself in Act 3 Scene 1. The Vice character was associated with the Devil and linked to sin, hell and damnation, as well as being the source of much comic energy on the stage. Shakespeare's Richard uses similar verbal trickery and punning, shows the same triumphant glee in his deceptions and has a similar relationship with the audience as did the Vice character, who moved easily from the world of the play to the world of the audience.

Although Richard dominates the play, the other characters also shape our response to him. Richard's colloquial and informal language is contrasted with the formal rhetoric and elaborate language of the women in the play. The triad of women — all of them queens — who clearly see Richard's evil intentions, are brought together in scenes of grief and madness. The former Queen Margaret's mad curses, Richard's mother's shame at having borne such an evil son and Queen Elizabeth's grief-induced insanity are all testimony to another perspective on Richard. Their highly rhetorical speeches create patterned and rhythmic sequences, and offer a contrast to Richard's informal language.

While thinking through the range of possible written responses, you may find it helpful to consider the performance possibilities offered by the play. Your own perspective will develop as you make connections between its dramatic, contextual, linguistic and thematic features.

Creative writing

At different times during your study of *King Richard III*, you may be writing about the play and about your personal responses to it. Creative responses, such as those encouraged in the activities on the left-hand pages in this book, allow you to be as imaginative as you want. This is your chance to develop your own voice and to be adventurous as well as sensitive to the words and images in the play. This is a rich, multi-layered text that benefits from many different approaches, both in performance and in writing. Don't be afraid of larger questions or implications that cannot be reduced to simple resolutions. The complex issues are often the most interesting.

- Richard's asides and soliloquies allow him to engage with the audience in a sophisticated yet informal manner. Try to write asides and soliloquies for another character so that they also develop a relationship with the audience. What difference does this make to your understanding of the character?

- What happens to the characters who live on after the play has finished? Choose one of the characters and write their version of events. Write this as a first-person narrative, a monologue or a script.

Essay writing

Other responses, such as essays, have a set structure and specific requirements. Writing an essay gives you a chance to explore your own interpretations, to use evidence that appeals to you, and to write with creativity and flair. You can approach the play from a number of critical perspectives or in relation to different themes. You will also need to explore the play in the social, literary, political and cultural contexts of its production (Shakespeare's day) and reception (today or at any point since Shakespeare's day).

An essay can be seen as an exploration of the play in which you chart a path to illuminate ideas that are significant to you. It is also an argument that uses evidence and structural requirements to persuade your readers that you have an important perspective on the play. You must integrate evidence from the script into your own writing by using embedded quotations and by explaining the significance of each quotation and reference to the play. Some people like to remember the acronym PEA to help them here. P is the POINT you are making. E is the EVIDENCE you are taking from the script. A is the ANALYSIS you give when using this evidence, which will reflect back on the point you are making and contain your own personal response and original ideas.

The following titles are typical essays based on *King Richard III*:

1. Shakespeare's representation of Richard III is influenced by historical accounts of the last Plantagenet king and by dramatic characters from medieval drama. How do you understand this character and the impact he has on the stage and in the events of the play?

2. Choose two or three central themes and explain how each is developed linguistically and dramatically through the play.

3. Write about an aspect of language that interests you in *King Richard III*.

4. The figure of Vice (and other representations of evil on stage) from medieval drama is an important influence on the character of Richard. Discuss the effect this has on your understanding of characters and events in the play.

5. Do you see Richard as the play's hero or as its villain? What evidence can you find in the play that suggests you could argue that he is both?

- Pick at least two of these essay titles and sketch out an essay plan for each. Swap plans with two other students in your class, giving constructive feedback and making suggestions for improvements.

- Select the two essay titles that you think are the most difficult to answer. Try to pinpoint which aspects of the questions you find most challenging. Then get together with a partner and share ideas about how to address these challenging aspects.

King Richard III 理查三世

Royal family tree 王室家谱图

m = married

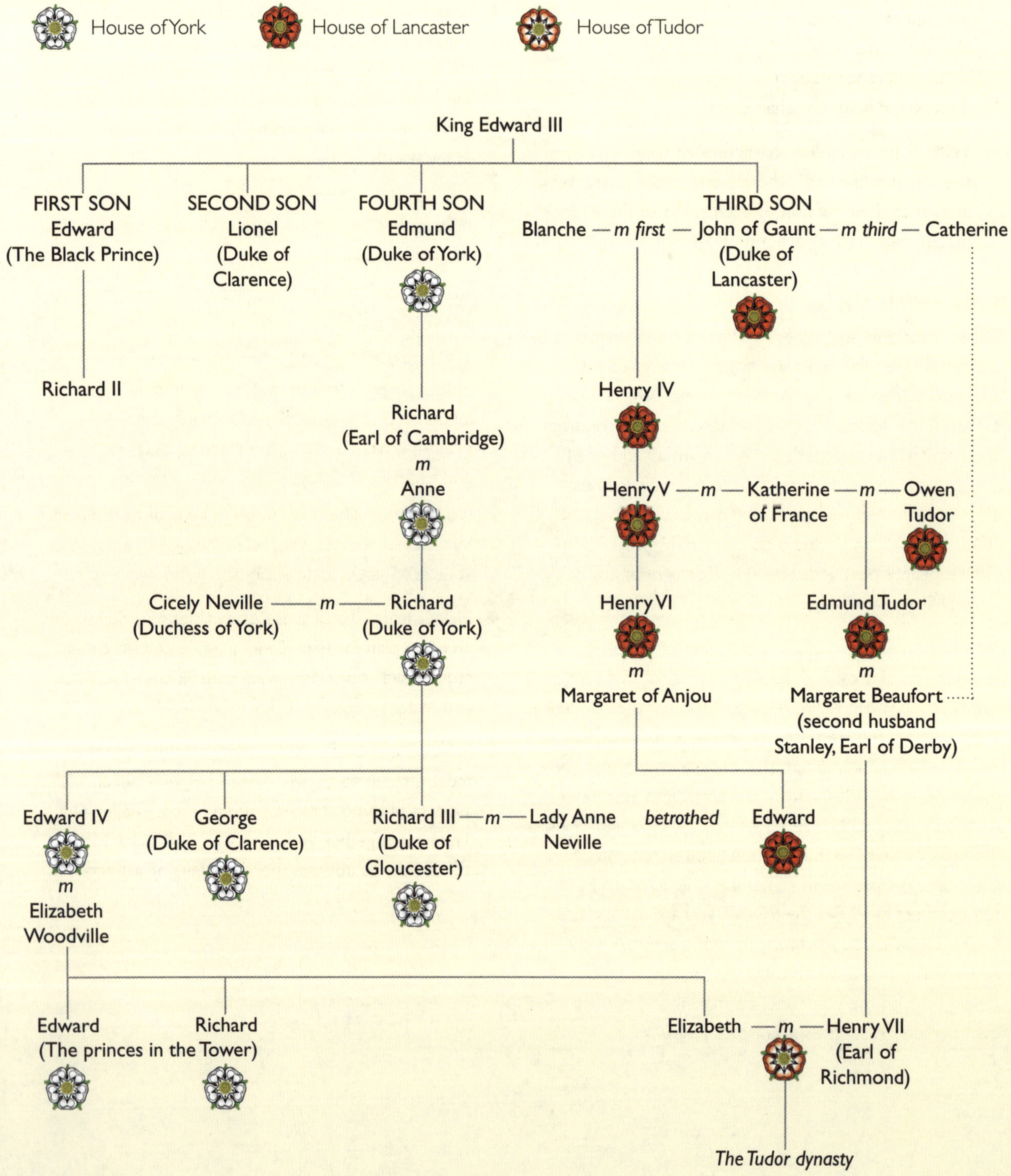

- House of York
- House of Lancaster
- House of Tudor

```
                                King Edward III
        ┌───────────┬───────────┬──────────────┬──────────────────┐
    FIRST SON   SECOND SON  FOURTH SON              THIRD SON
     Edward       Lionel      Edmund      Blanche — m first — John of Gaunt — m third — Catherine
  (The Black    (Duke of    (Duke of York)                    (Duke of Lancaster)
    Prince)    Clarence)
        │                        │                        │
    Richard II                Richard                  Henry IV
                        (Earl of Cambridge)
                                m                        │
                               Anne              Henry V — m — Katherine — m — Owen Tudor
                                │                              of France
                                │                        │
          Cicely Neville — m — Richard              Henry VI              Edmund Tudor
         (Duchess of York)   (Duke of York)              m                     m
                                                   Margaret of Anjou    Margaret Beaufort
                                                                         (second husband
                                                                         Stanley, Earl of Derby)

  Edward IV   George       Richard III — m — Lady Anne    betrothed    Edward
      m    (Duke of        (Duke of         Neville
  Elizabeth   Clarence)    Gloucester)
  Woodville

  Edward    Richard                                   Elizabeth — m — Henry VII
  (The princes in the Tower)                                          (Earl of Richmond)

                                                              The Tudor dynasty
```

266

William Shakespeare 莎翁年表
1564–1616

1564	Born Stratford-upon-Avon, eldest son of John and Mary Shakespeare.
1582	Marries Anne Hathaway of Shottery, near Stratford.
1583	Daughter Susanna born.
1585	Twins, son and daughter Hamnet and Judith, born.
1592	First mention of Shakespeare in London. Robert Greene, another playwright, described Shakespeare as 'an upstart crow beautified with our feathers'. Greene seems to have been jealous of Shakespeare. He mocked Shakespeare's name, calling him 'the only Shake-scene in a country' (presumably because Shakespeare was writing successful plays).
1595	Becomes a shareholder in The Lord Chamberlain's Men, an acting company that became extremely popular.
1596	Son, Hamnet, dies aged eleven. Father, John, granted arms (acknowledged as a gentleman).
1597	Buys New Place, the grandest house in Stratford.
1598	Acts in Ben Jonson's *Every Man in His Humour*.
1599	Globe Theatre opens on Bankside. Performances in the open air.
1601	Father, John, dies.
1603	James I grants Shakespeare's company a royal patent: The Lord Chamberlain's Men become The King's Men and play about twelve performances each year at court.
1607	Daughter Susanna marries Dr John Hall.
1608	Mother, Mary, dies.
1609	The King's Men begin performing indoors at Blackfriars Theatre.
1610	Probably returns from London to live in Stratford.
1616	Daughter Judith marries Thomas Quiney. Dies. Buried in Holy Trinity Church, Stratford-upon-Avon.

The plays and poems

(no one knows exactly when he wrote each play)

1589–95	*The Two Gentlemen of Verona*, *The Taming of the Shrew*, *First*, *Second* and *Third Parts* of *King Henry VI*, *Titus Andronicus*, **King Richard III**, *The Comedy of Errors*, *Love's Labour's Lost*, *A Midsummer Night's Dream*, *Romeo and Juliet*, *King Richard II* (and the long poems *Venus and Adonis* and *The Rape of Lucrece*).
1596–99	*King John*, *The Merchant of Venice*, *First* and *Second Parts* of *King Henry IV*, *The Merry Wives of Windsor*, *Much Ado About Nothing*, *King Henry V*, *Julius Caesar* (and probably the Sonnets).
1600–05	*As You Like It*, *Hamlet*, *Twelfth Night*, *Troilus and Cressida*, *Measure for Measure*, *Othello*, *All's Well That Ends Well*, *Timon of Athens*, *King Lear*.
1606–11	*Macbeth*, *Antony and Cleopatra*, *Pericles*, *Coriolanus*, *The Winter's Tale*, *Cymbeline*, *The Tempest*.
1613	*King Henry VIII*, *The Two Noble Kinsmen* (both probably with John Fletcher).
1623	Shakespeare's plays published as a collection (now called the First Folio).

King Richard III
理查三世

Acknowledgements 鸣谢

Cambridge University Press would like to acknowledge the contributions made to this work by Rex Gibson and Pat and Tom Baldwin.

Extracts from 'Richard III: Shakespearean actors rake over the remains', The Guardian, 4 February 2013 on p. 247 copyright © Guardian News and Media Ltd 2013. Extract from programme notes from Nicu's Spoon Theater Company production of Richard III, 2007, on p. 247 reproduced with permission of Stephanie Barton-Farcas.

Picture Credits

p. iii: John Douglas Thompson as Richard in a Shakespeare & Company production 2010. Photo by Kevin Sprague; p. v top: Crucible Theatre, Sheffield 2002, © Donald Cooper/Photostage; p. v bottom: Richard III: An Arab Tragedy, RSC/Swan Theatre, Stratford-upon-Avon 2007, © Donald Cooper/Photostage; p. vi top: Shakespeare's Globe, London 2012, © Geraint Lewis; p. vii bottom: RSC/Barbican Theatre, London 1985, © Donald Cooper/Photostage; p. vii top: Richard III: An Arab Tragedy, RSC/Swan Theatre, Stratford-upon-Avon 2007, © Donald Cooper/Photostage; p. vii bottom: RSC/Barbican Theatre, London 1996, © Donald Cooper/Photostage; p. viii top: Richard III: An Arab Tragedy, RSC/Swan Theatre, Stratford-upon-Avon 2007, © Donald Cooper/Photostage; p. viii bottom: RSC/Barbican Theatre, London 1996, © Donald Cooper/Photostage; p. ix top: Jason Asprey (Hastings) and Ryan Winkles in a Shakespeare & Company production 2010. Photo by Kevin Sprague; p. ix bottom: RSC/Swan Theatre, Stratford-upon-Avon 2012, © Geraint Lewis; p. x: RSC/Barbican Theatre, London 1996, © Donald Cooper/Photostage; p. xi top left: RSC/Royal Shakespeare Theatre, Stratford-upon-Avon 2003, © Donald Cooper/Photostage; p. xi top right: RSC/Royal Shakespeare Theatre, Stratford-upon-Avon 2003, © Donald Cooper/Photostage; p. xi bottom: RSC/Courtyard Theatre, Stratford-upon-Avon 2007, © Geraint Lewis; p. xii left: Northcott Theatre Company/Ludlow Festival 2008, © Donald Cooper/Photostage; p. xii right: RSC/Royal Shakespeare Theatre, Stratford-upon-Avon 1984, © Donald Cooper/Photostage; p. 14: © Donald Cooper/Photostage; p. 22: RSC/Young Vic Theatre, London 2001, © Donald Cooper/Photostage; p. 26: Leia Espericueta (Anne) and John Douglas Thompson (Richard) in a Shakespeare & Company production 2010. Photo by Kevin Sprague; p. 38: Bridge Project/Old Vic Theatre, London 2011, © Geraint Lewis; p. 46: RSC/Royal Shakespeare Theatre, Stratford-upon-Avon 1980, © Donald Cooper/Photostage; p. 60: Shakespeare's Globe, London 2003, © Donald Cooper/Photostage; p. 67: RSC/Royal Shakespeare Theatre, Stratford-upon-Avon 2003, © Donald Cooper/Photostage; p. 70: RSC/Royal Shakespeare Theatre 1980, © Donald Cooper/Photostage; p. 78: A Noise Within, Los Angeles 2009, © Craig Schwartz Photography; p. 88: Judah Piepho (Duke of York) and Anne Miller (Duchess of York) in a Shakespeare & Company production 2010. Photo by Kevin Sprague; p. 95 top: RSC/Swan Theatre, Stratford-upon-Avon 2012, © Geraint Lewis; p. 95 bottom: A Noise Within, Los Angeles 2009, © Craig Schwartz Photography; p. 102: Northcott Theatre Company/Ludlow Festival 2008, © Donald Cooper/Photostage; p. 108: Richard III's boar emblem, © PA Photos/Topfoto; p. 116: Temple University, Philadelphia 2009. Photo by Ian Paul Guzzone; p. 120: RSC/Royal Shakespeare Theatre, Stratford-upon-Avon 1995 © Donald Cooper/Photostage; p.126: Richard III: An Arab Tragedy, RSC/Swan Theatre, Stratford-upon-Avon 2007, © Donald Cooper/Photostage; p. 132: RSC/The Other Place, Stratford-upon-Avon 1992, © Donald Cooper/Photostage; p. 136: Lyttelton Theatre/National Theatre, London 1990, © Donald Cooper/Photostage; p. 147: 'Children of Edward' by Paul Delaroche, © DEA/G. DAGLI ORTI/Getty Images; p. 156: RSC/The Other Place, Stratford-upon-Avon 1992, © Donald Cooper/Photostage; p. 158: © Donald Cooper/Photostage; p. 160: 'The Murder of the Princes in the Tower', © Getty Images; p. 172: RSC/Swan Theatre, Stratford-upon-Avon 2012, © Geraint Lewis; p. 176: RSC/Royal Shakespeare Theatre, Stratford-upon-Avon 1984, © Donald Cooper/Photostage; p. 197: Apollo Theatre, London 2012, © Nigel

Acknowledgements

Norrington/ArenaPAL; p. 204: A Shakespeare & Company production 2010. Photo by Kevin Sprague; p. 210: Companhia Bufomecanica, World Shakespeare Festival/Courtyard Theatre, Stratford-upon-Avon 2012, © Donald Cooper/Photostage; p. 212: RSC/Barbican Theatre, London 1996, © Donald Cooper/Photostage; p. 218: RSC/Aldwich Theatre, London 1981, © Donald Cooper/Photostage; p. 229: John Douglas Thompson as Richard in a Shakespeare & Company production 2010. Photo by Kevin Sprague; p. 231: Crucible Theatre, Sheffield 2002, © Donald Cooper/Photostage; p. 233: *Richard III: An Arab Tragedy*, RSC/Swan Theatre, Stratford-upon-Avon 2007, © Alastair Muir/Rex Features; p. 235: A Noise Within, Los Angeles 2009, © Craig Schwartz Photography; p. 236: Portrait of Richard III, © Topfoto; p. 238: RSC/Royal Shakespeare Theatre, Stratford-upon-Avon 1984, © Donald Cooper/Photostage; p. 241: John Douglas Thompson as Richard in a Shakespeare & Company production 2010. Photo by Kevin Sprague; p. 245: © Donald Cooper/Photostage; pp. 252–3: 'The Long View of London from Bankside' by Wenceslaus Hollar; p. 253: RSC/Royal Shakespeare Theatre, Stratford-upon-Avon 2003, © Donald Cooper/Photostage; p. 254: David Garrick playing Richard III by William Hogarth 1745, © The Granger Collection/Topfoto; p. 255 left: RSC/Royal Shakespeare Theatre, Stratford-upon-Avon 1984, © Donald Cooper/Photostage; p. 255 right: RSC/Young Vic Theatre, London 2001, © Donald Cooper/Photostage; p. 256 top: Shakespeare's Globe, London 2003, © Donald Cooper/Photostage; p. 256 bottom: Apollo Theatre, London 2012, © Geraint Lewis; p. 257 Clowns Shakespeare, Porto 2013, © Diogo Baptista/Demotix/Corbis; p. 258 top Manchester Opera House 1945, © ArenaPAL; top: p. 258 bottom: *Richard III* directed by Frank Benson 1911, © Cooperative Cinematograph/The Kobal Collection; p. 259 Ian McKellan in *Richard III* 1995, © Moviestore Collection/Rex Features; p. 261: RSC/Barbican Theatre, London 1989, © Donald Cooper/Photostage.

Produced for Cambridge University Press by
White-Thomson Publishing
+44 (0)843 208 7460
www.wtpub.co.uk

Managing editor: Sonya Newland
Designer: Clare Nicholas
Concept design: Jackie Hill